Praise for *UNBUILD*

"*Unbuild Walls* is a vital intervention! The freedom to move around and the freedom to stay put are central to abolitionist vision. Silky Shah shows, with lively detail, how abolitionist political analysis is both preparation for and guidance through complex, difficult struggles."
— **RUTH WILSON GILMORE**, author of *Abolition Geography: Essays Towards Liberation*

"Silky Shah has written a crucial history of the nexus between draconian immigration enforcement and the criminal legal system. Rather than framing the cruelties of the Trump administration as the result of a single man's nativist designs, Shah exposes the decades-long bipartisan project to quickly incarcerate and deport immigrants. Shah avoids the all-too-easy claim that these two systems should be disentangled, arguing that this narrative pits immigrants against other marginalized groups—including people affected by the prison industrial complex—and instead deftly argues for abolition."
— **GABY DEL VALLE**, cofounder of BORDER/LINES

"This book is an essential tool to build abolitionist analysis within the migrant justice movement, and to bring people who are already mobilizing for police and prison abolition into the fight for migrant justice. Anyone interested in social change and in the most pressing questions about social movement tactics needs to read this book."
— **DEAN SPADE**, author of *Mutual Aid: Building Solidarity During This Crisis (and the Next)*

"Silky Shah's excellently crafted book, *Unbuild Walls*, refreshingly busts through the persistent and predictable debates about border and immigration enforcement. This fast-paced read is well written, well researched, often personal and insightful, and a must for anyone concerned about immigration and connections to struggles for economic and racial justice."
— **TODD MILLER**, author of *Build Bridges, Not Walls: A Journey to a World Without Borders*

"This book is an extraordinary call to action that urges anyone who cares about immigrant justice to embrace abolition. Silky Shah writes from her unique perspective as an organizer and leader in the movement to end immigration detention, sharing the abolitionist lessons she has learned from her journey. *Unbuild Walls* is a gift to those who are ready to learn from the past and build a better future that uplifts the dignity of all people."

—**ALINA DAS**, author of *No Justice in the Shadows: How America Criminalizes Immigrants*

"*Unbuild Walls* opens our eyes to the ways the criminal punishment and immigration enforcement systems are fully intertwined. Grounded in stories of immigrants impacted by immigrant detention, as well as her own courageous organizing journey fighting against the deportation machine, this book inspires us to embrace the call for the abolition of mass incarceration and immigrant detention. This book is a must-read for anyone committed to building a democracy where freedom and justice is a reality for all."

—**CRISTINA JIMÉNEZ MORETA**, MacArthur fellow and cofounder of United We Dream

UNBUILD WALLS

WHY IMMIGRANT JUSTICE NEEDS ABOLITION

SILKY SHAH

Haymarket Books
Chicago, IL

Published in 2024 by
Haymarket Books
P.O. Box 180165
Chicago, IL 60618
www.haymarketbooks.org

ISBN: 979-8-88890-084-0

Distributed to the trade in the US through Consortium Book Sales and Distribution (www.cbsd.com) and internationally through Ingram Publisher Services International (www.ingramcontent.com).

This book was published with the generous support of Lannan Foundation, Wallace Action Fund, and Marguerite Casey Foundation.

Special discounts are available for bulk purchases by organizations and institutions. Please email info@haymarketbooks.org for more information.

Cover design by Rachel Cohen.

Printed in Canada by union labor.

Library of Congress Cataloging-in-Publication data is available.

10 9 8 7 6 5 4 3 2 1

For the members of Detention Watch Network,
past, present, and future

Those who build walls are their own prisoners. I am going to go fulfill my proper function in the social organism. I'm going to go unbuild walls.

—Ursula K. Le Guin, *The Dispossessed*

CONTENTS

Foreword *by Amna A. Akbar*   ix
Prologue   xiii
Introduction   1

Part I: Immigration in the Era of Mass Incarceration
  Chapter 1:   The US Prison Boom and
               the Growth of Immigrant Detention   17
  Chapter 2:   Obama, Criminalization,
               and the Limits of Reform   44
  Chapter 3:   Deterring the Crisis: Prosecutions, Prisons,
               and the United States-Mexico Border   68

Part II: Organizing for Immigrant Justice
  Chapter 4:   From Legalization to Racial Justice:
               The Evolution of a Movement   97
  Chapter 5:   Private Prisons and the Demand to Defund   126
  Chapter 6:   Communities Not Cages   148

Part III: Making Abolition
  Chapter 7:   Abolitionist Approaches to System Change   185
  Chapter 8:   Beyond "Abolish ICE"   197

Acknowledgments   211
Notes   216
Index   243

FOREWORD

The 2020 uprisings marked a popular rebirth of radical imagination. Estimates suggest between 15 to 26 million people across 2,000 cities and towns in the United States protested in the weeks after George Floyd's and Breonna Taylor's murders. Calls to defund the police and cancel rent howled within the summer-long rebellion and the early days of the pandemic. Radical critiques of police and capitalism had taken root for countless young people. Imagination was back in a growing left. We wanted a society focused on care and mutuality rather than violence and exploitation. No one had it worked out with all that much detail, but that was the point—not to draw permanent blueprints, but to conjure enough of a horizon to shift our understanding of what was possible, and to identify that horizon as a guiding star in the long haul and daily grind of movement building.

These are the moving parts of a theory of social change: critique, horizon, and practice. Critique is where we articulate our understanding of what it is we are deconstructing and delegitimizing—the alienation, exploitation, violence, and dispossession produced by capitalism and colonialism. Horizon is the place for freedom dreams, where we develop affirmative visions of the social, economic, and political relations that anchor the world we are fighting to build. Practice is the place of active struggle: where we experiment with strategies and tactics—organizing, protesting, running campaigns, and building mutual aid projects—that will bridge the world in which we live to the more just world of our horizon. In *Unbuild Walls*, Silky Shah manages to hold in view all three.

On critique, Shah argues we must understand the US immigration system vis à vis the criminal legal system as intertwined systems of racialized violence and exploitation, defined by long histories of capitalism and colonialism, met always by the resistance of ordinary people. We must understand relevant histories like the incarceration of people of Japanese descent in the United States during World War II, the rise of the war on drugs and the ascent of neoliberalism in the 1970s and 1980s, and the North American Free Trade Agreement of 1994. We must situate the United States and its migration policies in the context of its rise as a global superpower and its accumulation of land and wealth on the backs of Black people, within the homes of Indigenous peoples, and all the while dependent on the degradation of and uneven differentiation among working-class and poor people.

We must also understand the present. Shah details the failures of "comprehensive immigration reform" in 2013 that continue to define the brutal terrain of immigration enforcement today. The Obama administration deployed tropes of "good" and "bad" immigrants to expand detention and deportation, including via partnerships with police departments, sheriffs, county jails, and capital: private prisons and the industries that service the carceral state with all manner of goods. Programs like Secure Communities that were touted as public safety reforms ultimately juiced the power of the prison industrial complex.

Shah's critique echoes a generation of young people, people of color, and a growing cohort of radical activists, progressives, and questioning liberals who are connecting seemingly disparate systems of exploitation and violence: between family separation at the border, in prisons and jails, and through family policing and family courts; between militarism and environmental destruction and migrant crises. These problems exist beyond Trump and the Muslim Ban. Instead they are a product of a bipartisan consensus about a state and an economy built on violence and dispossession—the brutality of which is on display moment to moment in virtually any direction you look.

Mirroring the intersectional critique, on horizon, Shah argues immigrant justice requires the abolition of the prison industrial complex. Immigrant justice entails not simply the tearing down of carceral spaces but the building of a world where all people's needs are met. "Communities not cages" of the immigrant justice movement belongs next to other abolitionist refrains such as "Divest, invest" and "Defund the police, refund communities." Racial justice movements must understand the centrality of ending immigrant detention and deportation alongside prisons, police, surveillance, and a carceral economy.

Shah's lucid critique and horizon remind us to center the connections of our struggles in the United States and around the world, across "issue areas," organizational formations, and political tendencies. Shah adds to the growing calls that link incarceration, securitized borders, and the state form in our critique and horizon. In her telling of the immigrant justice movement, we see the necessity of what organizers and activists in the Stop Cop City campaign call "multiple grammars of struggle" to build strong movements—and movements of movements—to take on and win on the urgent questions of our times. The difficult work of building solidarity makes us stronger.

What makes this book essential reading is Shah's disciplined commitment to practice, the essential bridge between critique and horizon. Shah urges us to think about abolitionist steps, or nonreformist reforms: campaigns that aim to shrink the power and legitimacy of detention, deportation, and surveillance; that provide relief to people detained or those under surveillance; and that emerge from and are exercises of budding movement power. Central to the book are a series of campaigns that Shah dubs "site fights." These are campaigns to shut down detention centers or prevent new ones from opening, mirroring the growing No New Jails (and prisons) campaigns all over the country. Shah details how organizers in Illinois, Texas, New Jersey, California, Alabama, and elsewhere have paved the way for a

more just world, battling against carceral creep, shifting consciousness, and building movement power.

While we agitate for our movements and analysis to grow in scale,
power, and ambition, we face extraordinary odds. Police and prosecu-
tor unions, billionaires and their lobbyists, and an empowered right-
wing are doing everything in their power to beat back emancipatory
people's movements. Shah identifies a range of actors invested in
immigrant detention and deportation: GEO Group and GEO Care,
ICE and county sheriffs, Democratic and Republican lawmakers, and
the many businesses that depend on precarious immigrant labor. She
reminds us that organizing means taking on concrete targets. This is
a necessary rejoinder to the liberal approach to politics: the idea that
we can all just get along—a dangerous position to take when there are
clearly identifiable opponents in our struggles.

Unbuild Walls is much more than a theoretical guidebook. It is
a tool and a sophisticated primer for activists, organizers, students,
and intellectuals who hope to change the world. It belongs on all our
shelves next to Jane McAlevey's *No Shortcuts* or Eric Blanc's *Red State
Revolt*—books that became essential readings for organizers and
activists understanding how to run labor and teacher campaigns.

Drawing from her involvement in decades of concrete, disciplined, and sustained political struggle—and from her work with
Detention Watch Network in particular—Shah provides a history
of the contemporary immigrant justice movement, featuring debates
and strategic flashpoints that have defined the terrain. By reading
about her experiences at local and national levels, we learn about the
messy and necessary political work it takes to contest the state, law,
and capital in our fight for a more livable and just world. It is here, on
the terrain of practice, that we must focus in the coming days, weeks,
years, and decades: strategies, tactics, and experiments that contend
with the world as it is as we attempt to build another.

—Amna A. Akbar
February 2024

PROLOGUE

Catalyst is good, but organization is better.
—Mike Davis

T he week the world changed, I spent my days in a cramped conference room with thirteen other people. It was something that I
wouldn't do again for quite some time. Each day as we attempted
to focus on our task at hand, the anxiety of the shifting conditions
began to seep into every conversation and decision on the table. It was
March 2020, and I was in Washington, DC, for a weeklong Detention Watch Network (DWN) staff retreat. Then-president Donald J.
Trump was on the verge of declaring a nationwide emergency and a
European travel ban due to the spread of COVID-19. The previous
year, his administration had expanded immigrant detention to the
highest level in US history; over five hundred thousand immigrants
had been detained over the course of 2019.

At the retreat, we were meant to plan DWN's biennial national
member conference. We knew bringing the membership together
was critical for keeping us going amid the relentless attacks from
the Trump administration. Since the founding of the organization
in 1997, the DWN conference had been a transformative space for
members to learn, strategize, and find camaraderie with others who
were also fighting the expansion of immigrant detention. But now,
with news of the pandemic, we had to cancel the conference. There
was a lingering sense of uncertainty among the team as we figured

out what would come next. We considered ways to fill the void left by canceling the event, like hosting a virtual conference. But then we each began to realize that whatever was to come of the impending spread of COVID-19, the conditions for people incarcerated would only worsen. Prisons, jails, and detention centers were notorious for spreading illness. (In 2019, nearly 900 immigrants contracted mumps after outbreaks at immigrant detention centers in nineteen states.) The confusion at the onset of the pandemic was hard enough for those free from incarceration—what would it be like for those inside? We knew at that moment we had to do anything and everything possible to free them all.

What are the strategies for getting people released? Who are the relevant decision makers? What resources will organizers need to ramp up pressure? How will we expose the impact of diseases and viruses in detention? How will we show what level of support exists for freeing people? What will immigrants need after being released? These were the questions we asked ourselves as we started developing a plan. By the end of the week, we all scattered back to our respective parts of the country to shelter in place, but we had already begun working on a #FreeThemAll toolkit and pivoting to focus most of our work on getting people out as the virus started spreading.

In one of the most challenging moments of our collective lives, organizers, advocates, lawyers, and ordinary people stepped up to do anything they could to protect and support immigrants detained. Almost immediately, from New Jersey to Washington State, hundreds of detained immigrants went on hunger strikes to protest the harshening conditions of confinement as the pandemic took hold. By March 19, 2020, over 750 organizations had signed a DWN-organized letter to Immigration and Customs Enforcement (ICE) demanding that the agency release everyone in immigrant detention due to the spread of COVID-19. That same day, in an open letter, 4,000 medical professionals also urged ICE to release immigrants from detention. Caravans of people in their cars began forming outside detention centers, honking and chanting to show their support for immigrants locked up. Attorneys filed lawsuits on behalf of the most vulnerable immigrants: those who were elderly or immunocompromised in some way. Journalists exposed ICE's negligence in providing protection from the virus and meeting basic hygiene needs inside detention centers. The call to #FreeThemAll was an organic one that echoed throughout the movement to end immigrant detention and other forms of incarceration. Soon #FreeThemAllforPublicHealth was trending, and #FreeThemAll chapters popped up across the country.

The pandemic brought new clarity to the fight against mass incarceration. Prisons and jails were not just ripe for spreading disease within their walls; their mere existence could also grow the virus in surrounding communities. The United States, the world's leading incarcerator, was itself a hotbed of infection. Soon, more Americans began to question why we incarcerate so many people in this country. People in jails and detention centers were mostly there awaiting trial—why keep them locked up, especially during a pandemic? Questions that we at DWN had been asking for years were gaining traction. The Overton window was shifting.

Two months later, these questions would take on new meaning. Once again, the nation watched in horror as another Black man, George Floyd, was murdered by Minneapolis police. Immediately people took to the streets. Hundreds of thousands of protesters in cities across the country chanted "Black lives matter" and "Defund the police." Calls for abolition began to grow. And again, questions about our current systems were raised. Why do we continue to witness people dying at the hands of the police? Why don't the police make us feel safe? Maybe these systems are fundamentally unjust. Maybe they can't be fixed.

In September 2020, a whistleblower report revealed that a doctor had performed hysterectomies and other gynecological procedures without consent on immigrant women locked up at the Irwin County Detention Center in Ocilla, Georgia. An immediate deluge of coverage, investigations, and congressional visits followed. In organizing and movement building, these catalyst moments come on like wildfire and sometimes fizzle out just as quickly. They are hard to predict, but at their core, catalyst moments usually come about when something happens that challenges our idea of what is right and just, something that goes so far beyond the bounds of what is acceptable that we must express outrage and do something in response. Often, their staying power and ability to create change depend on how prepared our movements are when these catalysts happen. In these moments, we must ask ourselves: What is our analysis of why this is happening? What solution are we offering? Is there a path toward that solution? What is the most useful direct action for people to take? For immigration, there have been a few catalyst moments in recent years, most notably Trump's signing of the Muslim Ban in 2017 and the family separations at the US-Mexico border in 2018. While the outrage and response were palpable and the policies were rolled back (to a degree), once the initial firestorm had subsided, little happened in the way of meaningful change to the underlying immigration system.

With Irwin, though, the situation was different. That summer, as many immigrant rights organizations had been planning for the 2020 election, hoping for Trump's defeat, and laying out blueprints for a potential new administration, the question of what to do about immigrant detention came up. For years, many establishment immigrant rights organizations had hesitated to call for the outright abolition of immigrant detention. But in the summer of 2020, for some, this demand didn't seem so unfathomable anymore. After nearly four years of Trump in the White House, after living through a pandemic that ravaged prisons, jails, and detention centers, after a summer of protests that laid bare the inherent racism within our systems of governance, many realized that calling for an end to immigrant detention might be the only answer.

The salience of detention abolition had entered the mainstream immigrant rights movement. In combination with a long history of inside and outside organizing against Irwin, documentation of abuses by advocates and journalists, and the election of a new administration, deeper shifts were possible. In May 2021, ten years after the facility first opened, the Department of Homeland Security ended the ICE contract with the Irwin County Detention Center. Despite president Joe Biden's abysmal record on immigration, one that continued many Trump-era policies, Irwin wasn't the only detention center to close. The Biden administration ended contracts at four additional detention centers over the next two years and requested less funding for immigrant detention in its annual budget. After forty years of constant detention expansion, we finally started to move the needle in the other direction.

That week in March 2020, we didn't know that the months to follow would open up space to make our case for detention abolition. We were, however, prepared for the moment. Our understanding of the system, the campaigns and strategies we employed, and our commitment to other movements were all informed by the framework of abolition. In the pages to follow, I share the story of how we got there, how the system came to be and has changed over time, how we started to understand it better, how the movement has evolved in response to those shifts, and how abolition can help guide us in the interconnected struggles for racial and migrant justice.

INTRODUCTION

On December 31, 2020, in the waning days of the Trump administration, Jesse Jerome Dean Jr., a fifty-eight-year-old man from The Bahamas, was set to be released from prison. Dean had been arrested and charged with drug trafficking in Florida in 1995, but he maintained his innocence and refused a plea bargain, which resulted in a thirty-year prison sentence. Over the course of more than two decades of incarceration, Dean was transferred to several federal prisons until he finally ended up at a privately operated immigrant prison in Baldwin, Michigan.

Upon his release, Dean was looking forward to reuniting with his family in The Bahamas, including his son, who had been only eight years old when his father was first taken into the custody of the US government. But Dean wasn't a US citizen. Instead of being freed that December day in 2020, he was transferred yet again to a county jail in Battle Creek, Michigan, where ICE rents bed space, to await deportation. During his thirty-five days in ICE custody, Dean's health deteriorated. He complained twenty-seven times about abdominal pains and lost seventeen pounds. Staff ignored his protests for medical attention. One nurse threatened him with a citation for "interfering with staff duties." On January 30, 2021, he told medical staff, "I feel like I'm going to die." And five days later, twenty-six years after he was first imprisoned by the federal government, Dean passed away.[1]

I had been organizing against immigrant detention for nearly two decades when I first learned about Dean's death. Yet I struggled

1

to make sense of it. My work as an organizer taught me things that should have explained a moment like this. From having read dozens of death reports over the years, I knew in detail how horribly immigrants were treated inside detention centers. I also knew that Black men dying in the custody of the US government was not an uncommon occurrence. Dean died less than a year after one of the largest series of protests in US history had been set off by the brutal murder of George Floyd. Jesse Dean was now another addition to the list of Black people dying at the hands of the state. Still, even knowing all of this, Dean's death rattled me. I couldn't accept that this man—who had spent most of his adult life behind bars and was finally going to be freed and reunited with his family—had just been left to die. And despite working at an organization that advocates for an end to immigrant detention, I knew that his time in ICE custody was only part of the injustice he had experienced over twenty-six years in prison.

Dean's story illustrates something that more people in the immigrant justice movement have come to realize in recent years: the US immigration enforcement system and the prison industrial complex are not separate, as is commonly understood, but are intertwined systems of repression. While some may see this relationship as a more recent phenomenon, accelerated by the post-9/11 crackdown on immigrant communities, migrants have long been labeled "illegal" or "criminal" as a strategy for controlling their movements and preventing their acceptance into US society. The harmful effects of these labels have only been compounded by the growth of mass incarceration. Today the United States incarcerates nearly two million people in prisons, jails, and detention centers.

To understand how these systems are intertwined in the ways they are today, we have to return to the 1980s and 1990s. As abolitionist scholars such as Ruth Wilson Gilmore argue, it was during this period that prisons expanded as a "solution" to the economic, social, and political conditions of the time, notably rising social inequality and the erosion of welfare. The policy approach to immigration began to follow a similar path, and immigrants became a central target of the nativist agenda in Congress. Dean's experience with the US criminal legal system was a direct result of these shifts. Laws that had been passed during the height of the war on drugs resulted in his multidecade prison sentence and required his detention and deportation after his sentence was complete. He should still be alive today.

Sharing Jesse Dean's story might be a grim way to start this book, yet I hope it doesn't turn you away. We don't have to resign ourselves to a system in which his life did not matter. It could be different, and it should be different. What if we didn't have to accept these tragedies, but actively prevented them? This is one of the questions that abolition poses for us. In recent years, the number of people locked up in the United States has stopped its upward trend as more communities have begun to question why we incarcerate so many people. As the harms of the prison system have come to light, the demand to end immigrant detention has gained momentum. If our goal is justice for immigrants and nonimmigrants alike, we must be willing to go further and embrace abolition of the prison industrial complex as a whole. Understanding the relationship between immigration enforcement and the criminal legal system is a critical part of the abolitionist struggle.

My own journey toward embracing abolition began in Texas. I grew up in Houston in the eighties and nineties. Sprawling and humid, a city of strip malls and highways, Houston is not particularly pretty. But it is affordable (or, at least, it was). Immigrants flocked to Houston for opportunity and the ease of being in a place where they could find others like them. Now the fourth-largest city in the United States, in recent years Houston has been named the most diverse in the country. For my parents, who moved there in 1973, the feeling of belonging grew as more and more South Asian, and specifically Gujarati, immigrants arrived in the following decades. The city expanded rapidly during this period. Despite never having moved, I went to five different schools across my childhood due to the booming population. If I had graduated one year later, it would have been six.

Each year, my class became more diverse. By the time I got to high school, my circle of friends felt like a veritable melting pot—immigrants themselves or kids of immigrants, like me, from all over the world: Mexico, Vietnam, Ecuador, Ghana, Pakistan, the Caribbean, and so on. Sometimes before school we'd walk across the street to the *panadería* to buy *conchas* for breakfast, and afterward we'd go down the road for cheap Indian buffet in what is now officially named the Mahatma Gandhi District. Later, many years after I graduated, my high school was featured in the show *Anthony Bourdain: Parts Unknown*. In the episode, Bourdain observes a class for students learning English as a second language. My school is now home to the largest immigrant student population in the Houston Independent School District.

But another side of Houston is not so welcoming to immigrants. In 1984, the Corrections Corporation of America built its first private prison, the Houston Processing Center, an immigrant detention center in the northeast part of the city. Its opening began a partnership between the federal government and private prison companies that has endured for decades. As the city grew, so did the immigrant detention capacity and the tools the federal government used for targeting immigrants. I started to get a sense of these changes when a close friend disclosed their undocumented status to me in high school and I became worried about what could happen if they were to be arrested. After we graduated in 1999, our school, with a majority Latinx student body, went on to start a group to support "Dreamers," or undocumented youths.

Later, in 2008, Harris County (where Houston is located) became the first county in the United States to pilot Secure Communities, a fingerprint database program that skyrocketed deportations under the Obama administration, earning him the moniker "deporter-in-chief." Prisons, jails, and detention centers now surround the city. Today, there is capacity to detain roughly 4,000 immigrants at any given time at four jails and detention centers within a seventy-five-mile radius of downtown Houston. Harris County has the second-highest rate of ICE arrests in the country, and the Harris County Jail continues to collaborate with ICE to target immigrants for deportation. Like other large urban jails, such as Cook County Jail in Chicago or Rikers in New York City, it has a long record of abuse and deaths in custody. Twenty-seven people died while incarcerated at the Harris County Jail in 2022 alone.

The immigrant detention archipelago in and around Houston is substantial, but not unique. Across the country, local law enforcement agencies and private prison companies collaborate with ICE to arrest, detain, and deport immigrants. Detention numbers have fluctuated during the pandemic, but on average ICE maintains a capacity of 34,000 immigrant detention beds and detains hundreds of thousands of immigrants over the course of each year. The people filling these beds range from undocumented immigrants to people seeking asylum to visa holders to legal permanent residents. Detention takes a terrible human toll on those in its grip. Immigrants in jails and detention centers are routinely denied medical and mental health care, lack access to the outdoors and nutritious food, and face abuse, including sexual assault, and retaliation by prison guards. To cut costs, immigrant detention functions on the exploited labor of those incarcerated, who often get paid only a dollar a day to keep the system running. ICE has national detention standards regulating conditions of confinement, but they are not codified in law; therefore, the standards serve as mere recommendations. All detention is essentially indefinite. There is no sentence. Immigrants are waiting either to have a hearing before a judge or to be deported and can sometimes spend years locked up.

When arguing against immigrant detention, advocates often focus on this point: immigrants are not serving a sentence for a crime. But the argument misses the ways that the immigration enforcement system, or more accurately the deportation system, relies on incarceration to function. In the immigration context, prisons and jails are not only a site of punishment in the name of compliance and deterrence; they have been key drivers of the rise in deportations. A recent study found that immigrants are 2.3 times more likely to be arrested in counties with a detention capacity of more than fifty people. In counties with a detention capacity of more than 850, the likelihood of arrest went up by a factor of 6.4.[2] The expanding infrastructure of detention created the conditions for more people to be deported.

—

As an undergrad at the University of Texas at Austin, my understanding of the prison industrial complex and its interconnections sharpened during events ranging from anti–death penalty protests at the Texas State Capitol to forums on the targeting of Muslims in the United States after the September 11 attacks. I started organizing on campus with a group advocating for university divestment from the private prison industry. In 2003, in my final semester, I accepted a position as an organizer with Grassroots Leadership, a southern-based nonprofit that had been leading the campaign against private prisons. My job involved organizing students nationally around the campaign, but stopping prison expansion in Texas also became a priority.

After I started the job, it soon became clear that a post-9/11 prison boom was taking place. The Department of Homeland Security had just been created, and the border was a key site of expansion. Private prison companies began seeking out rural counties to finance new prisons on speculation. It was an "if you build it, they will come" mentality—and it worked. The number of people being locked up for immigration infractions skyrocketed. In 2004, immigration crimes became the number one offense in the federal courts, and immigration-related imprisonment only continued to increase from there. The prevailing narrative explains that the growth of mass incarceration made immigrants a target, which is absolutely true—this is one of the core arguments of this book. But the converse is also true: the federal government's more punitive approach to immigration also amplified the prison and jail system in the United States.

In response to the increasing number of immigrants being prosecuted, the Federal Bureau of Prisons created separate immigrant prisons with fewer services like medical care and reentry programs, since people held in them would be deported after their sentence was complete. It was in one of these prisons that Jesse Dean spent the last years of his life. The federal government also financed local jail expansions across the country to solve its need for more pretrial detention capacity as Congress passed more tough-on-crime legislation. County jails expanded and found a regular source of revenue in detaining immigrants, creating a symbiotic relationship between federal agencies and local governments. An entire prison and jail economy developed, making the demand to reduce mass incarceration that much more difficult.

—

In April 2003, a month or so before I graduated from college and started my job at Grassroots Leadership, I traveled to New Orleans for the Critical Resistance South conference. Critical Resistance had been formed in late nineties in California by Angela Davis, Ruth Wilson Gilmore, and others to promote an abolitionist vision. The conference was an opportunity to meet my soon-to-be coworkers and immerse myself in the movement. Little did I know that it would fundamentally change the way I understood the world.

It was at Critical Resistance South that I first learned about prison abolition. Prisons had expanded rapidly in the decades prior, but this shift did not make us safer. While crime panics focus on random acts of violence, people are much more likely to be murdered or raped by someone they know. People believe that prisons and police protect them from violent acts like rape and murder, but these crimes are largely unreported or go unsolved. Most people in prison are poor and working class. They are also disproportionately people of color. Black people are incarcerated at a rate six times that of white people.[3]

Opportunities for steady income and housing are few and far between for people released from prison, and many end up back in the system.

Prisons did nothing to help society. They didn't prevent harm; they only caused more of it. What purpose did they serve? Why did they keep expanding? The framework of abolition and the questions it posed helped me make sense of the senseless. The Iraq War had started two weeks before I attended the Critical Resistance conference. So many of us who had marched in the streets and watched millions of people come out in opposition to the war across the world felt utterly defeated when the war began. Angela Davis saw the connections and addressed the conference attendees on opening night: "Any movement to stop the militarization and lock-down of our communities here at home must be linked to an international movement to stop US military aggression abroad." She urged us to imagine another way, insisting that "we must demand options for our communities other than joining the military or going to prison."[4] Abolition isn't just about what we don't want. Abolition is about the world we want to create.

Prisons are violence. That was always clear to me. But it wasn't until I started organizing around federal policy at Detention Watch Network in 2009, when Barack Obama had just taken office, that I began to better understand the nature of the abolitionist struggle—its arguments, its vision, and its practice. Abolition became a critical lens for our work at DWN and a theory of change. The Obama administration set out to reform the detention system early on, and in the process it engaged with advocates to consider what reforms would be best to pursue. We raised concerns about conditions and encouraged alternatives to detention. The administration attempted to address these issues, but in the end detention expanded, and deportations went through the roof. In response to the terrible conditions in detention centers, the Obama administration started contracting for even more private prison capacity, since the companies were willing to design facilities that ostensibly met their standards. During those years, private prisons went from operating less than half of the detention system to making up 70 percent of its capacity. And implementing alternatives to detention only widened the net of government surveillance. ICE started putting people on electronic monitoring who would otherwise never have been detained. Detention continued to increase, and now ICE had another tool at its disposal for keeping track of people. The reforms only served to make the machinery larger.

Abolition was more than just a vision. It helped us determine which reforms would further dismantle the system and which ones would only serve to fortify it. Once DWN adopted a detention abolition vision, our strategies and tactics became sharper. Our approach shifted from a focus on conditions and alternatives to an emphasis on defunding and closing detention centers, aligning with abolitionist demands. A decade later, we finally started to win our campaigns to end immigrant detention contracts, something that had never happened before we had taken the position of abolition.

—

Immigration discourse in the United States is dominated by the idea of the "good immigrant" versus the "bad immigrant." Good immigrants are usually accepted based on their proximity to whiteness and ability to supply certain types of labor. Bad immigrants are seen as a drain on government resources (often labeled a "public charge") and as diluting a traditional, albeit evolving, American identity. "Bad immigrant" has become synonymous with the term "illegal alien" and the view that immigrants are breaking the law merely with their presence on US soil. Who falls into which category is largely dependent on the economic and political conditions of the time, but race is an unequivocal factor. Moreover, the bad immigrant narrative reinforces the view that immigration itself is a public safety issue and that immigrants breed lawlessness, fueling xenophobic attitudes. It also serves to pit immigrant communities and other communities of color against each other.

To secure legalization for the millions of undocumented people living in the United States, the mainstream immigrant rights movement has fully endorsed the narrative of the good immigrant versus the bad immigrant. "We are not criminals, we are workers" remains a common refrain at immigrant rights action and rallies. It draws an immediate line between those who are deserving of citizenship and those who are not. Immigration reform advocates often portray immigrants as being relatively innocent and more productive than other working-class people and communities of color in the United States. Many organizations, for example, have elevated research pointing out how immigrants commit fewer crimes than citizens, without fully understanding the anti-Black racism that underlies such comparisons. This framing has not only hurt our ability to challenge racist and xenophobic immigration laws and policies, but it has also furthered division between the immigrant rights and racial justice movements.

This book aims to disrupt the notion that merely severing the ties between the criminal legal system and immigration system will result in justice for immigrants. As you will read in the coming pages, these systems are fully intertwined. The justifications used to target immigrants are based on the same long-standing beliefs that have criminalized other marginalized groups for decades. By addressing this relationship and embracing abolition, immigrant justice activists have been able to limit detention and the pipeline to deportation. As we continue to tackle the harsh political climate immigrants and people of color face, this book provides an anatomy of the last forty years of immigrant incarceration, an analysis of the successes and failures of the immigrant rights movement to come to grips with increasing criminalization, and strategies for dismantling both systems.

Part I of the book explores the history of the immigration enforcement system through a lens of mass incarceration. The first chapter tracks the growth of immigrant detention and its relationship to the US prison and jail boom from the early 1980s to after 9/11. Immigrant detention does not exist in a vacuum, and understanding where the American obsession with punishment and incarceration came from can help us determine how to undo mass incarceration and mass detention. Specifically, I lay out the ways that anti-Black racism, the drug war, and national security frameworks shaped immigration policy and subsequent detention expansion.

Chapter 2 covers the myriad ways that the Obama administration augmented the criminalization of immigrants, including the implementation of a range of ICE-police agreements, the consolidation of an increasingly privatized detention system, and the mistreatment of families arriving at the border in 2014, a precursor to Trump's family separation policy. It reveals how, despite early indications of an overhaul of the immigrant detention system into something "civil," his administration's reforms to immigrant detention were largely cosmetic. And the adjustments to immigration enforcement only served to make the system more efficient. The results were some of the highest detention and formal deportation numbers we have ever seen.

In recent years, the manufactured image of crisis at the border has sucked up all the oxygen on policy decisions about immigration and solidified deterrence as the overriding bipartisan agenda. Chapter 3 explains how a moral panic, in which immigrants are viewed as undesirable and an inherent threat, led to increasing prosecutions for unlawful entry and reentry at the US-Mexico border. The focus on deterrence and additional funding for border militarization have made the act of crossing the border one of the most prosecuted federal crimes, resulting in the growth of immigrant incarceration in the federal prison system (separate from and in addition to immigrant detention).

In part II, I turn to the immigrant rights movement and its evolution over the last twenty years. Chapter 4 examines the tensions within the movement over comprehensive immigration reform and the trade-offs on securing citizenship for more enforcement, specifically focused on the border. It shows how the Obama administration's focus on criminalization and the growing Black Lives Matter movement sharpened

immigrant justice organizing, leading to a reduction in mass deportations of immigrants currently living in the United States.

Chapter 5 addresses the role that money plays in immigrant
detention policy decisions and the campaigns and tactics that have
been employed over the years to address it, including an overemphasis
on private prisons. I also look at how the demand to defund ICE and
Customs and Border Protection emerged as an important counter to
the comprehensive immigration reform effort in DC and prevented
Trump's deportation agenda from reaching the heights he promised
on the campaign trail.

Local organizing has played a critical role in shifting federal policy and the overall debate on immigrant detention. Chapter 6 focuses
on the successes and challenges of "site fights," campaigns that aim
to close a specific detention center or prevent the opening of a new
one. I share case studies of various campaigns at the county, state, and
regional level that have employed multiple tactics among broad coa-
litions working in tandem with people in detention. Because of these
efforts (and the shifting terrain during the pandemic), immigrant
detention finally began to shrink for the first time in forty years.

Part III looks at what's on the horizon for the immigrant justice
movement and how we might approach organizing given the challenges ahead. Chapter 7 offers a critique of the reformist approach and
provides abolitionist steps, or "nonreformist reforms," that can help
us get closer to detention abolition. Chapter 8 makes the case for why
it is long past time for the immigrant justice movement to embrace
abolitionist frameworks to become more interconnected, accountable, and effective. I reflect on how divisions between movements
have limited our progress toward decarceration and why an intersectional approach will be critical to achieving racial and migrant justice.

—

After I started working at Detention Watch Network, a friend from
my previous organizing days said to me, "Silky, you were the criminal
justice person, but now you're the immigrant rights person. Why did

you decide to shift?" The cliché about being a hyphenated American is that it is hard to be your full self in whatever space you're in, and you often end up feeling out of place. Being a prison abolitionist in the immigrant rights movement has at times felt this way. I get the impression that the people I'm working with are missing a big piece of the puzzle—that if only they could zoom out and expand their worldview, they'd understand things better. I can't remember what my response to my friend was when they asked me that question, but I remember thinking to myself, Why can't I be both?

The title of this book, *Unbuild Walls*, references a quote from Ursula K. Le Guin's 1974 sci-fi classic *The Dispossessed*. In the story, the "walls" are both the physical wall that exists between the two societies and the invisible walls we put up that constrain us and prevent human connection. This book is about breaking down the literal prison, jail, and detention center walls as well as the border walls, whether tangible, imaginary, or digital. But it is also about unbuilding the walls between our movements for social change. These walls are often intentional; we are fighting for a specific cause and must make that specific case. Inadvertently, the divisions and lack of shared analysis because of these walls have resulted in harm to other causes and movements. Abolition helps us better understand that the struggle for immigrant justice is also a fight for racial, gender, and economic justice. By embracing abolition, maybe we can finally begin to bring the walls down.

PART I

Immigration in the Era of Mass Incarceration

CHAPTER 1

The US Prison Boom and the Growth of Immigrant Detention

The "nation of immigrants" incarcerates more immigrants than anywhere else in the world. Major milestones dot the history of the contemporary immigrant detention system in the United States. In 1980, when detaining immigrants was a rare practice, the arrival of Cuban and Haitian refugees by boat during the Cold War led to the birth of the modern system with the opening of the Krome Detention Center in south Florida. Later, during the height of the war on drugs, mandatory detention became law, stripping certain immigrants of due process rights. In 1996, the passage of two draconian immigration bills under president Bill Clinton expanded the grounds for deportation and doubled the existing detention capacity. But it was 9/11 that made immigrants an unequivocal target of the government in the name of protecting the "homeland," after which billions of dollars were funneled into the deportation machinery. In recent memory, Trump's wholesale attack on immigration led to a considerable expansion of the system, reaching a peak of half a million people detained in 2019.

But beneath these common points of departure lies another aspect of immigrant detention's history: the rise in mass incarceration. In

1970, the United States incarcerated less than two hundred thousand people; three decades later, that number had risen to over two million. The prison boom that took place over the last half-century is central to the story of immigrant detention in the United States. Critical Resistance defines the prison industrial complex (PIC) as "the overlapping interests of government and industry that use surveillance, policing, and imprisonment as solutions to economic, social, and political problems." As the PIC was fortified through various developments, including increased funding for law enforcement, harsher sentencing laws at the state and federal levels, and the promise of jobs and revenue derived from a growing prison economy, the response to unnaturalized immigrants living in the United States and those arriving at our borders increasingly took on a carceral logic. Since the 1980s, a combination of economic restructuring and increasing tough-on-crime policies have produced devastating results: the highest rates of incarceration in the world and the greatest number of deportations in US history.

In my experience organizing against immigrant detention, there is a tendency among advocates and politicians to acknowledge the problems with the system without questioning how the United States came to have the world's largest detention infrastructure. Many will boil it down to a simple product of racism and xenophobia. Others will focus on the profit motives. While these factors are certainly salient, what is often missing is a more critical perspective on the role of the US government in the PIC. In recent years, the Trump administration's promotion of white supremacy has generated interest in examining the roots of criminalization and deportation. Yet in this process of discovery, there is a risk of taking the wrong lessons from history. Certain narratives give the impression that nothing has changed, which can fuel passivity and make us feel like there is little we can do to make things better. But in reality, mass incarceration and mass immigrant detention are recent developments, and learning about their expansion over time helps us better understand how these systems might be undone.

In this chapter, I track the growth of the modern immigrant detention system through key moments in US history. I start in the 1960s, when a backlash against social movements and civil rights gains triggered an acute and misguided focus on the problem of crime. This development coincided with a watershed in immigration policy, when the racist national-origins quota system was terminated. The United States opened its door to some immigrants, but simultaneously limited migration from Mexico for the first time. This pattern of extending rights and opportunities to certain immigrants while tightening restrictions on others continued for more than two decades. The idea behind it was an old one: to support the "good" immigrants while keeping out the "bad" ones. In the 1980s, the combined circumstance of prison overcrowding and the arrival of Cold War–era refugees precipitated the initial transition of Immigration and Naturalization Service (INS) into a mass jail operator. This turn of events set the stage for the normalization of detention during the following decade when, amid the culture wars and influence of the New Right, immigrants became a central target in the war on crime. The rise of neoliberalism remade immigration as well as economies in the United States and around the world; meanwhile, the prison industrial complex grew to levels never seen before. It was in this context that the attacks on September 11, 2001, took place, creating the political will for expanding the detention and deportation machinery and restructuring it into the system we have today.

The Hart-Celler Act and the Dawn of the War on Crime

The 1960s proved to be a pivotal decade for changes to both the criminal legal system and immigration system. Amid civil rights protests and political unrest, concerns about rising crime were harnessed to a conservative political agenda. Barry Goldwater, Arizona senator and Republican nominee for president in 1964, stoked fears about the deterioration of law and order in his bid against president Lyndon B. Johnson.

Goldwater lost, but the focus on crime prevailed. Even though Johnson advanced civil rights and launched social welfare programs as part of his "war on poverty," he gave credence to the racist belief that crime was in part a result of the "breakdown of the Negro family structure."[1] In response to the right-wing moral panics over political uprisings, he "ushered in a new era of American law enforcement," which came to be known as the war on crime.[2] Johnson would go on to sign legislation to provide more funding for police and establish a crime commission later that year. Prior to leaving office, he created the Law Enforcement Assistance Administration, which furthered the federal government's role in building up state and local law enforcement to combat crime. In the wake of civil rights progress and the end of the Jim Crow era, where explicit and outward white supremacy had been inscribed into law, as Michelle Alexander notes, crime became a label through which we could "engage in all the practices we supposedly left behind."[3] Eventually, the war on crime would change the nature of the federal government's approach to immigration control.

The advancement of civil rights also played a role in the immigration debate. The US restrictionist policy on immigration dating back to the 1920s allowed some Europeans to migrate, but banned almost everyone else from the Eastern Hemisphere. As a result, the foreign-born population in the United States at the time was barely 5 percent. After World War II, this policy began to be perceived as outdated due to its racist nature, and during the civil rights movement an effort toward immigration reform progressed. These conditions led to the passage of the Hart-Celler Act of 1965, a revision of the Immigration and Nationality Act. The new legislation eliminated the national-origins quota that barred immigration from non-European countries, opening up migration for Eastern and Southern Europe in addition to Africa, Asia, and Latin America. Immigration quotas remained, but now they would be applied universally, and there were no limits on visas for family members. While lawmakers said that it would have little impact on the "ethnic mix of this country," the Hart-

Celler Act and its inclusions and exclusions fundamentally changed the demographics and the political landscape of the United States.[4]

The 1965 law ended discrimination in immigration policies based on "race, national origin, sex, place of birth, or place of residence." While it opened up migration from the Eastern Hemisphere, it introduced quotas—for the first time—for migrants in the Western Hemisphere. Ignoring the economic drivers of migration and citing "fairness" as the reason for its inclusion, the federal government capped visas at 120,000 for the entire region; for Mexicans, the quota was later limited to 20,000.[5] The previous year, the government had ended the exploitative Bracero Program, a decades-long policy that encouraged Mexican workers to come to the United States for short periods to address labor shortages. The restriction on the number of visas due to Hart-Celler coupled with the end of the Bracero Program in 1964 resulted in an unprecedented rise of unauthorized migration. At the time, some 200,000 Mexicans were coming to the United States for work annually. Now the first 20,000 immigrants from Mexico could be issued visas, but the 20,001st immigrant would not be; if they had to cross for work, they would be considered illegal.[6] Immigration-related apprehensions increased rapidly each year after the law passed, from 44,000 arrests in 1964 to over a million in 1977.[7] While the law is often perceived as a watershed moment for supporting immigration, it made Mexicans a target for deportation and situated "the US-Mexico border as the theatre of an enforcement 'crisis.'"[8]

In line with the narrative of good immigrant versus bad immigrant, another framework emerged in the 1960s that further divided communities of color in the United States. The model minority myth, which positions Asian Americans as superior to members of other marginalized communities due to their presumed education and submissiveness, has persisted for decades. Its framing intentionally erases the history, varied experiences, political agency, and class backgrounds of Asian immigrant communities. After all, some of the first laws restricting immigration, the Page Act of 1875 and the Chinese

Exclusion Act of 1882, were bans on Asian migrants. Nonetheless, while it may feel dated, the model minority myth continues to undergird race discourse in the United States. By emphasizing a model minority, it automatically implies a non-model minority, a group of people of color who are undesirable (most often Black people but also those who are criminalized or perceived as unproductive, including people with disabilities or illness and members of lower classes).

Preference categories in the Hart-Celler Act determined that people who did not have family already residing in the United States would require certain skills or education in order to be allowed to migrate. As historian Mae Ngai explains, "Political instability and lack of opportunities for professional advancement in many Asian countries . . . encouraged those of the professional and technical classes to emigrate." After they arrived, Asian immigrants sponsored their family members (what conservatives refer to as "chain migration"), which then often "replicated the class composition" of the first generation, advancing the myth.[9]

This change to immigration law in 1965 is central to my family's immigration story. My father came to the United States in 1968 for graduate school, and a few years later he sponsored my mother. Over the years, they would both go on to apply to bring their many siblings and their respective spouses and children along with them. It took time. My siblings and I often felt like interlopers when we traveled to India, the rare kids in the family who had been born in the United States, who didn't speak the language as well or know the appropriate ways to show respect. But then, by the nineties, many of our aunts, uncles, and cousins had migrated to join us. Family that once had felt far away was now within reach. As a result of Hart-Celler, the Asian American population grew from less than 1.2 million in 1965 to over 22 million in 2019. But even now, Asian Americans comprise less than 6 percent of the US population.[10]

While the civil rights era advanced the ability for Asians to migrate, the heightened focus on crime starting in the 1960s often served to pit communities of color against each other. Despite gains to civil rights,

Black communities continued to be positioned as a problem in the eyes of the American public. Media highlighted the successes of Asian Americans in comparison to African Americans and the lack of "delinquency" in Asian communities. An article from *U.S. News & World Report* from 1966 reported, "Visit 'Chinatown U.S.A' and you'll find an important racial minority pulling itself up from hardship and discrimination to become a model of self-respect and achievement in today's America." It goes on to focus on crime specifically: "In crime-ridden cities, Chinese districts turn up as islands of peace and stability."[11] The singling out of Asian Americans as superior not only promoted the model minority and good immigrant stereotypes, but advanced anti-Black racism.

In 1968, presidential candidate Richard Nixon employed the "southern strategy" to win: he galvanized white Democrats in the South to shift to the Republican Party, utilizing post–civil rights tensions and increasing support for tough-on-crime policies, including a call for a war on drugs. Nixon's domestic policy adviser John Ehrlichman later admitted that the war on drugs was a political tool used to discredit antiwar activists and Black communities: "By getting the public to associate the hippies with marijuana and blacks with heroin, and then criminalizing both heavily, we could disrupt those communities."[12]

The focus on drugs also fomented tensions at the border. In 1969, Nixon implemented Operation Intercept, ordering border agents to stop and search all northbound vehicles from Mexico for marijuana, immobilizing the economies of border towns from Texas to California in the process. A drug enforcement agent stationed in Mexico, Joe Arpaio, helped develop the plan, which served to further the idea that all Mexicans were smuggling drugs and therefore needed to be surveilled.[13] Decades later, in the early 2000s, Arpaio would become a leader of the anti-immigrant movement as the sheriff of Maricopa County, Arizona.

As a result of restrictions on Mexican migration through Hart-Celler and the beginning of the war on drugs, media began to stoke concerns about "illegal" immigration, giving rise to the idea of a

"Latino threat."[14] The passage of the Rockefeller Drug Laws in New York in 1973 increased prison time for a drug offense, including, in some cases, lifetime sentences. Other states soon passed similar laws. From 1970 to 1980, the US prison population grew from less than 200,000 people behind bars to 315,000—a 60 percent increase.[15] While considerable, the sharp rise would be far outpaced by what was to come in the following two decades.

The Birth of the Modern Immigrant Detention System

Immigrant detention was a rare practice from 1954, when the federal government stopped detaining immigrants at Ellis Island, through the 1970s. Though some egregious cases existed, for the most part, if someone was detained, it was usually only for a day or two. Law enforcement agents would then release immigrants on parole while they went through immigration proceedings. In the 1980s, that started to change. While president Ronald Reagan's rhetoric on immigration remained largely supportive, his administration's policy toward people seeking asylum was anything but. The war on drugs and the crime panics of the period transformed the prison and jail system, leading to prison overcrowding. As a result, the federal government opened new detention centers and started passing laws to support its agenda of mass immigrant detention.

In 1980, Congress passed the Refugee Act, adopting international conventions around refugee and asylum admissions, which were ostensibly "rooted in principles of humanitarianism and objectivity."[16] It was still the era of the Cold War, and the US government outwardly supported refugees, especially those who were leaving communist countries, such as Cuban and Vietnamese people. However Haitian migrants fleeing a US-backed dictatorship were almost universally denied asylum. The federal government labeled them "economic migrants" undeserving of relief, and developed a plan for the INS to start using federal prisons to process and detain Haitians.[17]

A month after the Refugee Act's passage, the Mariel Boatlift began, a seven-month period named after Cuba's Mariel Harbor in which approximately 125,000 Cubans and 25,000 Haitians arrived on the shores of Florida. In response to the arrivals, the government erected shelters at several military bases across the country to detain immigrants. One of these locations outside Miami, the Krome Avenue Detention Center, eventually became a permanent detention center that is still in operation today.

Anti-Black racism drove the response to the arrival of Cubans and Haitians during this period. The Mariel Cubans were darker and more working class than the Cubans who had previously migrated. As a portion of those arriving had at some point been incarcerated in Cuba (nearly 20,000, according to some sources, including some who had been criminalized for sex work and for being queer and transgender), the media and elected officials played up Cold War tensions to amplify claims that Fidel Castro was casting off "criminal aliens" to the United States, creating an "illegal immigration crisis."[18] Because of the political conditions of the time and the racialized labels given to the arriving migrants, the Mariel Boatlift and the increasing number of Haitians who arrived by boat to seek asylum are considered the main catalysts of the system of mass detention we have today.

Although Krome was meant to be a temporary detention site, in 1981, the Reagan administration issued a directive to INS to indefinitely detain Haitians, making Krome a permanent detention center. The facility quickly became overcrowded, and conditions at Krome were abysmal, including many health and sanitary code violations.[19] Yet resistance inside prisons has existed as long as prisons have, and the situation was no different with immigrant detention. Haitian migrants locked up at Krome went on multiple hunger strikes in 1981 and around Christmas caught the attention of national Black leaders, including Reverend Jesse Jackson, who would later visit Krome and tour the facility.[20] Multiple antidiscrimination lawsuits were brought against the government for the systemic detention of Haitians. Anti-Black logics that conflated the

Mariel Cubans and Haitians with "bad immigrants" led to detention expansion.[21] Historian Brianna Nofil notes that in order "to make the optics less damning," given the racial implications of detaining only Black migrants, they started "detaining different groups of people alongside the Haitians."[22] As more immigrants arrived from Central America in the 1980s, fleeing US-backed counterinsurgent wars and violence, the Reagan administration increasingly saw detention as a tool for deterrence. The result was a de facto policy of mandatory detention that stimulated the warehousing of immigrants in detention. In 1983, the Reagan administration issued a Mass Immigration Emergency Plan that encouraged the building of more detention centers that would allow for a capacity to detain up to ten thousand at any time.[23]

Before his days as law-and-order mayor of New York City and Trump lackey, Rudolph Giuliani oversaw the expansion of detention during this period as associate attorney general. Since federal prisons were overcrowded, he started pushing for the Federal Bureau of Prisons (BOP) and INS to locate "contingency space" for future Mariel-type situations.[24] So began a competition among multiple sites from Oklahoma to Louisiana to Virginia to build a new INS detention center. In the end, Oakdale, Louisiana, won the battle. Located in Allen Parish, Oakdale had the highest levels of unemployment in the state after a nearby paper mill had shut down, and it was looking for new forms of revenue.[25] The mayor had pulled out all the stops to lure INS and Giuliani to the town, including garnering support from members of Congress. Senator J. Bennett Johnston told the mayor to let the Justice Department know "that if Oakdale cannot be considered, the appropriations for the Center will be taken out of the bill legislatively."[26] Giuliani noted that "the overwhelming community support at Oakdale means it is highly unlikely that lawsuits would be brought in an attempt to block our efforts."[27] After securing the contract, the mayor claimed, "The mood of this town changed from depression to euphoria," calling the new detention center a "recession-proof industry."[28] Oakdale was one of the first instances of immigrant detention being perceived as an economic development strategy, setting a new model that helped drive growth.

It was in this period that the first modern private prison company, Corrections Corporation of America (CCA), was founded. With prisons overcrowded, private prisons appealed to Reagan's free market and small government agenda as a way to build "at a faster rate with more innovation."[29] Private prisons were parasites ready to benefit from the government's growing desire to confine more people, and were not necessarily the central drivers of mass incarceration. After all, it was federal policy, resources, and practices that created the conditions for mass incarceration. The corporate face fit small government ideologies, but the government footed the bill. In the case of immigration enforcement, however, private prison entanglements created a unique and enduring relationship with the federal government. In January 1984, CCA converted the Olympic Motel in Houston, Texas, into a makeshift immigrant detention center by adding barbed wire around the perimeter and iron bars to the windows. At the same time, the company was building its first permanent private prison, the Houston Processing Center, an immigrant detention center.[30] That same year, Wackenhut Corrections Corporation was founded, seeing an opportunity to profit as federal immigrant detention capacity expanded. In 1987, Wackenhut opened its first prison, the Aurora Processing Center, outside Denver.[31] Wackenhut rebranded as the GEO Group in 2004, and CCA changed its name to CoreCivic in 2016. Both are still in operation today.

—

The war on drugs was in full swing by the 1980s. States passed harsher sentencing laws and built more prisons, while a bipartisan agenda in Congress further entrenched the federal government's role in the prison boom. Democratic senator and future president Joe Biden was a key champion in growing the federal response to drugs and crime, along with the notoriously racist Republican senator Strom Thurmond of South Carolina. Together they helped pass an omnibus package of bills referred to as the Comprehensive Crime Control Act of 1984, which eliminated federal parole and limited bail. As a result, people spent much more time in prisons and jails.[32] The system snowballed: federal prosecutors more aggressively pursued drug charges and, due to overcrowding, the new legislation facilitated the expansion of the US Marshals Service's pretrial jail system, which included both federally run jails and the use of county jails.[33] The *Los Angeles Times* reported a year after the law went into effect that it had led to a 32 percent rise in the prison population and that bail had been denied in more than 82 percent of cases.[34] While the act was not directly related to immigration, it did advance the belief that pretrial detention was necessary for preventing future crime, which is one of the main arguments for detaining immigrants with criminal histories.[35]

The arrival of the Mariel Cubans and Haitian migrants in 1980 also fed into the broader war-on-crime narratives in the United States at the time. Democratic governor of Florida (and later senator) Bob Graham labeled the Black and working-class migrants "illegal criminal aliens" and subsequently sued the federal government for overcrowding Florida's jails with immigrants.[36] In New York, Republican senator Alfonse D'Amato also attributed the overcrowding of prisons and jails to the increasing immigrant population. As a New Yorker, D'Amato promoted the idea that the problem of prison overcrowding was in part due to the increase in undocumented immigrants, as revealed by the Mariel crisis, and thus it was not merely an issue for the state of Florida, but in fact a national crisis. Both Graham and D'Amato were major proponents in Congress of passing harsher immigration laws that would grow the detention system significantly.

A key piece of legislation was what many now refer to as Reagan's amnesty bill, the Immigration Reform and Control Act (IRCA), passed in 1986. Despite his policy of detaining people seeking asylum, Reagan outwardly supported immigration by proclaiming, "We cannot erect a Berlin Wall across our southern border," alluding to Cold War–era dynamics.[37] The push for legalization of undocumented immigrants residing in the United States had been gaining steam, especially as the undocumented population grew after 1965. However, much like the Hart-Celler Act, IRCA has a complicated legacy. While it is often remembered as the bill that provided legal status to 2.7 million undocumented immigrants living in the United States—the last time such a bill was passed—other provisions in IRCA only reinforced harsher immigration crackdowns, including a sanction on employers who hired undocumented immigrants. IRCA also passed during the height of the war on crime, in which federal and state governments were increasingly managing overcrowded prisons and jails. Senator D'Amato of New York continued to stress the issue of prison overcrowding by claiming that "criminal aliens" were "savaging our society."[38] In response, lawmakers incorporated language in IRCA requiring that "in the case of an alien who is convicted of an offense which makes the alien subject to deportation . . . [officials may] begin any deportation proceeding as expeditiously as possible after the date of the conviction."[39] This change in law led the INS to increase coordination with local law enforcement and state corrections departments to deport immigrants.

Reagan and Congress began using the war on drugs to deport "criminal aliens" and make mandatory detention, which had received pushback in the courts, into law. The same year IRCA passed, Congress also passed the Anti-Drug Abuse Act (ADAA) of 1986. The law is notorious for creating a racially motivated sentencing disparity between possession of crack versus powder cocaine and expanding mandatory minimums, leading to longer stays in prison. A lesser-known provision authorized the use of "detainers," or immigration holds, that allowed INS to request that local law enforcement agencies hold immigrants until they were transferred to INS custody if arrested for a drug crime.[40]

Sociologist Patrisia Macías-Rojas underscores the role that prison overcrowding played in the shift toward harsher immigration policy: "Congress proposed deporting 'alien felons' swept up in the drug war as a way to free up more detention space and prison beds

for native-born Black and Latinx youth who would fill them."[41] Here
we see how the snowballing of the criminal legal system that brought
about the prison boom also furthered the mechanisms for detention
and deportation. The "solution" to prison overcrowding for the federal government became ramping up deportations.

In 1988, an update to the ADAA reinstated the federal death
penalty and expanded mandatory minimums. It also advanced the
Reaganite anti-immigrant agenda in several ways. The ADAA created the legal category "aggravated felony," which applied to certain
offenses. At the time, only a few crimes were considered an aggravated felony: murder, firearm trafficking, and drug trafficking. The
law required that an immigrant convicted of an aggravated felony be
subject to mandatory detention while in immigration proceedings
and prior to deportation. Mandatory detention meant that a judge
could not exercise discretion and that detention would be required
regardless of the individual's circumstances. Law professor Alina Das
notes that the "invention of the aggravated felony breathed new life
into the the longstanding frenzy over 'criminal aliens,'" leading to the
number of crimes classified as such expanding considerably over the
next decade.[42] The ADAA also created the Alien Criminal Apprehension Program and Institutional Removal Program, both predecessors
to programs that still exist today that enhance cooperation between
different law enforcement agencies to expedite detention and deportation. The legal category of aggravated felony and requirement for
mandatory detention expanded the tools that the federal government
could use for targeting immigrant communities, melding the criminal legal system and immigration system in startling new ways.

Neoliberalism and the Fear of the "Criminal Alien"

The Clinton era would prove to be the most consequential for the
growth of mass immigrant detention. The 1990s are often remembered
for the "culture wars," in which polarization deepened over certain

social and political issues, such as religion, sexuality, and abortion. Despite these divisions, Democrats and Republicans aligned in a number of areas, including crime, immigration, and the economy. Neoliberal policies that favored the so-called free-market approach and small government, like the North American Free Trade Agreement (NAFTA) and the rollback of welfare, furthered economic disparities in both the United States and Mexico, increasing tensions around immigration. Terrorist attacks during Clinton's first term instigated fears around national security and the need to defend ourselves against the "criminal alien." In response, Congress greatly expanded the legal framework for mandatory detention and deportation. And, perhaps most memorable in the history of mass incarceration, the passage of the Violent Crime Control and Law Enforcement Act of 1994 led to a considerable expansion of law enforcement and a surge in the prison boom. These heightened conditions—neoliberalism, anti-immigrant sentiment, tough-on-crime rhetoric, and national security initiatives—created the perfect storm for building up the prison industrial complex and deportation machine to levels never seen before.

Barely a month after Clinton's inauguration in 1993, a bomb exploded at the World Trade Center, killing six people and injuring another thousand. One of the men who planned the attack, Ramzi Yousef, had claimed asylum when arriving in the United States in 1992. After initially being detained at an overcrowded INS jail, he was released on parole while awaiting a hearing on his case. That Yousef had been let go by the INS incensed Clinton and other politicians.[43] Several months after the bombing, the Golden Venture, a cargo ship carrying nearly 300 Chinese immigrants, docked offshore in Queens, New York. Chinese arrivals had skyrocketed in the 1990s to nearly one hundred thousand per year. News media heavily covered the arrival of the Golden Venture, raising questions about how INS would respond. Clinton homed in on the smuggling networks that brought the Golden Venture to shore and issued a directive to "preempt, interdict, and deter alien smuggling." The memo also specified that migrants who enter with assistance from "criminal syndicates" shall be detained as a deterrent to smuggling "to ensure repatriation if asylum status is denied."[44] Even though both incidents took place in New York, Clinton emphasized the idea that securing the southern border would be critical to stopping these types of events from taking place: "The simple fact is that we must not and cannot surrender our borders to those who wish to exploit our history of compassion and justice.... We must say no to illegal immigration."[45]

INS decided to send 154 Chinese migrants who had arrived on the Golden Venture to York County Prison in Pennsylvania.[46] York County opened its prison in 1979 with a capacity to hold 200 people, but after the incarceration rate skyrocketed, the population in the prison reached almost 600 people a decade later. Anticipating federal use, the county expanded to an even greater capacity of 1,200. After INS began using the jail, York County officials noted that its "capability to house federal prisoners and INS detainees has been so successful that the County decided to further expand the prison facility." York continued its expansion spree in the late 1990s, becoming the largest INS detention center in the United States at the time.[47] Many of the immigrants who'd arrived aboard the Golden Venture spent years locked up at the York County Prison until Republican representative Bill Goodling pressured Clinton to release the fifty-three remaining immigrants in 1997, citing the hypocrisy of raising concerns over human rights in China while detaining Chinese asylum seekers.[48]

—

The market-based political ideology of neoliberalism, which encouraged reduced government spending, had been heavily promoted by Reagan but advanced considerably in the 1990s under Clinton. Despite opposition from labor unions, Clinton ratified NAFTA during his first year in office. NAFTA was touted as a tool to help curb "illegal immigration," yet the agreement instead spurred a major rise in Mexican migration to the United States. In NAFTA's first decade, "1.1 million small farmers—and 1.4 million other Mexicans dependent upon the farm sector—were driven out of work." The number of Mexican migrants arriving in the United States each year more than doubled by the end of Clinton's time in office, reaching 770,000 in 2000.[49] While the media and politicians instilled panic over the "border crisis," as activist and writer Harsha Walia reminds us, the "cumulative impacts of NAFTA led to a crisis of displacement."[50]

Economic restructuring and growing income inequality left many rural communities financially strained. As manufacturing was offshored and agribusiness made small farms obsolete, struggling rural towns viewed prison and jail expansion as a source of economic development. Antiprison advocate Tracy Huling notes the degree to which prison building became the economy of choice for these communities: "Between 1990 and 1999, 245 prisons were built in rural and small-town communities—with a prison opening somewhere in rural America every fifteen days."[51]

Neoliberal focus on individualism and human competition only served to increase the number of people considered disposable. As social inequality grew, waning support for public benefits left poor and working-class communities reeling. These changing conditions were showcased in California in the 1990s. Many Californians became unemployed after the end of the Cold War and subsequent downsizing of the defense industry. The beating of Rodney King by Los Angeles police resulted in both uprisings by communities of color and more police on the streets.[52] With the downturn in the economy and racial tensions at the forefront, immigrants became an easy scapegoat for the nativist right as well as for Democrats. In an op-ed in the *Los Angeles Times*, California Democratic senator Dianne Feinstein singled out immigrants with criminal convictions when she wrote that "rather than having our taxpayers underwrite the prison costs," the government should return them "to their home countries for imprisonment."[53]

In 1994, California passed two ballot initiatives that would advance both the war on crime and anti-immigrant policy. Proposition 184, or the three-strikes-and-you're-out law, imposed longer sentences

on people with repeat offenses, expanding the California prison population. California voters also approved Proposition 187, which would
have denied health care to undocumented immigrants and prevented
schools from letting them enroll. The initiative also focused on the
notion that immigrants commit crimes: "The [people of California]
have suffered and are suffering personal injury and damage caused by
the criminal conduct of illegal aliens in the state."[54] The proposition
passed in a landslide, but was challenged in the courts and days after
it passed was prevented from being fully implemented. Clinton came
out in opposition to Proposition 187 by proclaiming, "If you turn the
teachers and other educators into instruments of a sort of a state police
force, it's like bringing Big Brother into the schools."[55] However, he
would eventually agree to cutting other benefits. Two years later he
went on to sign the Personal Responsibility and Work Opportunity
Reconciliation Act, more commonly known as welfare reform. It drastically curtailed public benefits for poor and working-class people, in
addition to denying immigrants and anyone with a felony drug conviction access to welfare and certain federal medical benefits.[56] Providing
welfare became a proxy for aiding the "racially undeserving," and the
campaign against it relied on divisive anti-Black and anti-immigrant
discourse. Clinton was a true believer in the neoliberal hocus pocus
of competition and every man for himself, which drove not only his
economic policy but also his approach to crime and immigration.

The same year that California voters approved Propositions 184 and
187, Congress passed the Violent Crime Control and Law Enforcement
Act, otherwise known as the crime bill, which some consider "the most
extensive federal crime legislation ever passed."[57] Future president Joe
Biden continued his tough-on-crime agenda and championed the bill in
the Senate. The new law funded one hundred thousand more police officers, expanded the federal death penalty to an additional sixty criminal
offenses, and increased funding for prisons. The funding was partially
earmarked for states that enacted "truth-in-sentencing" laws, which prevented people from being granted parole. As with previous drug- and

crime-related legislation, the crime bill resulted in a ballooning of the prison system and included immigration provisions. Much of the framing around immigration restrictions focused on the "criminal alien," which became common vernacular that was often interchangeable with "illegal alien." Again, the provisions on immigration focused on boosted funding, expedited deportations, and greater coordination between federal and local law enforcement. These reforms to immigration policy in the crime bill further entrenched the fusion of the criminal legal system and the immigration enforcement system. Then came 1996.

For immigrant justice activists, the effects of the year 1996 linger like a perpetual dark cloud. Following a decade of laws that expanded the grounds for detention and deportation via the criminal legal system, the 1996 laws supersized the immigration enforcement system. Both the Antiterrorism and Effective Death Penalty Act (AEDPA) and the Illegal Immigration Reform and Immigrant Responsibility Act (IIRAIRA) were passed that year. Together they changed the paradigm on immigration to one that emphasized citizenship rather than residency and laid the legal foundation for the expansion of the deportation machine that emerged following 9/11. New York University law professor Nancy Morawetz describes the severity of the 1996 immigration laws, "Overnight, people who had formed their lives here—came here legally or had adjusted to legal status, were working here, building their families . . . suddenly, because of some conviction, weren't even allowed to go in front of a judge anymore. They were just fast-tracked to deportation."[58]

After the 1995 Oklahoma City bombing perpetrated by Timothy McVeigh, a white US military veteran, Clinton and Congress went into high gear to pass legislation to quell the country's fears about domestic terrorism. AEDPA has turned out to be one of the most harmful pieces of legislation passed in recent history. Its most notorious provision limits the use of habeas corpus, or the ability to appeal wrongful imprisonment. It also requires the Supreme Court to defer to state rulings, preventing the federal government from intervening when there are constitutional errors, even in capital punishment cases. On immigration, AEDPA greatly expanded the scope of what is considered an aggravated felony to a whole host of crimes, including misdemeanors with sentences as little as one year, down from the previous five-year threshold. Many crimes that were not technically felonies and would not be considered aggravated in the criminal context became aggravated felonies, including "bribery, counterfeiting or mutilating a passport, obstruction of justice, gambling offenses, and transportation for the purposes of [sex work]."[59] Upon signing AEDPA, Clinton said that it stood "as a tribute to the victims of terrorism and to the men and women in law enforcement who dedicate their lives to protecting all of us from the scourge of terrorist activity."[60] The singling out of law enforcement as being uniquely endangered by doing their jobs to protect citizens reinforced the idea that ensuring police safety is more essential than protecting civil liberties.

While AEDPA was another instance of bipartisan efforts in Congress to incorporate anti-immigrant provisions into crime-related legislation, IIRAIRA was a concerted Republican strategy to create an even harsher immigration system. Prior to its passage, legal permanent residents, or green card holders, were still able to make their case against being detained if they were convicted of an aggravated felony, but now they were required to be locked up while they went through immigration proceedings. The law applied retroactively, meaning that if you had committed a crime in the past and served your time, you could still be detained and deported. As the law expanded the scope of who could be targeted and imprisoned it effectively manufactured a growing number of "criminal aliens." IIRAIRA also took collaboration between law enforcement and INS one step further by creating the 287(g) program, which gave local police the authority to enforce immigration laws.

IIRAIRA made it much more difficult for immigrants to obtain legal status, ensuring that the undocumented immigrant population would grow. Rather than allowing immigrants to apply to adjust their status while in the United States, IIRAIRA introduced three- and ten-year bars, as they are commonly called. It required immigrants to "leave the United States to apply for their green card abroad, but as soon as they depart, they are immediately barred from reentering the country for a period of time"—three years for those who had been in the country without status for six months, ten years for those who had been in the United States for over a year without status.[61] The provisions resulted in many migrants being trapped in the United States, living without status out of fear that they would not be able to come back if they were to leave.

Combined, the 1996 laws normalized mandatory detention as a legitimate way to treat noncitizens. INS began pushing for more detention to manage deportations. In 1997, Doris Meissner, INS commissioner, explained to Congress, "We do very well on deporting those people who are in detention. It is very difficult and labor intensive to deport people who have orders of deportation who are not in detention. It's crucial. That's why we ask for it."[62] Meissner's quote shows how detention served to facilitate deportation. As capacity grew, so did deportations.

INS continued its expansion plan and, in 1998, opened the Batavia Detention Center near Buffalo, New York, far from the southern border, but where prisons were omnipresent. After the 1996 laws, the average daily population in detention more than doubled from 7,475 in 1995 to 15,447 in 1998.[63] In response to these shifts, in 1997, Detention Watch Network was founded by a group of legal service providers who afforded counsel to immigrants and who felt the immediate impact of the laws on their clients. Attempts were made by advocates to "fix '96" in the late nineties by rolling back some of the harsh provisions. And in president George W. Bush's first year in office, a growing effort toward another amnesty was also gaining steam. However, the events of September 11, 2001, stalled the reform attempts.

The Homeland Security State Takes Shape

It is difficult to fully comprehend the impact of the September 11th attacks on US institutions, culture, and social life. With almost no debate, the United States became a fortress state focused on limiting the rights of both citizens and immigrants in the name of national security. The "war on terror" permeated all facets of domestic law enforcement and resulted in deadly wars in Iraq and Afghanistan—invasions that took years to end and had generational impacts. In the wake of 9/11, every aspect of the existing immigration enforcement infrastructure expanded, from the number of immigration agents to immigrant detention capacity and miles of border wall. The legal framework for immigrant exclusion preceded the attacks, but 9/11 created the political and institutional will to build up the massive border enforcement and deportation apparatus we have today. While Islamophobia was nothing new in the national discourse, after 9/11 it became a core component of the federal approach to immigration. The implementation of the National Security Entry-Exit Registration System, which required men sixteen and older from twenty-five predominantly Muslim countries to register with the government, resulted in over 13,000 Muslim men being put into deportation proceedings.[64] Domestically, the war on terror became an extension of the war on crime.[65]

But, as previously noted, much of the groundwork for expanding the detention and deportation system had been laid by the time 9/11 happened. The detention capacity of INS and US Marshals Service (USMS) was overburdened because of harsher sentencing and an increase in policing. Months before the attack, attorney general John Ashcroft established the Office of the Federal Detention Trustee (OFDT). The goal of the OFDT was to strengthen detention operations and secure more bed space for INS and USMS. Its creation further strengthened the symbiotic relationship between the federal government and local counties for immigrant detention. The OFDT identified the need to "form strategic alliances with state and local governments and private industry to develop proactive 'results oriented' acquisition practices" and to use "long-term contracting vehicles to stabilize government costs."[66] To increase pretrial federal jail capacity, the federal government provided funding to certain counties to expand local jails and contracted with private prison companies. During the decade it existed, the OFDT expanded the federal jail system (pretrial criminal and immigrant detention) to an average daily population just shy of one hundred thousand people, which was roughly half the total number of people who were incarcerated in the United States in 1970.[67]

The growth of detention was aided by the establishment of the Department of Homeland Security (DHS) in 2002, which consolidated power across multiple federal agencies and normalized the idea that immigrants are a security threat. The INS, previously housed under the Justice Department, shifted to DHS and was split into three separate agencies: Immigration and Customs Enforcement (ICE), Customs and Border Protection (CBP), and Citizenship and Immigration Services (USCIS). Upon its creation in 2003, ICE adopted a strategic plan called Operation Endgame, which further solidified the relationship between national security and immigration. Its new mission became to "promote the public safety and national security by ensuring the departure from the United States of all removable aliens through the fair and effective enforcement of the nation's immigration laws."[68] Unlike INS, which existed to both enforce immigration law and process migrants through adjustment of their status, ICE's sole purpose is to arrest, detain, and deport immigrants.

While much of the post-9/11 discourse focused on combating terrorism, since the undocumented population had grown after NAFTA, Latinx immigrants were disproportionally impacted by the ramp-up of immigration enforcement under Bush. Wisconsin Republican representative Jim Sensenbrenner led legislative efforts to further restrict immigration and target immigrants living in the United States. The proposed legislation galvanized Latinx immigrant communities to protest in opposition, resulting in the largest immigration-related mass mobilizations in US history. But the protests did little to deter DHS's deportation agenda. Just weeks after the mass mobilizations on May Day 2006 in which millions came out for immigrant rights, ICE unleashed Operation Return to Sender, and "within a month, the operation swept away nearly 2,200 immigrants in raids across more than thirty states."[69] ICE conducted worksite raids throughout the Bush administration. One of the largest took place in 2008 at a meatpacking plant in Postville, Iowa, in which ICE agents detained some 400 immigrant workers. Of those arrested, 297 were charged with document fraud and sentenced to five months in prison before being deported.[70]

Prior to 9/11, private prison companies had been struggling. CCA was on the verge of bankruptcy and Wackenhut had been court ordered to shut down its youth jail in Jena, Louisiana, due to "animal-like" conditions of confinement.[71] The future of the private prison industry was in question. Then the events of 9/11 provided the windfall the industry needed to keep going. Steve Logan, CEO of Cornell Corrections, exposed the parasitic nature of the industry in a conference call with stakeholders later that fall: "What we are seeing is an increased scrutiny, a tightening up of the borders. . . . So I would say that's positive. And if anything, the federal system—that is already overburdened—is indicating to us that they need even more help as a result of 9/11. So that's a positive for our business."[72] The government shifting immigration into a "homeland security" paradigm proved to be quite lucrative for the prison industry. Companies began building facilities on speculation, anticipating growing demand from the federal government.

In addition to private companies, sheriff's departments also emerged as key beneficiaries of increased deportations and expansion of the carceral state. Many sheriffs and county commissioners entered into agreements with the federal government to rent out bed space in local county jails or to play intermediary between the federal government and private prison companies. While 287(g) agreements, which deputized local police to enforce immigration laws, had been codified in IIRAIRA, the first agreement didn't take effect until 2002, when the Bush administration began implementing it given the "new urgency" after 9/11."[73] Sheriffs are dubious entities among law enforcement agencies, as journalist Jessica Pishko points out: "Long tenures with limited oversight allow some to run their counties as small fiefdoms, subject to their own rules."[74] Joe Arpaio, who served as sheriff of Maricopa County, Arizona, for twenty-four years, is a prime example of how sheriffs use ICE–police collaboration programs to advance their anti-immigrant agendas. ICE entered into a 287(g) agreement with Maricopa County in 2007 and trained 160 deputies to enforce immigration law. Eventually, the county had the highest rates of apprehensions in the United States. Alessandra Solar, ACLU of Arizona executive director, explained, "The federal government gave Arpaio his power, and it turned him into a monster that terrorized our community for years."[75] Arpaio was notorious for detaining immigrants in a sweltering "tent city" detention complex, where they were required to wear pink underwear and cartoonish black-and-white-striped prison uniforms. The tent city had been constructed as a temporary solution to jail overcrowding in 1993, but endured for over twenty years.

Aided by Congress and increased federal funding for immigration enforcement, ICE continued its expansion spree throughout Bush's tenure. In 2005, the Bush administration announced an end to the practice of "catch and release," repeating something that elected officials periodically claim to do to show their toughness on immigration. The term can mean many different things in terms of policy. In this case, ICE contracted with CCA to open the Hutto Detention Center in Taylor, Texas, to detain immigrant parents with their children. The expansion of Hutto, which had a capacity for roughly five hundred people, signaled a new terrain for immigrant detention. Later, in 2008, the GEO Group (formerly Wackenhut) converted its shuttered youth jail in Jena, Louisiana, into an immigrant detention center, which is still open today.[76] Dozens of jails opened for immigrant detention after 9/11, growing the average daily population of detained immigrants from twenty thousand to thirty-two thousand during Bush's tenure.

Abolitionist Lessons

Contrary to popular thinking on the issue, the expansion of immigrant detention was not merely a xenophobic response to increasing undocumented immigration. It was a direct outgrowth of the rise in mass incarceration in the United States. While the 1960s were a moment of relative inclusivity, with the advancement of civil rights and the passage of the Hart-Celler Act opening the door to some immigrants, since then, a backlash to the shifting demographics has led to an exponential rise in incarceration and deportations. The tough-on-crime agenda of the 1980s and 1990s, employing racist logics and often working through economically challenged communities, permeated immigration discourse and policymaking throughout the period. As a result, the US government's mass deportation agenda started to extend the carceral state into new territory. This was not inevitable. In taking stock of how the United States came to have the largest detention infrastructure in the world, we can better explain the arbitrary and contingent nature of its existence.

Immigrant detention has often been described as particularly immoral and inexplicable because immigrants in custody are not serving a sentence for a crime. But when examining the growth of the system from the early 1980s, the fact that immigrants are not serving a sentence is almost beside the point. We know from studies of the PIC that prisons became a space for warehousing the undesirable. Rather than being purely a tool for compliance with the legal system or for ensuring deportation, immigrant detention functioned similarly to warehouse undesirable migrants. This dynamic became more pronounced as the prison boom took place. The arguments used to expand immigrant detention cemented xenophobic beliefs that migrants are undeserving of rights, and over time the law changed to support the belief. But immigrants are not unique in this regard; the same logic has been used to strip rights from Black, brown, Indigenous, and poor and working-class white communities in the United

States. While the story often told about "crimmigration" is that of a merger of the systems that should be disentangled, as laid out in this chapter, the systems have become so enmeshed that it has become impossible to think of them as separate. Immigrant detention is part of the broader carceral landscape in the United States, and thus abolition of immigrant detention must be seen as concurrent with the demand to abolish the prison industrial complex.

CHAPTER 2

Obama, Criminalization, and the Limits of Reform

Even as we are a nation of immigrants, we're also a nation of laws. Undocumented workers broke our immigration laws, and I believe that they must be held accountable— especially those who may be dangerous. That's why, over the past six years, deportations of criminals are up 80 percent. And that's why we're going to keep focusing enforcement resources on actual threats to our security. Felons, not families. Criminals, not children. Gang members, not a mom who's working hard to provide for her kids. We'll prioritize, just like law enforcement does every day.
—President Barack Obama, Address to the Nation
on Immigration, November 20, 2014

Many aspects of president Barack Obama's immigration policy are worth critiquing, but perhaps the most impactful—and one that helped set up what the Trump administration unleashed in the years following—was how he convinced the public that sorting immigrants into two groups, criminals and noncriminals, was a progressive reform. In fairness, this approach was also heavily promoted by well-resourced immigration advocacy organizations, but Obama fully realized and perfected it. While Clinton before him solidified the relationship between the criminal legal system and the immigration enforcement system, after nearly eight years of Bush's domestic war on terror, Obama said he would be different. He campaigned on the promise of hope, after all. He was going to help immigrants "get out of the shadows" by finally passing comprehensive immigration reform.[1] He was going to "crack down on employers abusing undocumented immigrants."[2] He was going to address the conditions that had led to numerous deaths in immigrant detention centers across the country.[3] But instead, by claiming to prioritize "felons, not families" for deportation, President Obama reinforced the idea that criminalizing and deporting certain immigrants was essential to fixing the "broken" immigration system.

By the end of Obama's tenure in office, over three million people had been detained and formally deported—more than under any other president.[4] It was also under Obama that prosecutions for immigration in the federal courts reached their highest levels before Trump took office (more on this in chapter 3). How did Obama, the bearer of hope and change, end up with one of the highest detention and formal deportation numbers in United States history? Many have pointed to Obama's desire to pass comprehensive immigration reform as a core reason. In an effort to secure legalization for undocumented immigrants, the Obama administration ramped up immigration enforcement to placate Republicans who criticized him for being soft on the issue. While this was certainly part of Obama's play, it was also clear, as with most Democrats, that he was fully invested in the war-on-crime approach to governing. Thus many of the reforms he proposed further legitimized the narrative of the good immigrant versus the bad immigrant and the use of detention and deportation as a "tool for public safety."

In response to outcries over mass worksite raids and reports of deaths in detention, DHS announced two major reforms to immigration enforcement during Obama's first year in office. The administration prioritized the nationwide implementation of Secure Communities, a database system that identified immigrants in local jails for deportation, which was touted to improve public safety by targeting "criminal aliens." By retreating from the mass raids of the Bush era and more effectively commandeering the vast existing network of police departments, sheriffs, county jails, and private prisons to arrest, detain, and deport immigrants, Obama made the system bigger and more effective. Turning to the massive penal apparatus in the United States, the largest in the world, drove the number of deportations higher and higher.

DHS also announced sweeping changes to the immigrant detention system to improve conditions and consider release for some "low risk" individuals. The detention reforms emphasized the need to move away from the punitive nature of immigrant detention in recognition of the fact that immigration proceedings are technically civil in nature. The administration responded by building new facilities with better conditions. Despite the insistence that detention was not punishment, the administration continued to argue that it was targeting only "dangerous criminals." As a result, the reforms under Obama served to expand and extend detention and deportation.

I started working as an organizer at DWN in 2009, shortly after Obama took office. While I had already embraced prison abolition as a vision, it wasn't until this time that I fully understood how essential it was to our strategy as a movement. DWN had joined the ICE-NGO working group that DHS had set up under Obama to push for administrative reforms. However, early on it became clear that ICE's goal was not to reduce the number of people in detention or deportation proceedings, but rather to create nicer cages and to justify the deportations taking place. The mystique around Obama made it even more difficult to challenge the reforms being put forth. Despite their claims of transparency and accountability, rules around the working group were dubious, with access often removed on a whim. Many advocates had bought into the hype and the supposed access to power afforded by having a seat at the table, failing to acknowledge that each reform ICE implemented served to either legitimize the existing system or expand tools to further criminalize immigrants. As the system grew amid reform efforts, it became clear to me that it wasn't enough to just call for the end of detention. We needed a way to discern which strategies would get us closer to abolition.

The story of Obama-era immigration enforcement policy is an important cautionary tale for the immigrant justice and prison abolition movements. Advocates and the Obama administration affirmed the idea that immigration was a "public safety" issue, reinforcing the narrative of immigrants as criminals. Our experience during the Obama years underlined for me the way that reformist reforms setting out to "improve" prison and detention actually serve to expand it. This is a critical lesson to carry forward that explains why we must redirect our movement energy to abolitionist and decarceral reforms that dismantle and defund the system rather than try to make it "more humane."

Early Promises of Reform

Prior to Obama's presidency, the immigrant detention system operated much like so-called black sites or clandestine jails. The detention system existed to isolate and disappear people, and it did that at a tremendous scale, with over 350 detention facilities, mostly county jails, in use. Little information was available about how to find immigrants who had disappeared into the system and were being transferred frequently between facilities. A Human Rights Watch report found that more than three hundred thousand transfers had taken place in 2008 alone.[5] At the time of Obama's election, DWN's online map of detention center locations had been the sole centralized resource for lawyers, journalists, and family members looking for clients or loved ones in detention. In response to the inability to locate people in detention, ICE created the Online Detainee Locator System in 2009. The ICE locator was one of the most significant improvements of the Obama administration. But all it did was inform people about where a person was located in detention. It didn't let people out of detention, reduce the scale of the system, or even improve detention conditions. It was a procedural, not substantive, reform.

In addition to the locator tool, ICE announced a set of reforms to the immigrant detention system in Obama's first year, some of which were received positively. Most welcome was the announcement that ICE would no longer detain children at the Hutto Detention Center in Texas, one of two family detention centers in the United States at the time. After a sustained three-year campaign against the practice by local organizers, attorneys, and national advocates, the end to family detention at Hutto gave the movement some of that hope Obama had promised on the campaign trail. But the jail was converted into a women's detention center, and there was no net reduction in immigrant detention.

In spring 2009, former Arizona governor and newly confirmed DHS secretary Janet Napolitano brought on prison reformer Dora Schriro as a special adviser to assess and review the immigrant detention system and develop a report on her findings. The two had previously worked together when Schriro was the director of the Department of Corrections for Arizona. Schriro, a licensed social worker, had a long history in state-level prison management. An unfavorable 2004 profile of her in the *Phoenix New Times* described her approach: "In Schriro's world, parolees are called 'clients,' not criminals. . . . She's selling ice cream sandwiches to prisoners, with profits going to victims' groups."[6] The weekly newspaper chided her for being too academic for prison management and described her as living in a "parallel universe." Schriro's reputation as a reformer made her an ideal candidate for reviewing the immigrant detention system, according to Napolitano, but in doing so, Schriro soon discovered that it served a different purpose than prisons did. The core framework for her eventual report focused on the distinction between the administrative purpose of immigrant detention and the punitive nature of criminal incarceration:

> As a matter of law, Immigration Detention is unlike Criminal Incarceration. Yet Immigration Detention and Criminal Incarceration detainees tend to be seen by the public as comparable, and both confined populations are typically managed in similar ways. Each group is ordinarily detained in secure facilities with hardened perimeters in remote locations at considerable distances from counsel and/or their communities.[7]

For Schriro, the fact that immigrant detention was a civil proceeding and not criminal punishment meant that the government should provide a higher standard of care for those in ICE custody. Despite her acknowledgment of the supposed divergent objectives between immigrant detention and criminal incarceration, she never questioned detaining immigrants for civil purposes. In the report, Schriro noted that "ICE operates the largest detention and supervised release program in the country." While not explicitly calling for a reduction in detention, throughout the report Schriro called attention to the fact that noncriminals were often detained, and she indicated that Secure Communities "has the potential to identify large volumes of aliens with low level convictions or no convictions,"[8] which could grow the system unnecessarily.

This idea—that immigrant detention was not the same as criminal incarceration—became the driving force behind the Obama-era detention reforms. Her recommendations focused on population management through risk assessment, expanding "alternatives to detention," improving conditions of confinement to create a "truly civil" system, and increasing oversight and data tracking. As a result, ICE created an Office of Detention Oversight to regularly inspect detention centers and investigate deaths of immigrants in ICE custody. Notably, even though Schriro differentiated the nature of the criminal and immigration systems, all her proposed reforms had been tried ad nauseam in the criminal legal system, and most had done little to reduce the number of people incarcerated in the criminal sphere.[9]

Advocates initially welcomed the detention reforms but stressed the need to reduce the government's reliance on immigrant detention. However, by the time the report was released in October 2009, Schriro had left her new post as the director of the ICE Office of Detention Policy and Planning and had moved on to lead New York City's Department of Corrections and oversee the massive jail complex on Rikers Island. Despite Schriro's departure, creating a different civil detention system remained the administration's publicly stated goal.

The Detention Bed Quota and the Federal Budget

Even if Schriro's recommendations had called for a reduction in detention, this was unlikely to happen for a few reasons. First, the implementation of Secure Communities meant that more people were being funneled into the system than ever before (as explained in the following section, "A Growing Deportation Dragnet"). Trying to reform a system while increasing the number of people in it undermined the very possibility of reform. The administration also hit a wrinkle in Obama's first year in office when senator Robert Byrd, a Democrat from West Virginia, incorporated language into the fiscal year 2010 appropriations bill that essentially functioned as a quota for detention beds. The language, which came to be known as the detention bed mandate, stated that the administration "shall maintain a level of not less than 33,400 detention beds." The bed quota, which was later raised to 34,000, would remain a feature of the federal budget for eight years, facilitating the expansion of the detention system. Byrd had a long history as a racist politician with former ties to the Ku Klux Klan. While he renounced his white supremacist origins and even voted against the Iraq War resolution in 2002, he was always staunch in his anti-immigrant agenda. He died in 2010.[10]

A former aide to Byrd shared that "the senator wanted to ensure that cost increases [to detention contracts] wouldn't lead ICE to fund fewer beds."[11] Democratic senator Richard Durbin of Illinois, someone many consider one of the Senate's immigrant rights champions, presented the goals of the detention bed mandate to the Appropriations Subcommittee on Homeland Security:

> No. 1, securing our borders and enforcing our immigration laws; No. 2, protecting the American people from terrorist threats and other vulnerabilities; No. 3, preparing and responding to all hazards, including natural disasters; No. 4, supporting our State, local, tribal and private sector partners in homeland security with resources and information; and finally, giving the Department the management tools it needs to succeed.[12]

The quota acted as an artificial floor, propping up the size of the detention system as part of the evolving "homeland security" paradigm.

Democrats put the bed quota in place, but Republicans became its defender. A battle between the Obama administration and Congress emerged regarding the relationship between bed numbers and immigration enforcement. In February 2013, right before a three-week period of sequestration in which the federal government required agency funding cuts, ICE released some immigrants from detention. Ironically, these cuts had been orchestrated by the Tea Party, a right-wing nativist movement. ICE director John Morton came under fire from Republicans after initially claiming a few hundred people had been released but later revealing that 2,228 immigrants had been freed from detention. Republican representative Bob Goodlatte of Virginia claimed that "the Administration is needlessly endangering American lives."[13] Obama's emphasis that they had been targeting only criminals for detention gave Republicans fodder for the attacks. The quota became a tool by which to measure whether the administration was doing enough to deport immigrants. Napolitano's response was, "All

I can say is, look, we're doing our very best to minimize the impacts of sequester. But there's only so much I can do. I'm supposed to have 34,000 detention beds for immigration. How do I pay for those?"[14] The sequestration episode revealed the arbitrary nature of detention and the role funding plays in decisions about how many people are detained.

"Civil" Detention and the Return of Family Detention

To address concerns from media and advocates that conditions in detention centers were leading to unnecessary deaths, the Obama administration concentrated on improving the national detention standards. Advocates pushed for better conditions that could ostensibly have an impact on the day-to-day lives of those detained. In 2013, for example, Jorge García-Mejia, age forty, and Elsa Guadalupe-Gonzalez, age twenty-four, both Guatemalan nationals, committed suicide within three days of each other at the Eloy Detention Center in Arizona, which was then the deadliest detention center in the country.[15] It was soon revealed that Eloy, operated by CCA, had not updated its standards and was still operating under previous standards that did not include updated suicide prevention protocols—or improvements to medical care, protections from sexual abuse, or access to family and counsel.[16] This incident underlines the inefficacy of efforts to improve detention standards: The existing detention standards didn't protect García-Mejia or Guadalupe-Gonzalez. Further, the focus on revising standards did nothing to diminish the size of the detention system itself. Facility inspections often gave a pass to detention centers, no matter how they were functioning. The fact is, the national detention standards are merely recommendations. They are not a real tool for accountability; immigrants can't enforce them in court. The way that standards work is actually antithetical to reducing immigration detention—instead, they lead to improved pretenses for detention, legitimizing the system.

ICE owned and operated only six of its detention centers at this point. All other facilities were subcontracted out to county jails and private prison companies. (See chapter 5 for details on the different kinds of contracts.) The central reform goal based on the Schriro report was to create a more civil detention system, which meant setting new standards. Improving standards at the many county jails where ICE rented bed space alongside local jailed populations proved to be quite difficult because of the numerous and varied actors running those jails. Private prisons designed exclusively to detain immigrants became even more attractive to the administration. For their part, the private companies were more willing to play ball and provide ostensibly better conditions for detention, such as outdoor recreation, which many county jails meant for short-term stays did not provide.

In 2010, ICE started to send out feelers to local governments to either build or acquire new bed space. The intended goal was to create a "civil detention system that is not penal in nature." The new detention centers would ideally be located near urban centers to reduce the number of transfers to remote communities and to afford more access to counsel. "Civil" was never really defined. ICE used vague language to market aspects of the new facilities like "softer construction techniques with traditional brick and mortar penal structures" that would supposedly help reduce costs while "promoting the least restrictive detention environments."[17] Advocates had long pushed for detention centers to be located near metropolitan areas so that detained people would be in closer proximity to counsel, family, and medical services. ICE focused on consolidating the system away from the hundreds of county jails used for detention and expanding in the Chicago area as a hub for the Midwest, New Jersey for the Northeast, and outside Miami for the Southeast.

One such facility was Delaney Hall in Newark, New Jersey, operated by the private prison company Community Education Centers. In 2011, as part of an ICE stakeholder engagement, I joined a tour of Delaney Hall along with other advocates. The facility, a former

halfway house located next door to the Essex County Jail, was surrounded by barbed wire. Upon entering, visitors were inundated with
self-help signs with messages such as "stop lying" and "admit when
you are wrong," which ICE referred to as artwork. As we made our
way through the jail, taking in the dim environment (there were few
windows) and bleak living conditions, many of us questioned what
made the facility civil. Throughout the tour, ICE public advocate
Andrew Lorenzen-Strait continuously stated, "This is not a jail," in
what seemed to be an attempt to convince himself as much as the
advocates present.

Attempts to expand in the Midwest and Florida were less successful because of strategic organizing campaigns that stopped ICE proposals from moving forward. (We'll come back to this in chapter 6.)

Many detention centers opened or expanded under Obama's
watch, but no other facility exemplified the dog and pony show that
ICE employed to promote civil detention more than the Karnes
County Civil Detention Facility in Texas. ICE entered into a contract
with Karnes County with very little opportunity for public comment.
And Karnes County, which is located about an hour southeast of San
Antonio, signed another contract with the GEO Group, which owned
and operated the new immigrant detention center. Journalists and
advocates were invited to the opening, and organizers coordinated an
action and press event after the tour ended. The *New York Times* covered
the opening and described the scene at the detention center: "Unarmed
staff members, dressed in blue polo shirts and khaki trousers, are
known as 'resident advisers,' not guards." Much of the media coverage
affirmed ICE talking points about the civil aspects of the facility. The
Times story continued, "The gentler approach is immediately evident
in the center's modernist facade, which is painted in bright primary
colors—a far cry from the dreary bunkerlike structures that have characterized the system."[18] Karnes was purportedly designed to "improve
confinement conditions" with "enhanced recreational opportunities
and . . . contact visitation."[19] Those eligible to be held there were "low

custody" immigrants, meaning they were deemed low flight risks and had no or minor criminal histories. Based on ICE's own assessment of risk factors at the time, they should have been eligible for release, calling into question the purpose of the facility altogether. Karnes came to exemplify not only how senseless the expansion of civil detention was but also how detention reforms proliferated new kinds of facilities, all in the name of more humane treatment of immigrants.

In 2014, the number of families arriving at the border began to increase. Instead of responding by offering support to families seeking refuge, the administration ramped up mass detention at the border with an intention to deter future migrants. First, ICE opened a temporary site for detaining families at the Federal Law Enforcement Training Center in Artesia, New Mexico. Then, in what was perhaps one of the most infuriating detention-related developments of the Obama era, the administration chose to convert Karnes, their model civil detention center, into a center for detaining parents with their children. The administration further expanded family detention when it quickly contracted with CCA to open the 2,400-bed South Texas Family Residential Center in Dilley, Texas.

An end to family detention at Hutto in Obama's first year in office indicated a shift from the previous administration, but by the end of his time in office, Obama had completely retreated on his earlier position. He had expanded family detention from a capacity to detain 600 people to 3,000 at any given time. By bringing back family detention and emphasizing the need for deterrence, the Obama administration laid the groundwork for Trump's attack on families in 2018. Senior ICE officials, including Thomas Homan, even proposed family separation as a tool for deterrence in 2014 as the Obama administration was considering how to respond to families. Homan went on to serve under Trump, where he ultimately succeeded in helping implement the policy four years later.[20]

During Obama's tenure, ICE consolidated the detention system from 350 facilities made up mostly of contracts with county jails to roughly 200 detention centers, with high-capacity private prisons holding the most people. In 2009, 49 percent of ICE beds were operated by private prisons; by the time Obama left office in 2017, that figure had risen to over 70 percent.[21] The Obama administration's detention reforms served to fortify the system and entrench private prison companies even further. Now ICE had multiple new detention centers that were a "model." When the Department of Justice announced a phaseout of private prisons in the federal system in 2016, DHS concluded that the same phaseout wasn't possible for ICE because of the agency's dependency on them.

A Growing Deportation Dragnet

While ICE was "reforming" detention, it also began expanding ICE-police collaborations. Secure Communities was one of several programs ICE used to target people for deportation with the aid of local law enforcement; other such programs included 287(g), which deputizes police as immigration enforcers, and the Criminal Alien Program (CAP, renamed the Criminal Apprehension Program under Biden), which houses ICE agents within local, state, and federal jails and prisons across the country. Unlike 287(g) and CAP, which relied on ICE agents or local police, Secure Communities automated sharing data between agencies. When police took someone to jail, as part of the regular booking process, they scanned the person's fingerprints through FBI and DHS databases to determine whether they could be subject to an ICE hold. This in turn could lead to that person being transferred to immigration detention and eventually deported. The integration of different databases made booking processes at local jails a gateway to the federal immigration process. Secure Communities was the beginning of ICE's shift toward a more digital, surveillance-driven approach to immigration enforcement that paved the way for greater expansion of criminalization.

Obama's calculated use of the criminal legal system to apprehend immigrants not only increased the scale of the system but made deportations more severe. Many terms are used to describe the act of deportation: removal, departure, return, expulsion. They have varying consequences for those deported. The particular legal form of deportation that was dominant under Obama, known as removal—where immigrants are placed in formal deportation proceedings—came with some of the harshest consequences for immigrants. After someone is formally deported, they typically have at minimum a five-year bar from reentering the country. If they reenter without authorization again, they could face prosecution, resulting in sentences ranging from several months to twenty years in federal prison. By contrast, the same bars to reentry do not apply to immigrants who are coerced into "voluntary departure" or those who are turned away at the border or expelled. While expulsions had been higher under previous administrations, formal deportations increased dramatically during Obama's tenure, earning him the moniker "deporter-in-chief." The emphasis on formal deportations meant that immigrants attempting to return to the United States after deportation would have a more difficult time doing so and faced lengthy prison sentences if they were caught trying to reenter.

Secure Communities debuted in 2008 in Houston, Texas. By 2013, the program had been implemented in more than 3,000 counties in all fifty states. After the creation of DHS under Bush, formal deportations had already more than doubled, from 165,000 in 2002 to 360,000 in 2008. Obama essentially followed suit, and formal deportations reached a record high of 438,000 in 2013. The continued increase in deportations under Obama, which were already high in the late Bush years, dealt a major blow to immigrant communities nationwide.[22]

As the number of people funneled into the deportation pipeline grew, so did the immigrant detention system. In 2010, Immigration Centers of America, a small private prison company, was awarded an ICE contract for the one-thousand-bed Farmville Detention Center in Prince Edward County, Virginia. ICE assistant director Robert Helwig

commented that Farmville was opened "to address the impact of Secure
Communities. . . . We do anticipate a surge in detainees."[23] One of the
largest detention centers in the mid-Atlantic, Farmville became a hub for
the region. From 2008 to 2012, the number of people detained annually
grew by 26 percent, from 378,582 to 477,523.[24] In Obama's second term,
these numbers started to reduce as more local communities fought back
against rising deportations (more on this in chapter 4).

As more and more people were rounded up, Secure Communities became increasingly controversial. Advocates pointed out that
in Obama's first two years in office, more than 75 percent of people
arrested and deported under Secure Communities were either noncriminals or those who had low-level criminal convictions and that
the administration had "failed to target violent and dangerous criminals."[25] Some 3,600 US citizens had even been arrested by ICE because
of the program.[26] Obama's emphasis on targeting "dangerous criminals" became the opening for advocates to reveal how the program
was scooping up people indiscriminately. Instead of critiquing the
narrative of good immigrant versus bad immigrant, advocates argued
that the law was being applied too broadly, accepting that criminal
history should be a determining factor for detention and deportation.

Despite the growing concerns about police violence being highlighted through Black Lives Matter protests, advocates focused on
how collaborations between ICE and local police made immigrants
less likely to seek assistance from police. For example, immigrant
women might not report instances of domestic violence for fear of
being deported. Ignoring the racist and sexist frameworks that undergird policing in the United States and result in deportations in these
situations, advocates emphasized that Secure Communities prevented police from doing their purported job of protecting women.
These types of carceral feminist frameworks, in which people believe
that police and prisons are necessary tools for stopping gender-based
violence, disregard the violence these institutions perpetrate on
women and nonbinary people. Abusive partners have been known to

use the police to lock up and punish survivors, including threatening to call ICE. And rates of domestic violence are two to four times higher among police officers.[27] Despite these concerns, emphasizing a need to restore trust in police became an easy argument to fall back on as the movement fought the expansion of Secure Communities. While these arguments seemed persuasive to many decision makers, they often served to reinforce the idea that some immigrants deserved arrest and furthered divisions between the immigrant rights movement and those organizing against discriminatory policing.

The Morton Memo

During this period, many advocates and organizers pushed to increase prosecutorial discretion as a tactic for stopping deportations. Prosecutorial discretion that deprioritizes certain immigration cases has two justifications for its use in enforcement proceedings: first, to prioritize the time and resources of ICE to focus on high-priority cases; second, to provide protection for those who are potentially vulnerable or whose cases have humanitarian factors that should outweigh the pursuit of deportation. In 2010, the Obama administration released a set of priorities meant to guide ICE's discretionary decisions on whom to target for deportation, commonly referred to as the Morton Memo after ICE director John Morton. While some advocates and organizers found the memo to be a useful tool in waging individual deportation defense campaigns, it soon became clear that it was failing to significantly reduce deportations. A year after its implementation, only 1 percent of deportation cases had been closed because of the memo.[28] For example, data from the Transactional Records Access Clearinghouse documented that in Baltimore, only 230 of 5,256 pending cases were closed; in Denver, only 186 of 7,579 pending cases (excluding detained individuals) were closed as of March 2012.[29]

The memo and prosecutorial discretion did provide protection from deportation for some seventy-five thousand immigrants under

Obama.[30] But deportations continued to rise. The memo as written in a 2011 update included a laundry list of factors to consider for granting prosecutorial discretion. Positive factors included, for example, whether someone was a veteran or pregnant, and negative ones followed predictable categories of purported dangerousness, such as national security concerns, past criminal activity, gang affiliation, and risk to public safety. An additional category included people who had a "record of egregious immigration violations, including those with a record of illegal reentry."[31] This category was where the impact of Obama's commitment to formal deportations was increasingly felt, because when people attempted to return to the United States and rejoin their families, they violated the bar on their reentry.

In 2011, reentry prosecutions accounted for nearly a quarter of all federal criminal prosecutions. The number of reentry prosecutions rose significantly under Obama's tenure, from just over 20,000 in fiscal year 2008 to 37,000 in fiscal year 2012.[32] At the same moment that the Obama administration was supposedly providing more discretion for deprioritizing some deportations, it was simultaneously increasing the criminalization that would make it harder for many immigrants to get relief. Chapter 3 explains further how Obama's focus on building up the infrastructure for migrant prosecutions helped lay the groundwork for Trump's weaponizing of entry violations during the family separation crisis.

The Morton Memo did not provide the relief to immigrants that some believed it would. Activists evolved their strategies and started to push for expansive sanctuary policies at the local and state level to limit ICE's reach. Alongside these actions, a growing movement of undocumented youth continued to pressure the administration (more on this in chapter 4). In 2012, Obama announced Deferred Action for Childhood Arrivals (DACA), which provided work authorization and some protection from deportation to over eight hundred thousand immigrants. DACA was Obama's most positive reform to the system during his eight years as president. Even with all of its exclusions (including of people with criminal records), it became an effective tool for providing relief to large numbers of immigrants.

The ICE-NGO Working Group and the Illusion of Reform

As deportations increased, advocates continued to push the Obama administration to address the issues with immigrant detention. The Schriro report promoted the expansion of alternatives to detention (ATD) and the implementation of a risk assessment tool for determining whether someone should be detained or not. These reforms were the central focus of the ICE-NGO working group, a space for advocates to engage with the administration on ICE operations and policy. Advocates spent countless hours meeting with ICE and developing recommendations for tweaking these reforms. But ICE's goal remained the same: detaining and deporting immigrants in large numbers.

ICE developed the risk classification assessment tool over Obama's first term in office and implemented it nationwide in 2013. According to the Schriro report, the risk assessment tool was essential to determining whether someone could be released on an alternative to detention rather than become subject to formal detention. Assessment tools are often touted as more "objective" than individual determinations because "the predictive information they produce is free of the taint of racial bias."[33] As with other supposedly scientific enforcement tools, such as predictive policing, risk assessments seem to come straight out of *Minority Report*. In the science fiction novella and later film, mutant "precogs" determine who will commit a crime and then share the information with the police in advance of the criminal activity. Similarly, risk assessment tools, often trained on data drawn from racist systems, decide if someone should be detained based on the projection of whether they will abscond or commit a future crime.

At the time, there had been little data on how risk assessments might impact immigration enforcement. Advocates in the ICE-NGO working group saw the development of the risk assessment tool as an opportunity to provide recommendations that could result in fewer people being detained. The risk assessment tool considered three central factors: whether someone was especially vulnerable in detention (i.e., people with medical conditions, elderly people, LGBTQ people), whether they were a public safety risk, or whether they were a flight risk. Based on discussions with ICE, many advocates had thought that the risk assessment tool would apply to everyone who was subject to detention. But as the tool was being rolled out, an additional category was added that had not been discussed: whether the person was subject to mandatory detention. When someone is mandatorily detained, their detention is required based on their criminal record. Under the statute that first became law in 1988, the number of people subject to mandatory detention has fluctuated, but the existence of mandatory detention law continues to be a main driver of detaining immigrants with criminal histories and keeping them in detention during the entirety of their immigration proceedings. This exclusion meant that most people detained would be immediately disqualified from being considered for release.

The research of legal scholars Kate Evans and Robert Koulish illuminates how ICE's risk assessment tool "became a vehicle to impose detention on the executive branch's least favored migrants, regardless of whether they presented a risk to public safety or a risk of flight."[34] ICE agents locally had full discretion to override the decisions of the risk assessment tool, and they did. As a result, enforcement became even harsher.[35] Ultimately, the risk assessment tool did nothing to reduce detention, and low-risk people continued to be detained. It served to further entrench the tools available to the federal government for making the case that someone should be detained rather than released. These types of data-driven technologies are designed so that once someone has any interaction with the criminal legal system, they "continue to be criminalized in the future, whether or not they break any laws."[36]

The other major reform, alternatives to detention, has evolved considerably over time, but in those days, ICE was still figuring out the technology. Ravi Ragbir, an immigrant leader from Trinidad, was on an ATD when I met him in 2009 in New York City. He was speaking at an event organized by the American Constitution Society. When I went up to introduce myself, he lifted his leg to reveal an ankle monitor. Ragbir had been previously detained for nearly two years at jails in Alabama and New Jersey. Now he lived with a shackle on his leg. While I was aware of the problems with electronic monitoring, learning about Ragbir's day-to-day life on an ATD helped me understand more. Ragbir later married Amy Gottlieb, a longtime immigrant rights advocate with American Friends Service Committee. On their honeymoon, they had to stay close to home, given Ravi's limited travel range. Gottlieb recalls the experience: "The Saturday after we got married, we went to the Rockaways. We went to the beach and the next thing we know, we start hearing something say, 'You have exited your master zone. You've exited your master zone.' And it's beeping."[37]

The newlyweds had crossed over to Nassau County, which is not part of New York City's five boroughs and technically outside of his movement radius. The reference to "your master zone" evokes the era of chattel slavery. In doing so, it recalls a long and disturbing history of racism, exclusion, and exploitation in the United States; ATDs are now another tool for the deprivation of liberty. Ragbir often talked about how he would charge the ankle monitor while he was sleeping so that he wouldn't have to be tethered to the wall during the day. It wasn't a jail cell, but it remained its own type of confinement.

Disregarding concerns raised by Ragbir and others, advocates continued to push for the expansion of ATDs as a tactic for reducing detention. Once it became clear that ICE had settled on electronic monitoring as the best way to expand ATDs, the GEO Group pounced on the opportunity and acquired the company BI Incorporated, which had been contracting with ICE to operate its ATD program. Once again, ICE saw the private prison industry as a resource for employing their carceral agenda, evidenced by their invitation to the CEO of GEO, George Foley, to an ICE-NGO working group meeting. In the

meeting, when DWN's policy director, Emily Tucker, posed a question to Foley about how the shift from physical detention to electronic
monitoring might affect GEO's profits, ICE public advocate Andrew
Lorenzen-Strait immediately removed her from the meeting. The
meeting further revealed how the federal government and private
companies' interests aligned, promoting a neoliberal approach to governance that favored privatization and outsourcing. Many former ICE
officials from this period, such as David Venturella and Julie Myers
Woods, went on to work for or sit on the board of the GEO Group,
creating a revolving door between the agency and industry.[38]

In light of the concerns about electronic monitoring, or what
some have dubbed e-carceration, advocates began proposing a more
humane model of case management that would provide immigrants
with both a lawyer and a social worker to support them through their
proceedings. After endless conversations within the working group,
in February 2015, ICE finally posted a request for proposals for a five-
year case management pilot program to be rolled out in five regions:
Baltimore/Washington, Chicago, Los Angeles, Miami, and the New
York/Newark area.[39] The idea was that NGOs could submit proposals
for programs that would be much more humane than immigrant detention. Groups such as the Lutheran Immigration and Refugee Service
and the US Conference of Catholic Bishops, both service providers,
submitted proposals. In response to the potential for a new contract,
the GEO Group created a new subsidiary, GEO Care, and also submitted a proposal. In September 2015, ICE awarded the contract to GEO
Care. Advocates who had pushed for the program had no idea this was
a possibility. Mary Loiselle, another former ICE employee, became the
director of GEO Care's family case management program.[40]

The case management program itself was minuscule: fewer than
a thousand families were served over the year and half it existed. (The
Trump administration ended the program in 2017.)[41] As we've seen
with other types of ATDs, it only widened the net of who would be
under some form of ICE surveillance. Case workers provided support

but also functioned as a check on immigrants. Instead of being used as a strategy for releasing people, case management became another tool for expanding control over a greater number of people.

From 2015 to 2016, the Obama administration nearly doubled the number of people under ATDs from 26,625 to 46,777.[42] The focus on ATDs under Obama laid the groundwork for their explosion in the years to follow. The technology continued to evolve. As advocates cautioned against the use of ATDs, GEO adapted. The current ATD of choice is a phone app called SmartLINK. (Smartwatches have also been rolled out as a possible ATD.) Under Biden, detention capacity finally began to retreat, but ATDs skyrocketed sixfold to over 300,000 in 2022, through a mix of people on ankle monitors, SmartLINK, and telephonic reporting.[43]

Despite Dora Schriro's emphasis on the difference between "civil" immigrant detention and criminal incarceration, every single reform she proposed in her review of the system had been tried before by criminal justice advocates. Ultimately, the intention to improve conditions only served to expand detention, consolidate the system, and benefit private prison corporations. The implementation of a risk classification assessment tool did little to release people from detention and reinforced existing racist frameworks. Along with ATDs, such reforms have repeatedly failed at reducing the number of people incarcerated or improving the lives of those subject to incarceration. By the time Obama's tenure came to an end, many of us questioned whether the purpose of the ICE-NGO working group was to engage advocates or merely to provide cover for an administration bent on expanding detention and deportation.

Abolitionist Lessons

Secure Communities and the detention reforms illuminate the core failures of the Obama administration on reforms to immigration enforcement and advocates' responses to them. These two efforts, the

expansion of Secure Communities on the premise of targeting "criminal aliens" and the shift toward a model of "civil" detention to improve
conditions, ultimately operated in contradiction to each other. On
one hand, ICE claimed that Secure Communities would protect communities by taking "dangerous criminals" off the streets. At the same
time, the administration stressed that immigrant detention was not
the same as criminal incarceration, since it was not intended as punishment, and that immigrants in ICE custody deserved better treatment. As deportation numbers went up, many advocates argued that
the problem with Secure Communities and the existing detention
system was that innocent and vulnerable immigrants, not deserving of harsh treatment, were caught in the cross fire. Instead of challenging the idea of deportation as a public safety policy, the focus on
"innocents" threw those with criminal records under the bus, along
with any critique of the criminal legal system that had deemed them
disposable in the first place.

In reflecting on Obama's eight years in office, two key lessons
emerge. First, by accepting that the use of the criminal legal system
for targeting immigrants was tolerable and warranted, the immigrant
rights movement treated the PIC as natural and normal, rather than
a source of injustice. The reforms proposed further fortified both the
criminal legal system and the immigration enforcement systems,
leading to more deportations. Beyond that, the Obama administration expanded and set up a powerful machinery for Trump to exploit
by plugging in the detention and deportation system much more
closely to criminal law enforcement across the country. While some
of this relationship has been reduced in recent years due to growing
movement pressure, people continue to be deported every day due to
ICE's access to prison and jail systems at the state and local levels. The
abolitionist lens becomes critical, not only in fighting back against
growing criminalization of Black, brown, poor, and working-class
immigrants but also for ensuring that proposed reforms don't lead to
more detentions and deportations, as they did under Obama.

Political scientist Naomi Murakawa argues: "Liberal notions of racial violence and agendas for race-neutral machinery actually propelled development of a punitive carceral state."[44] It was Obama's approach to reform, to make the system more effective at targeting "criminals," that drove detention and deportation numbers up to their dramatic heights in the twenty-first century. Obama continued a path that had been laid out before him by previous administrations. The quote from his speech that opens this chapter even mirrors Clinton's framing of immigration in the 1996 State of the Union address: "We are still a nation of immigrants; we should be proud of it. We should honor every legal immigrant here, working hard to become a new citizen. But we are also a nation of laws."[45] The focus on legality, while also signaling support for (good, hardworking) immigrants, is a common theme among Democrats. Obama accepted nativist arguments that immigrants were threats to national security and public safety and enabled racial profiling through strengthening the ties between immigration enforcement and the criminal legal system, just as Clinton had done before him. In doing so, he not only oversaw more formal deportations than any other president, but likewise gave credence to Republican attacks on immigrants.

CHAPTER 3

Deterring the Crisis

Prosecutions, Prisons, and the United States-Mexico Border

> *If you cross the southwest border unlawfully, then we
> will prosecute you. If you smuggle illegal aliens across
> our border, then we will prosecute you. If you are smug-
> gling a child, then we will prosecute you, and that child
> will be separated from you as required by law. . . . So,
> we're sending a message to the world, really, the border
> is not open.*
> —Attorney General Sessions, remarks discussing
> the immigration enforcement actions of the Trump
> administration, May 7, 2018

In 2018, the Trump administration implemented a zero-tolerance policy in which families were separated upon arrival at the southern border. Much of the nation watched in horror as border patrol agents ripped young children from their parents' arms. Parents were locked up in federal jails, while their kids were shipped to faraway shelters or detention camps. They had no idea where their children were being taken. About 5,500 children were separated from their parents during the height of family separations.[1] Many remained apart for months—in some cases, years—after the policy was enacted. Some remain separated to this day.

As outrage over family separations escalated that summer, the call to abolish ICE gained steam among activists and even some politicians, who introduced legislation to do away with the agency. Family separations had become a flashpoint that exposed the harms of the system, leading many to focus on the agency that carries out mass deportations. What the demand to abolish ICE failed to acknowledge, however, was that the zero-tolerance policy went far beyond ICE's purview.

Family separations under Trump emerged directly from a long-standing strategy aimed at deterring migration through use of the criminal legal system to punish people for the act of immigration itself. For three decades, federal agencies have prioritized the criminal prosecution of border crossing. Through five consecutive presidential administrations, an interagency deterrence strategy has prosecuted thousands of people for unlawful entry and unlawful reentry each year. In the process, and unbeknownst to most Americans, immigration offenses became the most commonly prosecuted crimes in US federal courts. As a result, a parallel system of prisons and jails arose to incarcerate immigrants serving criminal sentences. The Trump administration used the structures already in place to carry out the family separation policy, or what was essentially state-sanctioned kidnapping and torture.[2] At a capacity reaching over fifty thousand in 2019, the size and scope of the immigrant population in federal criminal custody began to mirror that of the "civil" immigrant detention system.[3]

In the past thirty years, the United States government has created a crisis at the southern border. The "border crisis" is a right-wing project that over time has been accepted by the Democratic Party and the mainstream media. Beginning in fringe Republican circles in the 1970s, the narrative of the "Latino threat" and invasion at the border has since moved ever closer to the political center. This has spurred new types of opportunism and a feeding frenzy of lucrative political contracting.

There is no clearer place where the prison industrial complex and the military industrial complex intersect than at the US-Mexico border. Journalist Todd Miller has referred to this phenomenon as its own border industrial complex. As he puts it, government investment plus fearmongering over the border equals a "formula of a perpetual 'border crisis': the bigger the crisis, the more need for border infrastructure, generating more revenue."[4]

During this period, the amount of money Congress appropriated to border patrol increased tenfold, from $363 million in 1993 to nearly $5 billion in 2021.[5] The number of border agents, who operate as a cross between soldiers and police, grew from 4,000 to 20,000. Over the years, prison, surveillance, and defense contractors, such as Northrop Grumman, G4S, and CoreCivic, have secured over one hundred thousand contracts totaling $55 billion to build up border and immigration enforcement. As the apparatus expanded, the act of crossing became more perilous, as testified to by the remains of more than 8,000 migrants discovered in the borderlands since the 1990s.[6]

Politicians now use the so-called border crisis not only as a reason to grow the budget of Customs and Border Protection, but as an excuse to deny relief to the millions of undocumented immigrants living in the United States. But, in reality, the moral panic around the border, cynically used to garner votes, simultaneously obscures the actual causes of unprecedented levels of migration, namely the destabilization of the Global South and the climate catastrophe. With deterrence as the central goal, the southern border has come to represent who belongs and who does not, rather than a national boundary line or point of crossing. The United States is not unique in this regard. In reflecting on the era of nation-states after the fall of colonial empires, political theorist Achille Mbembe observes: "The idea is to make borders as the primitive form of keeping at bay the enemies, intruders, and strangers—all those who are not one of us."[7]

In spite of the militarization of the border and the gargantuan enforcement apparatus—agents, miles of border wall, prosecutions, prisons and jails, drones, new tech (such as robot dogs and surveillance blimps), and so on—people continue to cross the border to seek safety and opportunity in the United States, regardless of the harms they face. This fact illustrates the bankruptcy of the border industrial complex and the policies supporting it. Deterrence cannot address the root causes of increased migration; it just makes migration more harrowing, dangerous, and heartless.

While other authors (Joseph Nevins, Kelly Lytle Hernández) have offered important histories of the development of policing, surveillance, and military-style practices at the border, this chapter takes a closer look at the buildup of criminal law enforcement and federal prison systems related to border control. In the following pages, I share the history of border enforcement through migrant prosecutions and how they have been used by politicians to harden the border and advance the anti-immigrant agenda. In the process, the mass prosecution of migrants added new, often hidden, layers to both the carceral state and the US border regime.

When Immigration Became a Crime

Residing in the United States without proper immigration documentation is not technically a crime. When someone overstays a visa, for example, it is a civil violation of immigration law. Despite this, being undocumented can lead to punishment, such as detention and deportation. However, immigration is often treated as a crime too. The act of crossing the border without authorization is, under federal law, considered a misdemeanor crime. The act of crossing can lead to a period of up to six months in prison. If someone who was previously deported for a civil immigration violation or previously charged with the misdemeanor crosses without authorization again, they are subject to a felony charge carrying up to a two-year prison term. The sentence drastically increases to a potential maximum sentence of twenty years' incarceration when a previously deported person has also been convicted of other state or federal crimes. For years, criminal charges for these immigration offenses—unlawful entry and unlawful reentry—were the single leading driver of rising rates of prosecution in the federal system.

The story of how immigration became a crime begins almost a century ago in the 1920s. The decade was marked by extreme post–World War I racism and nativism. Several restrictive immigration laws had been passed in the decades prior that focused on excluding Chinese migrants, sex workers, people with disabilities, and those who were ill, among others. But in the 1920s, efforts to restrict migration were taken to another level. In 1924, Congress passed the National Origins Act, which barred Asian immigration and set restrictive quotas on immigration from Southern and Eastern Europe. These restrictions stayed in place for the most part until 1965. The law affirmed the strongly held belief that whiteness and European ancestry were defining factors of an American identity.[8]

White nativists in Congress and the executive branch ruled the day in most respects, and they clashed with equally powerful capitalists in one important way: because US employers had become dependent on Mexican labor, lawmakers excluded the Western Hemisphere, including Mexico, from the quota system. Agribusiness employers were also racist, but favored Mexicans as laborers over other migrant groups previously banned by exclusionary immigration laws. California businessman Fred Bixby testified to the Senate in support of Mexican migration, "We have no Chinamen, we have not the Japs. The Hindu is worthless; the Filipino is nothing, and the white man will not do the work."[9] But excluding Mexicans from the quota system frustrated the die-hard nativists, including the openly segregationist secretary of labor James Davis. Historian Kelly Lytle Hernández describes nativist objections: "Mexicans, they hollered, were 'peons,' 'mongrels,' and 'racially unfit for [US] citizenship.' Mexican immigration, they believed, threatened to degrade the nation's 'Aryan' stock."[10]

After Congress implemented the national origins quota, nativists continued their effort to limit Mexican migration. South Carolina senator Coleman Livingston Blease proposed a compromise.[11] Blease, a supporter of lynching and an "unrepentant white supremacist," according to Hernández, shifted his rhetorical focus away from racist fearmongering and toward the fact that many Mexican laborers crossed the border without authorization.[12] The Supreme Court had ruled that it wasn't technically unlawful for immigrants to be in the United States without status. But Blease found a work-around to remove them easily: criminalize crossing the border. Mexicans could still cross to pick crops, but the new law would allow the government to "prosecute and deport Mexicans *after* they're here—once the harvest is over."[13] It was a piece of subterfuge that used the pretense of "law and order" to streamline the process of deporting Mexicans.

Blease championed the Undesirable Aliens Act of 1929, which created the crimes of unlawful entry, a misdemeanor carrying a potential one-year sentence in prison, and unlawful reentry, a felony offense carrying a potential two-year prison sentence. Both included an additional one-thousand-dollar fine. The same eugenicists who had pushed for immigration quotas and bans in the 1924 law helped pass the 1929 measure in a "matter of weeks."[14] In the years following the passage of the law, the rate of prosecutions immediately spiked. Within a year, federal prosecutors had brought forward 7,001 cases of unlawful entry.[15] Mexicans made up the vast majority of those charged and imprisoned.

In 1952, the law was codified as part of the new Immigration and Nationality Act. At that time, the sentence for unlawful entry was reduced to six months, making it "easier to prosecute" by eliminating the requirement for a jury trial.[16] The two offenses are now commonly referred to as 1325 (unlawful entry) and 1326 (unlawful reentry) based on their sections in the United States Code.[17] After that, the number of prosecutions for unlawful entry fluctuated over time. For many years, criminal charges for unlawful reentry, which carried a longer sentence, were rarely pursued by US attorneys. Those crimes remained relatively dormant until another wave of politicians revitalized them for political gain.

—

The toughening of immigration and criminal law in the 1980s and 1990s helped shape the border enforcement regime we have today. The same politicians who advocated denying asylum claims to migrants and expanding detention, such as Bob Graham of Florida and Alfonse D'Amato of New York, also promoted the idea that immigrants attempting to return to the country after being deported should face harsher sentences. Legal scholar S. Deborah Kang addresses the history of 1326 prosecutions: "Whereas anti-Mexican racism informed the passage of the Undesirable Aliens Act and its 1952 revision, a combination of anti-Haitian and anti-Hispanic racism drove the enactment of the subsequent amendments in 1988, 1990, 1994, and 1996."[18] Through adjustments to criminal and immigration law via the Anti-Drug Abuse Act, the 1994 crime bill, and the 1996 immigration laws (detailed in chapter 1), Congress made punishment for unlawful reentry convictions more severe. These legislative changes along with stepped-up border enforcement resulted in an exponential increase in the number of immigrants incarcerated for criminal offenses in federal prisons and jails.

In 1994, the same year that the United States was opening its border to the so-called free trade of goods via the ratification of NAFTA, the border patrol adopted a new strategic plan. The plan inaccurately predicted that NAFTA would "reduce illegal immigration as the Mexican economy improves." It further claimed that "those attempting to illegally enter the United States in large numbers do so in part because of the weak controls we have exercised over the southwest land border in the recent past."[19] Henceforth, the official strategy for the border patrol became "prevention through deterrence," which aimed to make the conditions at the US-Mexico border so unwelcoming that migrants would hesitate in making the journey north. Through a series of operations utilizing war-related metaphors (Blockade, Hold the Line, Gatekeeper, Safeguard), the Clinton administration attempted to obstruct undocumented migrants from entering through ports of entry along the border. But rather than deterring migration, these initiatives only made the journey more treacherous, as migrants moved to harsh desert lands to cross.[20]

As immigrants became key targets in the wars on drugs and crime and the number of border patrol agents grew, migrant prosecutions also climbed sharply. In the 1980s, prosecution numbers remained in the hundreds. Under the prevention through deterrence approach, the government prosecuted nearly 34,000 migrants between 1994 and 2000.[21] Migrant prosecutions fluctuated until the creation of DHS, when both 1325 and 1326 prosecutions would reach levels so high that immigration offenses became the most prosecuted federal crime.

Operation Streamline and the Rise of Immigrant Prisons

About seventy-five years after the Undesirable Aliens Act passed in Congress, I found myself frequently trekking back and forth on Interstate 35 between Austin, where I lived, and Laredo, a border town in south Texas. In 2004, the United States Marshals Service solicited proposals for a 2,800-bed, privately operated jail, dedicated for migrants being prosecuted for unlawful entry and reentry. Local media dubbed it the Laredo superjail due to its size. I had recently graduated from college and was working as an organizer at Grassroots Leadership, a southern-based economic and racial justice nonprofit. My friend from college turned coworker Bob Libal and I had been coordinating a national campaign around university divestment from private prisons when rumors of the jail began spreading. Together with our comrade Carlos Villarreal of the Texas Criminal Justice Reform Coalition, we began traveling to Laredo to meet with community members in and around the city to gather information about the proposal and build a base of support against the jail. With local residents and statewide organizations, we came together to form the South Texans Opposing Private Prisons Coalition to block construction of the superjail.

Laredo was bigger than the other Texas border towns considering prison expansion at the time, but not so big that we couldn't secure a meeting with a county commissioner or the bishop. We would meet at various local haunts: Salsas, the Tex-Mex restaurant serving sushi, or Espumas, a downtown café with doilies for placemats that seemed to be permanently decorated for Easter. After ordering a round of *mariachis*, the Laredo term for breakfast taco, we would make our case against the superjail. We were met with a mix of reactions. The bishop told us he agreed with us but said he would not come out publicly against the jail. Some county commissioners were open to hearing us out.

Many private prison companies—often coordinating with local officials to finance the prison—vied for the contract, but, as usual, CCA and GEO were the most aggressive. At a public hearing on the jail, I remember feeling confident in the opposition group we had assembled and shown up with until a busload of CCA guards arrived and piled into the room to voice their support for the new jail. To persuade the public against the superjail, we employed various arguments over the course of the multiyear fight: that the jail would have a negative impact on the longer-term economic development of Laredo; that the jail would destroy the natural habitat of the local ocelot population; and, of course, that the jail was unnecessary, and the US government should instead deprioritize migrant prosecutions. Little did we know that the following year a new program would be rolled out in Del Rio, another Texas border town, that would make unlawful entry and reentry prosecutions a central component of the US border regime.

In 2005, an "enterprising Border Patrol chief," Randy Hill, proposed what became Operation Streamline, a joint initiative between DHS and DOJ to prosecute every migrant crossing the border without authorization in order to further deter migration.[22] Not only did Streamline increase prosecutions, it did so en masse; seventy or more people could be prosecuted daily in some border sectors, often a dozen or so at the same time.

Witnessing a Streamline hearing made it clear that due process within our criminal legal system is a farce. A dozen migrants lined up, shackled at their ankles and wrists, as a judge considered their cases, not on their individual merits, but often issuing a single ruling that applied to dozens of people all at once. Most of the migrants standing in the courtrooms took plea deals to minimize prison time. A 2015 report by the Migrant Border Crossing Study of people prosecuted through Streamline documented that "55 percent of respondents stated that their lawyer simply informed them that they needed to sign their order of removal and plead guilty."[23] Initially a ninety-day experiment in the Del Rio sector of the border patrol, Streamline expanded to every other sector along the border, except those in California, by 2010.

When someone is apprehended at the border, after a short stay in CBP custody, they can be sent to ICE detention for deportation proceedings or to a US Marshals Service jail, where they await trial for prosecution. Border patrol agents who were frustrated with the limits of immigrant detention capacity began targeting migrants for prosecution to ensure they would still be imprisoned.[24] It didn't matter to them whether migrants were sent to ICE or USMS as long as they were still being punished. As the prosecution of migrants for border crossing skyrocketed, filling federal courts, the federal criminal legal system found itself with a desperate need for beds. A Grassroots Leadership and Justice Strategies book on Operation Streamline points out that the prioritization of border-crossing prosecutions and the severe sentences handed out, often five or more years, "fueled a brisk market for additional capacity in the federal prison system, and resulted in lucrative contracts with a private prison industry that [was] ever eager to provide extra bed space."[25] The federal government once again looked to private prisons as the solution to their beds problem, this time in the criminal system.

In the late 1990s, as the Clinton administration was attempting to reduce the federal workforce, the Federal Bureau of Prisons (BOP) began contracting with private prison companies for the first time.[26] The federal government developed separate facilities for noncitizens serving federal sentences that would be exclusively operated by private prison companies, called Criminal Alien Requirement (CAR) prisons. These stripped-down prisons limited services such as drug treatment, education, and reentry programs under the justification that most people held in them would eventually be deported and therefore didn't need programs designed to promote successful reentry into society. Immigrants serving felony sentences would often spend years in CAR prisons.

As immigrant detention expanded under the George W. Bush administration, so did CAR prisons and USMS private jails. Despite local and statewide opposition, the Laredo superjail opened in 2008, with the GEO Group securing the contract, though with 1,500 beds, a smaller number than originally proposed. Bob Libal described the celebrations that accompanied the opening of the jail: "It was even more surreal than I could have imagined—complete with a high school mariachi band singing Spanish-language ballads, a cake in the shape of the GEO Group's corporate logo, and a slew of new GEO Group prison guards (many of whom looked to be eighteen or nineteen) wearing desert camo-style uniforms."[27] Later the jail expanded to 1,900 beds. It is still in operation today, incarcerating migrants in civil detention for ICE and in criminal detention for the US Marshals Service.

Paralleling the US prison boom, border prosecutions became a monster of their own making, and communities began to depend on the jobs and economy created by Operation Streamline and the growth of immigrant federal prisons and jails. One Arizona magistrate judge, Bernardo P. Velasco, described Streamline as a jobs bill, pointing to the economy it upholds: "We have Border Patrol officers who are employed, prosecutors employed, marshals employed, courtroom deputies employed, prison guards employed. A lot of people are making good money to support their families."[28]

This period during the Bush administration would set the course and build the infrastructure for the family separation policy in 2018. But it was the Obama administration that drove the number of prosecutions up into the tens of thousands each year. Obama ramped up both interior and border enforcement in an artless effort to get Republicans to support legalization. It was an ultimately futile exercise. A key component of this strategy was an evolution of the prevention through deterrence approach. While prevention through deterrence aimed to make border crossing more harrowing, through Operation Streamline, Obama prioritized prosecutions for people crossing the border, expanding the program to additional sectors. People seeking asylum were routinely charged with immigration crimes, making it more difficult for them to make a case for relief after serving their sentence. As deportations grew under Obama, so did the number of people who could be subject to prosecution. In 2013 nearly one hundred thousand people were prosecuted for immigration crimes, and unlawful reentry prosecutions carrying more severe sentences had increased by 76 percent since Obama had taken office.[29]

Federal immigrant prisons and jails are notorious for their lack of services and abysmal conditions. Journalist Seth Freed Wessler's investigations into CAR prisons and USMS jails have revealed how prison operators intentionally cut corners, especially on medical care. A review of seventy-seven deaths in CAR prisons found that in a third of cases, inadequacies in medical care "likely contributed to the premature deaths of prisoners."[30] Claudio Fagardo-Saucedo, a Mexican migrant who had been in and out of government custody for reentry, was repeatedly denied medical care and was not given a *required* HIV test until it was too late. Within a year of his time at a CAR prison in west Texas, he died of an HIV-related brain infection.[31]

Migrants incarcerated in CAR prisons grew frustrated with the limited services and long prison sentences and staged multiple uprisings during the Obama years, including one that destroyed the structure of a 3,000-bed prison in south Texas. Seemingly in response to media and government investigations exposing deaths and other problems with CAR prisons, Obama's Justice Department sought to phase out CAR prisons in 2016 (explained further in chapter 5). Though the Trump administration reversed that plan, Biden signed an executive order calling for a slow end to private federal prisons during his first few weeks in office. But jails like the Laredo superjail maintain contracts with the US Marshals Service and continue to jail immigrants despite the order. Meanwhile, migrant prosecutions and Democrats' defense of them remain a core element of the US border regime.

While the perception may be that those caught up in border enforcement are recent arrivals, the reality is that many people attempting to return after previously being deported have strong family ties in the United States. Most have already been filtered through the civil immigration enforcement system and separated from their families and livelihoods. Immigrants return despite the consequences they face. A National Immigrant Justice Center survey of fifty-four migrants charged with entry or reentry "found that more than 80 percent of the people interviewed had family members in the U.S. and indicated they were trying to rejoin them."[32] Antonio, a forty-two-year-old man who was deported due to Obama-era immigration enforcement initiatives, shared, "I have no choice, my family is there. I need to go back to my children who want me back."[33]

The Political Expediency of Moral Panics

Apart from the changes in administrative policy, migrant prosecutions became a way for politicians to push for harsher sentencing whenever a moral panic arose about an alleged criminal act by an undocumented immigrant. A few weeks after Trump announced his presidential run in the summer of 2015, Kate Steinle, a thirty-two-year-old white woman from the Bay Area suburbs, was shot by a stray bullet at the San Francisco waterfront and died soon after. José Inez García Zárate, a Mexican migrant with a criminal record (a point that politicians and the media emphasized repeatedly) was charged with murder and manslaughter.

The case set off a moral panic regarding both García Zárate's previous record and San Francisco's sanctuary policy. Due to the policy, instead of being transferred to ICE custody, García Zárate had been released to await a decision on a twenty-year-old marijuana possession charge when the incident involving Steinle took place. Law professor Jonathan Simon explains how, despite his felony convictions, García Zárate was not what lawmakers made him out to be, noting that "all but one of these felonies were for drugs or [unlawful] reentry," and that his "record is monument to how stretched the felony concept has become in our time."[34] After a trial, a jury eventually acquitted him of the murder charges.

García Zárate's case reveals how politicians from both parties easily seize upon crime panics to improve their standing and stoke fear around immigration. Disregarding concerns about rising deportations due to ICE-police collaboration, Democratic California senator and former San Francisco mayor Dianne Feinstein lambasted the city's sanctuary policy for allowing García Zárate to be released.[35] A few months after the incident, Republicans including senator Ted Cruz of Texas introduced what was dubbed "Kate's Law" after Steinle. It would have required a five-year mandatory minimum sentence for immigrants who attempted reentry and had certain prior convictions. The law was reintroduced multiple times but hasn't passed. Trump also used Steinle's story on the campaign trail to galvanize anti-immigrant sentiment leading up to the 2016 election, referring to García Zárate as an animal.[36] Despite García Zárate's eventual acquittal, his story continued to be used to attack sanctuary policies and garner votes for Trump.

The villainization of García Zárate harkens back to the 1988 election, when George H. W. Bush mobilized a moral panic over crime as a linchpin for presidential victory. To defeat his opponent, Michael Dukakis, then governor of Massachusetts, Bush repeatedly sensationalized the story of William Horton for political gain. Horton, a Black man serving a murder conviction, was charged with breaking into a house and raping someone while temporarily released from a Massachusetts prison on a weekend furlough. Prison furloughs were common at the time and viewed positively as a means of helping people serving time reacclimate to life on the outside. Previously, Reagan had defended the furlough program while he was governor of California, even after a murder raised questions about the program's efficacy. Reagan noted that the overall benefit of furloughs outweighed the rarity of such incidences, stating that "more than 20,000 already have these passes, and this was the only case of this kind, the only murder."[37]

But Bush used Horton to criticize furloughs and position Dukakis as soft on crime. Bush's campaign manager, Lee Atwater, a notorious racist, played up anti-Black stereotypes, renaming Horton "Willie" and using Horton's mugshot in political ads to instill fear. Horton later reflected on the experience in an interview with the *Nation*: "The fact is, my name is not 'Willie.' It's part of the myth of the case. The name irks me. It was created to play on racial stereotypes: big, ugly, dumb, violent, black—'Willie.' I resent that. They created a fictional character—who seemed believable, but who did not exist."[38] Bush took the presidency, and, as one scholar put it, the episode "taught the Democrats that in order to win elections, they have to mirror some of the racially inflected language of tough on crime."[39]

After the Horton episode, tough-on-crime agendas prevailed, eventually leading to a slate of harsher sentencing policies in the 1990s, including the 1994 crime bill and 1996 immigration laws. Similarly, Trump thrived on moral panics, not just about "dangerous immigrants" but also about the border itself. The border wall then became a symbol for his response to immigration. As he expanded on the infrastructure of previous administrations, the manufactured crisis around the border intensified.

Family Separation and the Carceral State

Migrant prosecutions for unlawful entry remained mostly out of the public eye until 2018, when they were used as a tool by the Trump administration to carry out the systemic separation of parents from their children at the border. While the family separation policy under Trump rightly provoked significant outrage, what it revealed most was the complete moral bankruptcy of the institutions that implemented it. Often the liberal critique of Trump's immigration policy sees him and his administration as an aberration, a departure from the basic norms of governing. This perspective ignores the fact that many of his polices were continuations and expansions of what previous administrations, especially since Clinton, had been seeding: the use of the criminal legal system to punish immigrants as a tool for deterring future migration.

When Trump came into office, much of the infrastructure for family separations was already in place. Under Obama, DHS had positioned migrant families as a problem in need of deterrence with the expansion of family detention. Operation Streamline had made migrant prosecutions a cornerstone of border enforcement, delivering layers of punishment on arriving migrants. In April 2017 under Trump, DHS and DOJ were directed to increase and prioritize prosecutions for border crossing.[40] This directive prompted Jeff Self, chief of the El Paso border patrol, to begin a pilot program for separating families by instructing agents to refer parents for prosecution. Children would be sent into the custody of the Office of Refugee Resettlement (ORR), while their parents would be imprisoned by the US Marshals Service.

The Trump administration had started separating families in 2017, but claimed otherwise. Data about separated families was collected in a haphazard manner or sometimes not at all. Children were sent to shelters or squalid detention camps several states away. Parents had no idea where their children were. Then, in April 2018, attorney general Jeff Sessions announced a zero-tolerance policy for all unlawful border crossings, expanding the El Paso pilot program throughout the Southwest. Family separations immediately began to spike as prosecutions increased exponentially. Prior to this shift, media coverage of the story had been steady, but boomed shortly after zero tolerance was implemented. In the *New York Times*, journalist Caitlin Dickerson reported on a list from ORR that revealed one hundred of the seven hundred children who had been separated were under the age of four.[41] The story blew up. Outrage over the policy grew as the public watched families being torn apart on the nightly news. Mobilizations and outrage reminiscent of the response to Trump's issuing of the Muslim Ban returned. Finally, Trump was forced to abandon the zero-tolerance policy, signing an executive order in June 2018 that ended it. But the damage had been done. Thousands of children had been separated from their parents, and information about how to reunite them was sparse.

Later, in retelling the story of family separations under Trump in the *Atlantic*, Dickerson exposed how mid-level career officials at DHS and DOJ just went along with the policy. These agencies had been ramping up prosecutions and targeting families for detention and deportation for years. This was a departure, but not by much. Some did question it on the grounds of it being "impractical" due to the lack of ORR capacity, but others, like Thomas Homan, who had worked in federal immigration enforcement since 1989, became its champions. Dickerson reported that Homan "wanted to apply the perceived lessons of Operation Streamline to migrant families . . . [triggering] an automatic family separation."[42] Homan, a former police officer from upstate New York, characterized his tenure at ICE as a continuation of his police career: "I've arrested aliens. I've sat on low houses. I've worked on the front lines. I'm a cop in a cop's job, and cops work for me."[43] He would later go on to contribute as a Fox News pundit. While much attention was placed on Trump and his senior adviser Stephen Miller, it was rank-and-file career officials in DHS and DOJ who carried out the family separations, many of whom were ready and willing.

Migrant prosecutions reached an all-time high during the Trump administration. In 2019 alone, over eighty thousand people were prosecuted for unlawful entry violations and twenty-five thousand for reentry.[44] Family separations at the border continued regularly but in smaller numbers. Under Trump, ICE also targeted migrants through mass raids, including one in Mississippi in which 680 immigrant workers were arrested and nearly a hundred were prosecuted for unlawful reentry or other immigration-related charges.[45]

Some politicians started to take issue with the role of prosecutions in immigration enforcement. At a Democratic presidential primary debate in 2019, candidate Julián Castro called for repeal of the law criminalizing unlawful entry: "Let's be very clear. The reason that they're separating these little children from their families is that they're using Section 1325 . . . which criminalizes coming across the border to incarcerate the parents and then separate them."[46] But many Democrats, including Joe Biden, argued that Section 1325 should remain: "If you cross the border illegally, you should be able to be sent back. It's a crime. It's a crime."[47]

—

Parents being separated from their young children is an everyday reality of both the criminal legal and immigration enforcement systems. In 2020, when Karina Cisneros Preciado, a twenty-one-year-old woman from Florida, called 911 to report domestic abuse, she was instead arrested by the police on the scene. She was detained at the Irwin County Detention Center in Georgia, a facility that came under fire due to the forced gynecological procedures conducted on women held there. During her time in Irwin, she experienced those procedures firsthand. She later testified in front of Congress: "My daughter was only four months old when the police took me from her. I was still nursing her at the time. Our separation was really traumatic for both of us. Being torn away from my baby, my mother, my family, for no fair reason, is overwhelming for me to think about."[48]

Beyond immigrant detention, when looking at state and federal prison systems, the number of parents separated from their children is alarming. A 2016 Bureau of Justice Statistics survey found that "nearly half (47%) of the approximately 1.25 million people in state prison are parents of minor children, and about 1 in 5 (19%) of those children is age 4 or younger."[49] According to the same survey, in the federal system, 57 percent of those incarcerated were parents to children under the age of eighteen. Incarcerated people who are pregnant while in prison are usually separated from their children shortly after birth, sometimes within twenty-four hours. And parents are often incarcerated hundreds of miles from their children, limiting the potential for visits and regular connection.[50]

The child welfare system, or what some now refer to as the family policing system, further reveals the various ways the state separates families of color. During the Obama era, the Applied Research Center found that in 2011, over five thousand children were in the US foster care system because their parents had been detained or deported.[51] Law professor Dorothy Roberts notes that the rate of children in the foster care system, at 576 per 100,000, mirrors the rate of incarceration for US adults, which is 582 per 100,000.[52] Black and Indigenous families are disproportionately impacted by family policing. More than half of Black children will be investigated by child welfare agencies in their lifetime.[53] Black children are "almost twice as likely to experience investigations as white children and are more likely to be separated from their families." Indigenous parents are "up to four times more likely to have their children taken and placed into foster homes."[54] The family separation moment under Trump revealed his particular brand of cruelty, but when looking at the broader PIC, including the family policing system, it is evident that family relationships, especially for poor, working-class, Black, brown, and Indigenous communities, are undervalued by these over-lapping carceral systems.

Biden, COVID-19, and the Border

After family separations in 2018, Trump senior adviser Stephen Miller continued his war on immigrants, combing through legal statutes to find something that would help his agenda of ending immigration as we know it. Miller attempted to invoke the president's public health authority to seal the borders, even in cases where agency neglect and mismanagement aided in the spread of illness: during a flu epidemic at a CBP detention center in south Texas, when a mumps outbreak spread through fifty-seven detention centers in nineteen states, and even after two migrant children died while in border patrol custody.[55]

In 2020, Miller finally got the chance he had been waiting for with the onset of the COVID-19 pandemic. On March 20, 2020, the Trump administration enacted Title 42, a section of federal law in the Public Health Services Act that allows the federal government to expel migrants at the border to prevent the spread of disease. While Trump downplayed the impacts of the pandemic, his administration simultaneously used it as a reason to turn away migrants and prevent them from seeking asylum at the border. Advocates and public health experts immediately criticized the policy, raising concerns that it would make the border and the journey to it even more dangerous for those seeking refuge.

With the election of a Democrat to the White House, many in the movement hoped Biden would welcome immigrants with open arms or, at the very least, give them a fair shot at asylum. Predictably, this was not the case. The Democrats, as they have operated for decades, toed the line of "securing our borders" as a necessity for deterring migration. However, the degree to which the Democrats took on Miller's playbook was unexpected, even for those of us who had worked against Obama's harsh immigration crackdown. While Biden's early days in office signaled a few positive reforms on immigration that limited ICE enforcement, by March 2021, Republicans had taken back the narrative, and Biden faltered on even those modest reforms. Demonstrating no clear vision for how to build an immigration policy or combat right-wing scapegoating of migrants, the Biden administration accepted the Republican script regarding the border. In doing so, the new administration made Miller's policies its own and continued to use the COVID-19 pandemic and public health as a guise for expelling migrants. By June of that year, vice president Kamala Harris, the daughter of immigrants, implored Central Americans to stay away, telling them, "Do not come. Do not come. The United States will continue to enforce our laws and secure our border. If you come to our border, you will be turned back."[56] Her words were as much a political message for US audiences as they were a warning to the would-be migrants. While targeting people in the interior of the country had become more politically controversial since the Obama years, border militarization was booming under Biden.

Despite this emphasis on border security, in Biden's first year in office, migrant prosecutions reduced significantly, and, consequently, for the first time since 2004, they were no longer the most prosecuted type of federal crime.[57] While it would be nice to believe the reduction was due to an intentional change in policy by the Biden administration to deprioritize prosecutions for unlawful entry and reentry, given how punitive they are, that was far from the case. Biden's insistence on keeping Title 42 in place meant that most migrants were immediately removed near ports of entry—they could not make it far enough to be referred for prosecution by border patrol agents. Instead, they were either expelled back into Mexico or taken to deportation staging sites to board flights back to their home countries.

The first year of the Biden administration almost felt like a throwback to decades prior, when the United States began building up its massive detention infrastructure in response to Black migrants seeking asylum. Within weeks of Biden taking office, flights ran nonstop from staging sites in Louisiana to Port-au-Prince to deport Haitians under Title 42. That September, images surfaced of border patrol agents in Del Rio violently chasing Haitian asylum seekers while on horseback. For some, the images harkened back to Jim Crow–era racial violence by law enforcement and revealed how little had changed about such agencies, regardless of who was president.[58]

Simultaneously, the Biden administration was still trying to signal its desire to reform immigration. DHS secretary Alejandro Mayorkas regularly met with immigrant rights groups to consider recommendations for making the current immigration enforcement system more humane. At a public discussion in April 2021, Mayorkas and UCLA professor Ahilan Arulanantham discussed migrant prosecutions. Arulanantham educated Mayorkas about the racist origins of the 1920s law that created unlawful entry and unlawful reentry crimes and asked him if it changed his view of the statutes. Mayorkas responded, "I am not familiar with that history at all. I was not aware of its racist origins. And those statutes need to be used quite advisably and certainly not in a way they were used over the past four years."[59]

In August 2021, the administration was provided an opening to deprioritize unlawful reentry as a federal offense. In a landmark case, a Nevada judge ruled that prosecutions for unlawful reentry authorized under Section 1326 were unconstitutional due to the statute's racist origins. The decision's timing was likely born from the moment—an aftermath of four years of Trump in office, combined with the broader racial reckoning taking place in the United States. Many historians and legal scholars, including Kelly Lytle Hernández, provided evidence to back up the claims. It was finally a golden opportunity to end the long-term prison sentences that mostly Mexican migrants received for reentering the country. But instead of embracing the ruling, Biden's Department of Justice immediately appealed the decision and argued to keep unlawful reentry as a federal law.[60]

Amid mounting pressure from immigrant rights and asylum advocates, the Biden administration announced it would finally phase out Title 42 in May 2022. But because Biden hesitated to end it as soon as he took office, Title 42 had taken on a life of its own. The moral panic around the border and the fear of losing in the midterm elections because of it led some Democrats to defend Title 42. Politicians from both parties criticized the administration's desire to end it because it could result in even more migrant "surges" at the border; Congress even proposed extending it indefinitely during budget negotiations. Litigation blocked the initial phase out, and Biden continued Title 42 throughout his second year in office until he was finally forced to end it when the public health emergency due to COVID-19 ended in May 2023.

The Biden administration offered a concession to opponents in exchange for ending Title 42—ramping up prosecutions. A year after Mayorkas learned of the nativist history of unlawful entry and unlawful reentry prosecutions, he doubled down on them in relationship to ending Title 42: "We will be increasing the number of criminal prosecutions to meet the challenge because the fact of the matter is there are more cases that warrant criminal prosecution than those cases that are being brought. We're a nation of immigrants, but we are also a nation of laws."[61] Mayorkas revived the familiar rhetoric of the Obama and Clinton years as a justification for ramping up detention, deportations, and prosecutions, all in the name of deterrence.

The Border Regime's Underbelly

While entry violations remain the most prosecuted federal immigration-related crimes, the moral panic around the border feeds on concerns over the smuggling of undocumented immigrants, drug trafficking, and human trafficking. In all these instances, the people perpetrating the crime are viewed as the main problem: members of drug cartels inflict violence in the border region and are contributing to the opioid crisis; smugglers take advantage of vulnerable immigrants seeking a better life and, in some extreme cases, have left them to die in eighteen-wheelers in the peak of Texas summer; human traffickers exploit migrants and keep them in bondage to turn a profit. Trafficking, in the commonsense views of Democrats and Republicans alike, thus justifies the need for entities like Homeland Security Investigations and is "often presented as an 'apolitical' topic about which everyone can agree."[62]

In our work to disrupt the narrative of chaos at the border, we must address the root causes of why migrants are able to be exploited. By examining the larger context of smuggling and trafficking, it is evident that the US government's restrictionist immigration policies and relentless agenda of border militarization have helped create unsafe conditions. Creating barriers to migration doesn't prevent people from needing or wanting to migrate to survive or reunite with family. The barriers only make the migration process more dangerous, enabling smugglers and traffickers to exploit migrants in the process. Sex worker activists Molly Smith and Juno Mac observe that "the vast, vast majority of people who end up in exploitative situations were *seeking to migrate* and have become entrapped in a horrifically exploitative system because when people migrate without papers they have few to no rights."[63]

Laws against harboring and smuggling are also used to target people who are trying to make the process of crossing safer. Scott Warren, a volunteer with the humanitarian aid group No More Deaths, was charged with two counts of harboring (Section 1324 of the US Code) and one count of conspiracy for providing aid, "food, water, and a place to sleep," to two migrants crossing a deadly stretch near the Arizona border. He faced twenty years in prison. After a mistrial, he won his case.[64] But prosecutions for harboring continue to be used as a tool for retaliating against activists and humanitarians providing help to migrants. It is our responsibility as immigrant justice activists to disrupt the belief systems that have resulted in more prosecutions

at the border, point to the context in which they occur, and put the
blame on the US government for exacerbating these conditions.

Abolitionist Lessons

The border now operates as a negative fantasy space for the political
right that Democrats have ceded to them for decades. In their 1978
book *Policing the Crisis,* cultural theorist Stuart Hall and his coauthors
explain how, to gain legitimacy and power, politicians use moral panics to spread widespread alarm over rising criminal activity by Black
and brown people.[65] The response to moral panics usually involves
an extension of social control by the government. In the case of the
US-Mexico border, the social controls in question had been ramping up since the 1990s. Public outrage over family separation under
Trump emphasized immigrant innocence to counter the moral panic
Republicans were attempting to stoke, but this approach ignored the
broader carceral machinery already in place. As Ruth Wilson Gilmore explains, "The system works . . . to move the line of what counts
as criminal to encompass and engulf more and more people into the
territory of prison eligibility."[66] Long before Trump, migrant prosecutions had already engulfed thousands of Mexican and Central American migrants into the federal prison and jail system every year. As
heartfelt as the response to Trump's policy was, the innocence frame
was never going to address the carceral and deterrence agendas at play.

For migrant justice activists, the discourse around the border
often feels insurmountable. Understanding the scope of government
entities involved in targeting, imprisoning, and deporting migrants
helps us better determine how and where we might be able to apply
pressure and intervene. Migration-related prosecutions illustrate that
the struggle for migrant justice and abolition of the prison industrial
complex are one and the same. As we advocate for humane treatment
of migrants seeking refuge and for those living in border communities, we must address the ways that the prison system and border mil-

itarization are intertwined. The issue goes far beyond ICE, and even beyond DHS. The Justice Department and a host of local and state agencies play a role in keeping the situation at the border carceral. Building power to defund those agencies and repeal the laws that have imprisoned thousands of migrants each year for the act of crossing the border will be critical to rolling back the reach of the prison industrial complex, at the border and beyond.

PART II

Organizing for Immigrant Justice

CHAPTER 4

From Legalization to Racial Justice

The Evolution of a Movement

We are all for detaining criminals.... What if we detained and deported only immigrants without documentation who pose a threat to public safety?

—Ali Noorani, executive director of the National
Immigration Forum, March 4, 2013

Shortly after ICE released more than 2,000 immigrants from detention centers nationwide, Ali Noorani of the National Immigration Forum (NIF) wrote the words of this chapter's epigraph in an article for Reuters. Republicans had attacked ICE for the releases, which took place before automatic funding cuts would go into effect during budget sequestration. Noorani was seemingly well intentioned in his attempt to defend the releases. Following the mention of detaining criminals, he wrote, "Miguel Hernandez, for example, had been detained after being pulled over for not using his car's turn signal. Not exactly a criminal offense." But he then went on to quell any concerns about Hernandez being free: "Neither Hernandez nor anyone else has

97

been entirely freed. Transferred detainees are supervised, must still appear in court and are still in deportation proceedings." In making these points, Noorani reinforced the idea that some immigrants deserve detention and deportation. His reasoning behind it: they have committed a crime that renders them unworthy of being in the United States. Miguel Hernandez wasn't one of the "real threats" that, according to Noorani, we, as a country, should be focused on. Noorani was attempting to expose the problems with mass immigrant detention, but he was also trying to influence the debate around comprehensive immigration reform (CIR) that was in full swing at the time. As he explains in the piece, "The politically charged reactions that followed the detainee transfer should be channeled into the productive conversation already under way in Congress about a better immigration process," referencing the 2013 CIR effort.[1]

The article exposes two common themes in the mainstream immigrant rights movement. First, it positioned most immigrants as "relatively innocent" and therefore undeserving of ICE's harsh treatment, while others are deemed criminals who should be deported. "We are not criminals," an all-too-familiar phrase in the movement, reinforces stereotypes about "good immigrants" who deserve relief versus "bad immigrants" who are disposable. This slogan has not only hurt our ability to challenge racist and xenophobic immigration laws and policies but also evokes anti-Black racism. The framing has thus furthered divisions between the immigrant rights movement and the broader racial justice movement. And a focus on criminal backgrounds affirms that immigration itself is a public safety issue. Despite many efforts to point out why saying "We are not criminals" is not only harmful to our movements but also bad messaging, the slogan endures.

Second, Noorani's piece alludes to what some immigrant rights leaders have referred to as the gold standard of the immigrant rights struggle: securing legalization for the eleven million undocumented immigrants living in the United States. For years, Democrats focused on passing CIR, meaning they have been willing to make significant trade-offs with Republicans in order to get legalization for a portion of the undocumented population. The trade-offs included ramping up border militarization and increasing interior enforcement to deport immigrants, justified by the narrative of the good immigrant versus the bad immigrant. Instead of questioning this line of thinking, well-resourced Beltway (those based in Washington, DC) immigration advocacy organizations championed the CIR framework and depictions of the hardworking and sacrificing immigrant who wants desperately to be an American versus the dangerous and lawless one who must be kept out.

The immigration debate is often centered on the notion that in order to get some legalization, we must also accept some enforcement. But during the Obama years, a growing contingent of the movement began to reject this viewpoint. I attribute this evolution to three key shifts that took place since Obama's first term in office. First, the Obama administration's more calculated use of the criminal legal system to arrest, detain, and deport immigrants revealed the broader problems with the prison industrial complex. Immigrant rights activists could no longer ignore the crisis of mass incarceration and racist policing in the United States. These became everyday realities for immigrant communities. Likewise, the movement's awareness of broader racial justice issues only grew as Black Lives Matter protests gained steam amid police killings in Ferguson, Baltimore, and beyond. Advocates who had shied away from talking about race, criminalization, and their relationship to the immigration system were now forced to reckon with the connections. A burgeoning group of antideportation and detention abolition organizations finally found its footing as these shifts took place. Then came the 2016 election. Trump's ascension to the presidency changed everything. Now not only were the fringes of the movement sharpening their understanding of the deportation system's intersections with the PIC, but the inherent racism of our immigration system was exposed, and even moderate national organizations had to acknowledge the conversation surrounding it.

In this chapter, I turn to the immigrant rights movement and track its successes and failures during the time when the most well-resourced organizations prioritized legalization over everything else. We must be sober about the right-wing forces that immigrant communities and those seeking to migrate are up against. The nativist right has grown more powerful over the last decades, and its xenophobic and restrictionist agendas have been mainstreamed. The impact has been alarming. When it comes to border enforcement, some Democrats have succumbed to the ideology of those who want to end asylum for good. This is why we must constantly examine our tactics and approach. How has the immigrant rights movement unwittingly reinforced the attacks by the right, adding fuel to the fire of their arguments? At the same time, how has it resisted and succeeded in pushing back against increasing detention and deportation? What I lay out in this chapter (and the following two chapters) only scratches the surface of the deep organizing and movement work that has taken place over the last twenty years. Even so, it shows that challenging criminalization and pushing beyond the legalization framework were the critical steps that enabled immigrant justice activists to finally turn the tide on mass deportations.

The Post-9/11 Immigrant Rights Movement

Pinpointing an exact scope of the immigrant rights movement is not an easy task. Since the early 2000s, the commonly held perception of the purpose of the movement is the effort to secure citizenship for the eleven million undocumented people living in the United States. This objective has often eclipsed every other goal. But there is much more to the movement than passing a legalization bill. For undocumented immigrants, these objectives have encompassed securing driver's licenses and accessing public benefits, in-state tuition, and fair wages. For both undocumented immigrants and those not naturalized, the movement has prioritized strategies for pushing back against the growing detention and deportation system: fighting individual deportation defense campaigns, ending ICE-police collaborations, stopping detention expansion, and repealing some of the laws that have made deportations skyrocket in recent decades. Other groups advocate for more refugee assistance, family reunification, better asylum policy, and humanitarian aid for those seeking safety at the border. The list goes on and on. Despite the varied nature of the immigrant rights struggle, the central demand for the most well-resourced groups and the foundations supporting them remains legalization. For them, in theory, if CIR were to pass, then many of the other issues immigrants face would be more or less solved.

CIR emerged as a framework in the early 2000s. At the time, president George W. Bush was considering a policy that would give amnesty to the undocumented immigrant population in the United States. The "grand bargain" would include a guest worker program and Mexico's support in controlling border crossings. It was dubbed the "whole enchilada" by Mexico's foreign secretary.[2] The logic of CIR, which trades legal status for some "good immigrants" in exchange for exclusion of "bad immigrants" has been central to immigration reform for decades. Both the Hart-Celler Act of 1965 and Reagan's 1986 "amnesty" bill had provisions that supported some immigrants, but they also included changes that made future migration more difficult and enforcement more severe. While amnesties continue to be seen as a positive development, they "are often one-time events that are coupled with a tightening of immigration controls."[3] They also always have stipulations that prevent certain people from benefiting, for example, because they may not meet a cutoff date or they have a criminal record.

DC-based immigration advocacy organizations remained steadfast in their commitment to securing legalization, which would require bipartisan support. The groups included the Center for Community Change, the National Immigration Forum, and the National

Council of La Raza (NCLR), among others. In an effort to build bipartisan support, CIR-focused organizations often avoided discussion of racism in relation to immigration and the root causes of migration, advising others to do the same. In a scene from *How Democracy Works Now*, a documentary about the legislative campaign for CIR in the early 2000s, Frank Sharry, then director of NIF, explained to a group of Iowa Democrats that "what doesn't work, for the most part, is calling your opponents racist." He then evoked a sanitized version of the civil rights era, arguing that Martin Luther King Jr. did not convince "a very skeptical American public about civil rights" by calling people "racist jerks" but by invoking "the American dream" and "who we are as a nation [as] welcoming to all people at God's table."[4]

Meanwhile, post-9/11 raids on immigrant communities were on the rise. In New York City, many legal permanent residents from countries in Asia and the Caribbean who'd had previous contact with the criminal legal system were increasingly being detained and put in deportation proceedings. Immigrant Defense Project, a legal nonprofit supporting immigrants with criminal histories, and Families for Freedom, an alliance of families fighting deportation, both formed in New York City after the shifts to immigration policy in 1996 and following 9/11. To equip immigrants to protect themselves when ICE came knocking at the door, the two organizations together developed a Deportation 101 curriculum. This type of partnership between organizers and lawyers has grown over the years and become a critical connection in fighting back against harsh immigration policies. DWN became an important hub for groups like Families for Freedom. The participation of community-based organizations and individuals who were directly impacted by new policies after 9/11 proved to be a crucial turning point on DWN's path to abolition.

On the opposite end of the country, the National Day Laborer Organizing Network (NDLON) was founded in 2001 in Los Angeles to support immigrant worker organizing. NDLON started to witness shifts in immigration enforcement as more immigrant workers were being rounded up by local police. Chris Newman, NDLON's legal director, first heard about the 287(g) program when he got a call from Salvador Reza, then an organizer with the Macehualli Worker Center and future founder of Puente, a grassroots immigration advocacy organization in Arizona. Reza called attention to Maricopa County sheriff Joe Arpaio and the new federal program that gave his deputies federal immigration authority. NDLON began following the expansion of ICE partnerships with local police as the Bush administration implemented several 287(g) programs to target day laborers from Alabama to North Carolina and beyond.

Networks like NDLON and DWN were critical for grassroots groups fighting back against the growing immigrant dragnet. During this period, I was working as an organizer at Grassroots Leadership in Texas, where very few people in the immigrant rights space knew about immigrant detention. We became members of DWN and attended our first conference in 2005. Suddenly, we didn't feel so isolated. DWN provided talking points, fact sheets, and legislative analysis that helped us advocate against detention in Texas. For my colleague Bob Libal and me at Grassroots Leadership, where we were often caught between immigration and criminal justice advocacy, DWN was a lifeline.

An organic movement of undocumented youth also began to emerge as they struggled with the hindrances to getting a university education and limited opportunities for employment. The DREAM Act, which would grant legal status to undocumented youths, had first been introduced in Congress in 2001, and variations of it continue to be a key site of advocacy for "Dreamers." Neidi Dominguez helped organize an on-campus group while a student at University of California, Santa Cruz, to support immigrant youth and workers. She explains the growth of the youth base: "Across the whole state, so many students were organizing to create these support groups on campus. Eventually there were about 32 different groups across the state."[5] With the support of the Coalition for Humane Immigrant

Rights of Los Angeles (CHIRLA), they formed the California Immigrant Youth Network. Later, a national network, United We Dream,
was founded to "transcend the CIR framework and a narrow focus on
legislation, and instead build a sustainable movement led by undocumented youth."[6]

On December 16, 2005, the House passed HR 4437, the Border Protection, Anti-terrorism, and Illegal Immigration Control Act (commonly referred to as the Sensenbrenner Bill after representative Jim
Sensenbrenner of Wisconsin, who introduced it). The provisions in
HR 4437 were so severe—among them, making it a felony to be in
the United States without documentation—that it brought hundreds
of thousands of people, mostly Latinx immigrant communities, to
the streets in opposition. The largest mobilizations took place in Los
Angeles and Chicago in the spring of 2006, but more than 200 cities
and towns across the country organized marches and rallies.[7]

For anyone working on immigrant rights at the time, it was an
unforgettable moment. In Austin, student walkouts against the bill
forced local organizations to coordinate better for the marches. In my
role at Grassroots Leadership, I helped organize two large mobilizations on April 10 and May 1, 2006. The local Spanish media promoted
the events, bringing thousands to the streets in some of the largest
protests Austin had seen since the Vietnam War. People chanted "El
pueblo unido jamás sera vencido" ("The people united will never be
defeated") and "Aquí estamos y no vamos" ("We are here, and we're
not leaving"). On April 10, I spoke in front of the state capitol to a
crowd of over ten thousand people.[8] I remember being at the podium
giving a speech about the growth of detention in Texas. I spoke about
the Laredo superjail and what the bill could do if it became law, and
called for an end to detention and deportations. As images from other
marches across the country emerged, we could hardly believe it; millions of people were in the streets demanding justice for immigrants.
It felt like a turning point.

The mobilizations against the Sensenbrenner Bill were precisely that: a defensive rejection of the bill and the growing nativist agenda in Congress. But many of the actions were also harnessed to a centrist message that pushed for CIR and didn't outwardly acknowledge the harms of detention and deportation. During the mobilizations, many of those marching engaged in the "politics of respectability," promoting immigrants' nationalism, innocence, and productivity. At the national level, DC-based groups, such as the Center for Community Change, called the actions "We are America" rallies. Abolitionist scholar Angélica Cházaro argues that CIR proponents in the movement did "their utmost to enhance the reputation of the undocumented and distance them from 'criminals' through constant appeals to immigrants' purportedly hard-working, law-abiding nature."[9] Throughout the mobilizations, protesters carried American flags and held signs that read, "We are workers, not criminals."

The primary objective for the Beltway organizations remained legalization. Immigrants with criminal convictions were not only the first to be thrown under the bus—they were often seen as a direct obstacle to reform. Andrea Black, DWN's founding executive director, told me that at one rally in DC, CIR organizations were so concerned about associating themselves with immigrants who had criminal convictions that they abruptly withdrew from a DWN-sponsored press event the night before the rally. DWN went ahead with the event, highlighting the stories of immigrants and their families impacted by the criminal legal system. The following day, DWN members successfully fought to be included in the speaker lineup at the CIR rally (though they were told not to mention criminalization). It was a small victory for the advocates fighting against detention and deportations.

In addition to tensions within the movement, certain Democrats in Congress were concerned with the rightward trend of CIR developments. In an incredible scene captured in *How Democracy Works Now*, during the failed CIR process in 2007, Democratic New Jersey senator Robert Menendez chides the DC immigration advocates for their willingness to bend over backward to get something passed. He begins by raising concerns about the state of the bill: "It seems we have bargained in a negotiation in which all the things that could moderate it are poison pills, dealbreakers." He goes on to address the role of the advocates: "I have to say I'm disappointed in all of you. And I think that the reason we're in this position, to be very honest with you, is because in the desire to get something, you've all been willing to cede and cede, and we've become a punching bag in the process."[10]

Alto Arizona and the Dreamer Movement

More than anywhere else in the country, the state of Arizona came to define the immigrant rights struggle during Obama's first term as president. Sheriff Joe Arpaio's assault on immigrant communities became a focal point for the movement. Through the 287(g) program that gave Maricopa County deputies federal immigration authority, thousands of immigrants were rounded up and detained at an inhumane and sweltering tent city jail. At the time, NDLON had been working with Salvador Reza and Carlos Garcia of Puente to raise concerns with DHS about the program. At a meeting with immigration advocates, including Chris Newman of NDLON, Obama brought up 287(g)'s problems and then insisted that despite its problems, it was necessary to get CIR to pass. Once again, Obama was making the argument for the "grand bargain" and ramping up enforcement in an effort to get legalization. These tensions around ICE-police collaboration in immigrant communities were further complicated by Obama's appointment of Janet Napolitano as secretary of DHS. As the former governor of Arizona, she had a friendly relationship with Arpaio. Arpaio had endorsed her in her first governor's race. Napolitano had often been silent about Arpaio's anti-immigrant initiatives and avoided intervening.[11] It took almost three years for her to finally rescind Arpaio's 287(g) agreement, and she only did it after considerable pressure from activists and lawyers.

Secure Communities, which Bush initially rolled out as a pilot program in 2008, was already on NDLON's radar when the Obama administration decided to make it the cornerstone of its reforms to the immigration enforcement system. In early 2010, NDLON filed a Freedom of Information Act request with the support of the Center for Constitutional Rights to better understand Secure Communities, dubbed SCOMM by activists, and to expose the racial profiling inherent to the program. CCR had recently filed a federal class action lawsuit against the NYPD's racist stop and frisk policy. Through understanding SCOMM's inner workings, immigrant rights activists began seeing more clearly the connections between different law enforcement agencies and the targeting of Black and brown communities. As deportations increased, groups across the country organized against SCOMM and pushed states such as Illinois and New York to opt out of the program. While ICE provided contradictory information about whether the program was voluntary or not, the agency eventually said that SCOMM would be mandatory.

Meanwhile, conservative states continued their own assault on immigration. In April 2010, Arizona passed SB 1070, a new law that encouraged racial profiling and criminal prosecution of undocumented immigrants. It was dubbed the "show me your papers" law by activists and the media. The combination of SB 1070's draconian nature with Arpaio's malice toward immigrants (and the federal government's enabling of it) made Arizona the cultural center of the movement and a hotbed of activist intervention. That organizing would eventually force the Obama administration to finally take executive action.

If you were an immigrant justice activist during this period, there was a good chance you would have at some point made the journey to Arizona to show support, and you would have left with "Alto Arizona" posters and a "Legalize Arizona" T-shirt. Communities across the country organized solidarity protests. Several mayors, including those in Los Angeles and Minneapolis, had city employees boycott by halting any travel to Arizona. Famous musicians like Shakira spoke out against the law, and others joined Sound Strike, which had per- formers boycott concerts and other events in the state, organized by Rage Against the Machine frontman Zack de la Rocha.[12] On May Day after the law passed, demonstrations took place in more than seventy cities.[13] Later that month, tens of thousands marched in the streets of downtown Phoenix, calling for the repeal of SB 1070. Puente kept the heat on Obama at the march. Salvador Reza spoke out at the rally: "If Obama lets this fester, we're going to have boycotts against the US, just like with South Africa in apartheid. I hope it doesn't get to that, but if it does, it's going to be on Obama's hands."[14] The Center for American Progress estimated that the Arizona boycott had cost the state's tourist industry $141 million within six months of the law being passed.[15]

While NDLON, Puente, and allies continued to raise the alarm about federal immigration policy and its relationship to SB 1070, groups advocating for CIR saw the attention on Arizona as an oppor- tunity to push their agenda. Frank Sharry, now at the communica- tions outfit America's Voice, wrote in an op-ed, "Having state and local governments pass laws that invite discrimination against citizens and legal residents who happen to be Latino is the wrong way. Having Congress enact comprehensive immigration reform that eliminates illegal immigration is the right way."[16] Sharry's framing affirmed the bipartisan narrative that "illegal immigration" is a problem in need of solving, but it was the role of the federal government, not the state of Arizona. The Obama administration agreed with this line of think- ing. Finally, after numerous protests, boycotts, and lawsuits against SB 1070, the Justice Department sued Arizona in July 2010 on the grounds that it was the federal government's responsibility to oversee immigration law.

The case eventually went to the Supreme Court. Legal journalist Linda Greenhouse noted how "utterly depressing" the oral arguments were: "Many casual followers of this case, *State of Arizona v. United*

States, no doubt assume it has something to do with the rights of undocumented immigrants. As the argument made abundantly clear, it doesn't. The question, rather, is which of two sovereigns, the United States or the state of Arizona, has the right to make the immigrants' lives difficult."[17]

—

The summer of 2010 was a turning point not only for those pushing back against increased enforcement but also for the immigrant youth movement, whose members were growing frustrated with the CIR debate. Earlier in the year, Tania Unzueta, an undocumented organizer with the Immigrant Youth Justice League in Chicago, organized the first National Coming Out of the Shadows Day. Immigrant youths, taking a page from the queer movement, were "coming out" as "undocumented and unafraid."[18] While the conventional narrative about Dreamers (a generation of activists associated with the DREAM Act) had often positioned them in the "politics of respectability," as the innocent hardworking young people who came to the United States at "no fault of their own," immigrant youth activists began disrupting this framework and critiquing the deportation system as a whole. Unzueta explained that a visit to Arizona helped her see that "the anti-immigrant strategy of attrition [was] about making everyday life difficult through laws and policies that, for example, block undocumented immigrants' access to public services, police patrols and raids through Latino neighborhoods, harassment of day laborers by the border patrol." Understanding the scope of enforcement helped her see the limitations of CIR. She and other Dreamers had begun pushing for a stand-alone DREAM Act.[19]

Beltway groups were less supportive of the decision of Dreamers to go out on their own, fearing it would look bad for their CIR strategy. Neidi Dominguez describes the reactions: "We got a lot of backlash from the right, from the left, from the middle. There were articles . . . calling us petulant children that only cared about ourselves. [We were] getting calls from international unions to other immigrant rights leaders or advocates on the ground to talk to us, to talk us down."[20] Despite this, the Dreamers forged ahead that summer. Activists started sitting in at congressional offices, bird-dogging political events, and organizing buses and marches from across the country to DC. The immigrant youth movement was not a monolith, and opinions about goals and tactics varied, but both immigrant youth activists and those fighting enforcement (two groups that frequently overlapped) started using civil disobedience as a strategy to pressure President Obama and members of Congress to take action.

In the fall of 2011, a radical group of immigrant youth activists escalated their tactics and began "infiltrating" detention centers. The National Immigrant Youth Alliance (NIYA) organized what they called break-ins, in which an undocumented youth activist would show up at a detention center to be detained as a strategy to assert their own agency. Marco Saavedra, an organizer with NIYA who was voluntarily detained at the Broward Detention Center outside Miami, explains: "We change the power dynamics and show that we are the ones to dictate our futures. . . . It isn't that ICE has the option to detain us; we are dictating whether we allow for them to detain us or not. We are the ones in control, regardless of what the authorities think." Once inside, Saavedra and other "infiltrators" started to communicate and collect information from other detained immigrants to expose how many of those inside could be eligible for prosecutorial discretion. NIYA began waging deportation defense campaigns for those locked up. Lawyers in the movement criticized NIYA's tactics, worrying they would complicate the immigration cases of detained individuals. Despite the naysayers, the degree to which undocumented youth were willing to go to expose the system proved to be effective at shining a light on the severity of Obama's immigration policy and what it was like inside immigrant detention, which had been hidden from the public.[21]

After the DREAM Act failed in Congress, Obama became the central target for undocumented youth efforts. Immigrant youth activists ramped up their tactics, even going so far as staging sit-ins at Obama's campaign offices during the 2012 election cycle. On June 15, 2012, the Obama administration finally relented with the announcement of Deferred Action for Childhood Arrivals (DACA). DACA gave certain immigrant youth protection from deportation and work authorization. It was a resounding victory for the immigrant youth movement, one that wouldn't have happened without their tireless efforts and actions. But it fell short in several ways, which Obama pointed out in his speech announcing DACA: "Now, let's be clear—this is not amnesty, this is not immunity. This is not a path to citizenship. It's not a permanent fix. This is a temporary stopgap measure that lets us focus our resources wisely while giving a degree of relief and hope to talented, driven, patriotic young people."[22] In addition to being temporary in nature and leaving many people out due to age restrictions, the program also excluded immigrants with felonies and some misdemeanors—that is, those on whom Obama planned to "focus our resources." Organizers like Dominguez said the announcement galvanized the movement to push the administration to go further: "The whole point was to win protection for all. We figured, if we can get him to say we deserve protection, what argument could they use to deny our parents?"[23]

For immigrant justice activists, the end of Obama's first term proved to be a crucial moment for abolitionist shifts in the movement. While DACA was a considerable concession for the administration, enforcement had reached an all-time high, with 478,000 people detained and 419,000 people formally deported over the course of fiscal year 2012.[24] DWN launched an effort to shut down detention centers (explained in chapter 6), but the organization had still not taken an abolitionist position when it came to detention. Then, in December 2012, after several often-contentious conversations within the membership, DWN adopted a vision of a world without detention, which undoubtedly helped clarify its purpose and strategies moving forward. NDLON, meanwhile, was figuring

out its next move. After DACA, it was clear that, while some people would be protected from deportation, many more would be left
out. It was in this moment that Marisa Franco, lead organizer with
NDLON, came up with the Not1More Deportation campaign. The
call for Not1More changed the conversation. Deportation was no
longer a given. Not one more meant not one more, and whether
activists realized it or not at the time, it was effectively calling for the
abolition of deportation.

The Senate Bill and the Campaign
for Not1More Deportation

While Obama had been ramping up interior and border enforcement
throughout his first term, as a ploy to pass CIR, congressional debate
at the time was largely focused on the Affordable Care Act, and due to
Republican opposition a CIR bill never moved. Obama's win in 2012,
with notable support from Latinx voters, meant that immigrant rights
groups would finally have another chance at securing legalization.
Several DC-based immigrant rights organizations—America's Voice,
NCLR, and Center for Community Change, among others—formed
the Alliance for Citizenship (A4C) in early 2013 to push for legalization and set their sights on the Senate to introduce a bill. A parallel
group of organizations, including DWN and NDLON, came together
to push back against the enforcement provisions that would inevita-
bly end up in a CIR bill, though with limited resources we were not
able to have any meaningful influence on the debate.

The core demand for A4C was a pathway to citizenship, but an
additional point in its principles included enforcement: "Ensure
enforcement measures protect American and immigrant workers,
advance due process and fair treatment, and are consistent with
American values."[25] A4C's messaging was in line with what polling
repeatedly told immigrant rights advocates: that in order to convince
the American public that legalization is worth supporting, we must

be patriotic and promote immigrants as productive and hardwork-ing. Often communications experts from these organizations would dissuade the rest of us from talking about why there was such a large undocumented immigrant population in the United States because it didn't poll well. The history of US-backed wars in other parts of world, neoliberal policies like NAFTA, and their impact on migration were things we weren't supposed to bring up.

In the Senate, four Democrats and four Republicans referred to as the Gang of Eight came together to draft the CIR bill. On April 16, 2013, Democratic New York senator Chuck Schumer introduced S.744, the Border Security, Economic Opportunity, and Immigra-tion Modernization Act, cosponsored by the rest of the gang. It was a behemoth of a bill—over 800 pages long. On legalization, while it included a pathway to citizenship, it would have taken undocumented immigrants thirteen years in total to achieve citizenship. Those who had been convicted of a felony or three misdemeanors would not be eligible.[26] On border enforcement, the bill included an additional $6.5 billion for DHS to "increase enforcement and extend fencing along the Southwest border." It also required the border security programs to be up and running before undocumented immigrants could apply for green cards.[27] Despite these and other anti-immigrant provisions, most immigrant rights groups celebrated the bill's introduction, they accepted bad provisions because mass legalization was on the table. For many advocates, it was a compromise—the "shit sandwich" or "bitter pill" we'd just have to take.

Then, in June, days before the bill came to a vote, Republican senators Bob Corker and John Hoeven introduced a "border surge" amendment. It took the border enforcement part of the bill and super-sized it from $6.5 to $46 billion. It would double the number of bor-der patrol agents to 38,000, build even more fencing at the border, and increase the use of drones and other surveillance technologies.[28] It would also triple unlawful entry prosecutions through Operation Streamline in Tucson to 210 people a day.[29] It was a terrifying pros-

pect. Most immigrant rights organizations, even those associated
with A4C, raised concerns about it, but it nonetheless passed in the
Senate and was included in the final bill. On June 27, 2013, the Senate
passed S.744 with a vote of 68–32 in favor.

The movement was divided. For the A4C groups, it was a victory despite the supersized border enforcement measures. Many CIR
advocates were present in the Senate the day of the vote, celebrating
and chanting "Yes We Can," Obama's campaign slogan, upon its passage.[30] In a statement, NCLR said that even though it wasn't "perfect,"
it "delivered a real solution to our broken immigration system."[31] Ali
Noorani of NIF expressed that increased enforcement was expected
for a bipartisan effort: "This bill has some really tough spots. Certain
[parts] of the movement don't feel it's part of the price of admission.
But winning legislation that's bipartisan means that not everybody
is going to be happy."[32] For others, the Corker-Hoeven amendment
was a step too far; some groups, including DWN, came out against
the bill. Gerald Lenoir, executive director of the Black Alliance for
Just Immigration, argued that the bill's passage pointed to larger systemic issues: "To those who hail the Senate bill as 'historic,' I say, yes,
it is historic in a distorted way. This War on Immigrants continues
the overall trend of militarization of U.S. society as a whole under the
guise of the War on Terrorism and the War on Drugs."[33]

In many ways, the Corker-Hoeven amendment was a sign of what
was to come in the discourse surrounding immigration. Since its
passage, the "crisis" at the border has driven policy decisions around
immigration more than anything else. While the movement's power
to secure legalization has since waned, the push for more border
militarization has only grown. After the Senate bill passed, reporter
Benjy Sarlin called the willingness to concede for legalization Democrats' "dirty secret," saying that as long as legalization is included
in a bill, "Democrats will meet any demand on border security—no
matter how arbitrary and misguided."[34] While Sarlin's comments
were focused on Democrats in Congress, the same could be said of

the organizations pushing for CIR. The propensity of groups involved in A4C to accept the "border surge" amendment gave Democrats a pass when it came to increased border enforcement, opening space for Republicans to advance their nativist agenda.

As the debate on immigration reform took place in Congress, the Not1More campaign launched to pressure Obama to end deportations. The campaign was broad in scope. It demanded an end to the 287(g) program and Secure Communities, as well as Operation Streamline and the mass prosecutions taking place at the border, bridging the gap between interior and border work. It also called for the expansion of DACA and prosecutorial discretion so that more people would be protected from deportation. It was an intentional affront to the CIR framework. The organizers put it this way: "The movement was designed not around advocating for those in our movements who were most sympathetic to the US mainstream, but around those who were criminalized and easily discarded by a messaging machine focused on 'hardworking' immigrants who were 'not criminals.'"[35] As the call for Not1More grew, #ShutDownICE actions took place across the country, which included a range of tactics: banner drops, bird-dogging events, and civil disobedience actions outside detention centers and ICE offices.

DWN had been working with NDLON regularly over the years, and as Not1More grew we coordinated to support local groups working to amplify the demands of immigrants going on hunger strike in detention centers. In October 2013, I attended a Not1More campaign convergence in Phoenix (we were in Arizona a lot those days). At some point, a woman stood up and began speaking with conviction about the GEO Group and conditions at the Northwest Detention Center (NWDC) in Tacoma, Washington. While detention was part of the conversation, it wasn't the central focus of these organizing spaces, and I knew I had to introduce myself to her. It turned out the woman speaking was Maru Mora Villalpando, who was organizing in Seattle with the group

NWDC Resistance to support detained immigrants. The organizing taking place around NWDC, which centered on coordinating with immigrants in detention, provided a new approach to antidetention and antideportation campaigns during Obama's second term.

One tactic Not1More employed was to block buses outside detention centers or deportation staging sites to prevent deportations from taking place. Not1More activists organized #ShutDownICE demonstrations to stop deportation buses across the country. In February 2014, in the cold and wet Pacific Northwest winter, ten organizers with NWDC Resistance locked arms and formed a human chain, blocking the driveway of the detention center. The organizers were able to stop one bus and two vans from carrying out deportations, preventing the deportation of 120 immigrants. The protest galvanized immigrants detained at NWDC: two weeks later, at least 750 immigrants began a hunger strike protesting detention conditions. Hunger strikes began to spread at other detention centers nationwide.[36]

The choice to situate Not1More civil disobedience actions at detention centers helped make the immigrant detention system more visible for the movement. For the most part, people felt the impact of ICE taking their loved ones away, but the role of immigrant detention had stayed hidden from the public and the larger immigrant rights movement. With these actions, something started to click, and more groups started seeing the connection between detention and the deportation pipeline.

Local- and state-level interventions to curb immigration enforcement, often referred to as sanctuary policies, became an important way to reduce the pipeline to deportation and to pressure the administration during this period. In 2011, the ICE Out of California Coalition came together to prevent the full effects of Secure Communities. During the Obama years, roughly 70 percent of ICE arrests had taken place at prisons or jails.[37] Cutting off ICE's ability to target immigrants through the criminal legal system would be essential to limiting deportations. The coalition focused on preventing detainers, which allow law enforcement agencies to hold immigrants even after they are eligible for release so that ICE can arrest them and place them in immigrant detention. The coalition supported the introduction of the TRUST Act, which would limit the use of detainers in California. The legislation initially failed to move, but the coalition started working with localities to opt out of Secure Communities and galvanized grassroots support across the state. Local organizers put pressure on sheriffs and other local entities to end ICE agreements and built a groundswell of support.

The shifting local terrain helped open space at the state level, and two years later, in 2013, the TRUST Act became law. Upon signing it and other immigration-related bills, Governor Jerry Brown proclaimed, "While Washington waffles on immigration, California's forging ahead. I'm not waiting."[38] Within the first year of the act's passage, the use of detainers to transfer immigrants to ICE custody decreased by 44 percent.[39] Eventually, in response to local and state resistance to Secure Communities, the Obama administration sunsetted the program. (The administration then launched a new program to attempt to address the concerns raised, though immigrant justice activists pointed out the similarities to Secure Communities and dismissed it as a rebranding effort.)

———

By early 2014, it had become clear that CIR had failed once again, with no hope for a bill moving in the Republican-controlled House. A4C groups were growing frustrated with the lack of action by the Obama administration as formal deportations hit two million under his tenure. While the campaign for Not1More deportation was often seen as a nuisance by many of the establishment immigrant rights organizations, since CIR wasn't going anywhere, some began to take on Not1More's messaging. In March, Janet Murguía, president of National Council of La Raza, spoke at a fundraising dinner: "For the president, I think his legacy is at stake here. We consider him the deportation president, or the deporter-in-chief."[40] It was something that NDLON

and affiliated groups had been saying for some time, and by the summer, Obama was receiving criticism from all sides. CIR groups and
those fighting enforcement demanded executive action. Meanwhile,
Republicans attacked the administration for being soft on immigration when the number of families arriving at the border increased. In
response, five years after ending family detention at Hutto, Obama
did a complete about-face on the issue as more families arrived at the
border, expanding the capacity to detain parents with their children
once again.

In November 2014, after continued pressure from Not1More
activists and CIR's failure, Obama announced the implementation of
Deferred Action for Parents of Americans and Lawful Permanent Residents (DAPA). The speech, at least in some parts of the movement,
has come to be known as the infamous "felons, not families" speech
(see chapter 2). DAPA would have given status to parents of US citizen children or of those with legal resident status, but, before it could
go into effect, Texas and other states sued, blocking its implementation. For many of us working to end deportations and detentions, the
speech only confirmed Obama's commitment to criminalization. Singling out "felons" and "gang members," Obama reinforced the good
immigrant versus bad immigrant frame. His administration then
went on to expand family detention, locking up nearly 3,000 immigrants, including children and babies, in new Texas jails under the
guise of "border security," revealing his hypocrisy on the issue. The
speech, despite the announcement of DAPA, was just another confir-
mation that Obama was no friend to immigrants.

A few weeks later, a St. Louis County grand jury decided not to
indict Ferguson police officer Darren Wilson in the killing of eighteen-
year-old Michael Brown. Once again, Black Lives Matter protesters
filled streets across the country. In a statement for NDLON, Marisa
Franco lamented: "Just days ago, President Obama announced relief
for families but not felons. But what are those terms in the context
of Ferguson? When our communities are already deemed criminal?

When the murdered are put on trial? And police forces like Ferguson's are the arbiters of this 'nation of laws?'"[41]

As Black Lives Matter protests spread across the country, United We Dream (UWD) started to connect with groups in the broader racial justice movement, including Dream Defenders and Black Youth Project 100. The young leaders of color came together to form Freedom Side, an homage to the Freedom Summer of the civil rights era, to amplify demands that spread across communities of color: ending the school-to-prison pipeline, ending deportations, ensuring public education for all and the right to vote, and so on.[42] Greisa Martínez Rosas, UWD executive director, describes the formation as a pivotal moment for the organization's understanding of the immigrant youth struggle as an abolitionist struggle: "It sharpened our analysis, it was putting a word to the thing we had been doing all along."[43]

As Obama's time in office came to an end and Trump became omnipresent, new organizations formed and embraced the racial justice aspect of the immigrant rights struggle in contrast to establishment groups that avoided it. In 2015, Franco and other Not-1More organizers formed Mijente to create a political home and "to confront the challenges of our time and respond to the growing threats to the Latinx community."[44] And in January 2016, the organization UndocuBlack Network was founded, with a vision "to have truly inclusive immigrant rights and racial justice movements that advocate for the rights of Black undocumented individuals, [and] provide healing spaces and community to those with intersecting identities."[45]

The Post-Trump Immigrant Rights Movement

For many of us in the immigrant rights movement, waking up the day after the 2016 election was reminiscent of when we first learned about the 9/11 attacks fifteen years earlier. It was impossible not to fear for the immigrant communities that would bear the brunt of the domestic policy shifts that were about to take place. While Trump is often seen as an aberration, he merely brought forward the existing racism of the system for the world to see. But even so, his administration's assault on immigrants was relentlessly cruel. From day one, Trump's agenda was clear: punish immigrants to the greatest extent possible and keep them out at all costs. The Trump era spurred the immigrant rights movement to sharpen its analysis and adapt its strategies to push beyond the legalization framework. However, having to constantly negotiate the onslaught of attacks was overwhelming, to say the least, and the movement has struggled in its aftermath.

CIR advocates were at a loss when Trump became president. With Republicans in control of the White House, Senate, and House, congressional strategies were few and far between. For those fighting enforcement, this political shift provided an interesting opening in Congress around the role of the federal budget, which I discuss in chapter 5. But for others who had spent years focused on currying favor with Democrats in Congress and the Obama administration, it was a disorienting moment. Many organizations turned their attention to defensive litigation as a tool to push back against some of Trump's harshest policies (such as the Muslim Ban), but legal strategies could only go so far, given the conservative nature of the courts. Others finally focused on debunking the racist and xenophobic narratives coming from the administration.

The greatest movement shift was the turn to state- and local-level strategies, which many groups had already been employing. Thanks to pressure from local organizers and advocates during the Obama years, many cities and states started implementing sanctuary policies like the TRUST Act. These limits on ICE's relationship to local law enforcement protected some immigrants from detention and deportation. Sanctuary policies combined with the implementation of DACA and other forms of relief helped bring down ICE interior arrests toward the end of Obama's second term from nearly 300,000 in 2009 to 110,000 in 2016.[46]

When Trump came into office in 2017, he immediately reinstated Secure Communities and gave ICE license to target all immigrants, moving away from the concept of enforcement priorities. He also resorted back to one of George W. Bush's most vicious tactics: having ICE conduct mass raids targeting immigrant workers. One of the largest took place in Mississippi in 2019, when ICE raided chicken processing plants in six cities on the first day of school. ICE arrested 680 immigrant workers, leaving many of their children reeling and terrified. About 300 immigrants were released, but the rest were detained at the nearby Adams County Correctional Facility in Natchez, Mississippi, and in other detention centers in Louisiana.[47] The raid and ICE's cruelty galvanized immigrant communities in Mississippi, and soon after the local group Immigrant Alliance for Justice and Equity formed in response.

Despite Trump's efforts to instill fear in immigrant communities, formal deportations did not skyrocket. In fact, in ICE's 2019 annual report, the agency noted that "one of the biggest impediments to [its enforcement operations] was the lack of cooperation from an increasing number of jurisdictions nationwide."[48] While raids continued, the number of deportations of those currently living in the United States failed to reach Obama-era levels because of the successful campaigns to limit ICE-police collaboration in states with large immigrant populations, such as California and New Jersey. The movement had successfully stopped an increase of formal deportations in the interior under Trump by blocking the reach of the criminal legal system in immigrant communities.

The border was another story. By the end of the Obama administration, border apprehensions had gone up, and ICE was detaining forty thousand immigrants at any given time, the highest capacity the system had ever reached. People arriving at the border to seek asylum were spending months incarcerated, despite having passed screenings that should have allowed them to be released. Humanitarian and antienforcement organizations criticized Obama's approach, as did those based in the border region, but for most of the movement border policy was not a priority. Years of accepting border militarization as a given for CIR finally caught up to the movement. Now the Trump administration had made draconian border policy the centerpiece of his anti-immigrant agenda. As a result, many Beltway organizations were forced to change their tune and no longer use the immigration enforcement system and its myriad harms as a bargaining chip. This reckoning led many of the CIR groups to turn inward and focus on visioning, something they were now open to doing with a broader range of organizations and perspectives, including those of us working against enforcement.

—

In early 2021, President Biden took office with a Democrat-controlled Congress. Many saw this as yet another opportunity for a pathway to citizenship for the eleven million undocumented immigrants. But the movement had changed and the status quo of legalization or bust had shifted—or so we thought. Several of the long-standing CIR groups and pro-immigrant labor organizations joined with younger movement leadership to launch We Are Home, a campaign urging the Biden administration and Congress to take action on immigration. The goal would be to protect the most people possible through passing legalization and curbing interior enforcement. Because it was the first time that the mainstream movement had publicly committed to winning cuts to detention and deportation alongside citizenship, the intentional focus on enforcement brought DWN and Mijente to the table to ensure we did not repeat the mistakes of past immigration reform efforts. It was potentially an important turning point for the movement. But one key element of immigration policy was left out: the border. We Are Home made a decision to focus solely on those currently living in the United States. The intention was to avoid the tenuous politics around the border and keep a narrow focus on winning legalization and interior enforcement reforms.

By March 2021, the Republicans had taken back the narrative around the border, and the administration faltered on ending Trump-era policies. Many groups within We Are Home hesitated to critique Biden because the campaign needed his full-throated support for the legislative play they were making on citizenship. While a parallel effort existed with groups focused on border and asylum policy, it mostly consisted of humanitarian and policy organizations with no grassroots base and little vision for how to combat the right-wing fearmongering over the border, limiting their power in pushing back against Biden's border militarization. We Are Home as an entity focused its resources on legalization and hesitated to raise concerns about border-related issues like Title 42, the Trump policy (continued by Biden) that resulted in mass expulsions of people seeking asylum at the border.

Having a large contingent of the mainstream immigrant rights movement support a reduction to detention and deportations gave weight to the demand, but many of us soon grew frustrated with the lack of investment by We Are Home on the antienforcement aspect of the campaign. With the central focus once again on legalization, We Are Home spent most of its energy and money trying to get something passed through Biden's Build Back Better bill, which ultimately failed. While many believed a post-Trump immigration policy would be more welcoming and supportive of immigrants, given how draconian Trump's administration had been as well as Biden's commitments on the campaign trail, the opposite proved true. Meaningful reforms to immigration were few and far between, in large part because Democrats feared that the issue would hurt them in the midterm elections. In the end, We Are Home failed to secure legalization, once again, and the prospects of doing so in the future felt even more limited than twenty years prior when CIR was first proposed.

Abolitionist Lessons

The most critical lesson here is that prioritizing relief for some immigrants at the expense of other immigrants has ultimately done more harm than good. The continued willingness of mainstream CIR groups and congressional Democrats to cede ground on enforcement has only reinforced the frames by which both parties argue over immigration. Years later, legalization continues to be out of reach, and tools for administrative relief, such as DACA, are being challenged. But legalization is not the be-all and end-all of immigrant justice. British activists Gracie Mae Bradley and Luke de Noronha explain that "while amnesties might provide material relief to one group of undocumented people, unless they occur within a broader context of abolitionist reforms to an immigration system, they do nothing to ease the lives of people who become undocumented in the future, or to break with the idea that being a citizen is the only way to live a dignified life."[49]

Immigrants can and should be able to live fulfilling lives, regardless of their status. The political disenfranchisement of undocumented and unnaturalized immigrants, an unspoken aspect of the political discourse on immigration, makes this goal much more difficult. This condition, it bears emphasizing, is something immigrants share with millions of people with felony convictions who also cannot vote. To remedy this inequity, some municipalities have started allowing residents, including undocumented immigrants, the ability to vote in local elections. While it's important to remember that voting is not the only way to exert political agency, this is a laudatory step. At both the local and federal level, a multifaceted approach to ensure the greatest rights to noncitizens should be the goal. Those actions include eliminating the fear of detention and deportation, advocating for a living wage and nonexploitative working conditions, providing access to public benefits, and ensuring the ability to travel outside the United States and return.

Obama's implementation of DACA is now lifted up as one of his most important legacies on immigration. But, as this chapter shows, it took a great deal to get him to do even that. The existence of DACA is a direct result of civil disobedience and mobilization organized by immigrant youths and those fighting immigration enforcement. Local sanctuary efforts also finally began to curb deportations and limit the damage done to immigrant communities. Despite all the political will and money that went into fighting for CIR, it was local organizing and movement building that started bringing relief to immigrant communities. This lesson is important to keep in mind as we tackle new challenges. Sharpening our analysis of what's happening at the border and the role it plays in immigration discourse will be critical to advocating for both people seeking to migrate and immigrants living in the United States.

CHAPTER 5

Private Prisons and
the Demand to Defund

*I agree with you. I'm working on it, man. Give me another
five days. Folks, you all know what they're talking about.
There should be no private prisons, period . . . none,
period. That's what they're talking about, private detention centers. They should not exist and we are working to
close all of them. . . . I promise you.*

—President Joe Biden, April 29, 2021

A hundred days into Joe Biden's presidency, he was disrupted at a drive-in rally marking the event outside Atlanta, Georgia. As he gave his speech, organizers yelled "End detention now" and "Communities not cages," their words painted on a large banner. He was promoting the coronavirus recovery bill to the 300 vehicles that had shown up. Among those chanting were Li Ann Sanchez, a transgender woman from Mexico who came to the United States to seek asylum, and Nilson Barahona, a father originally from Honduras who had lived here for over twenty years. Both had been detained at detention centers in Georgia and had protested their incarceration while inside. Biden responded, assuming they were focused on private detention, and promised he would soon end it. "Give me another five days," he said. The protesters cheered. A gaggle of cars honked in support.

By chance, I was watching coverage of Biden's speech on the news when it happened. Upon hearing Biden's response, I was surprised and confused. Months earlier, Biden had signed an executive order phasing out private prisons. The Obama administration had also tried to phase out private prisons in his last year in office, but the plan had been rescinded by Trump. The order only applied to the Department of Justice, which includes the Federal Bureau of Prisons and the US Marshals Service. The Biden administration (following the Obama order) excluded ICE from the phaseout. I wondered if Biden's promise meant they were going to extend the executive order to ICE's immigrant detention centers. As news of the incident spread, the movement was immediately abuzz. Jess Morales Rocketto of the National Domestic Workers Alliance called me right after the clip aired. She had heard from a reporter that ICE was planning to renew its contract with the Broward Detention Center, a GEO Group–run facility near Miami. Biden's statement didn't track with what we knew. We reached out to contacts in the administration, but they didn't know of any private prison–related announcements. In the end, Biden backtracked on his remarks to the protesters, telling reporters he was just "teasing" about something happening in five days.[1]

Private prisons had lost favor over the last several years, and Democrats had begun to renounce them. But despite the rhetoric, the Biden administration kept using them for immigrant detention. The decision to exclude ICE from the phaseout revealed how Democrats' shunning of private prisons wasn't an outright rejection of privatization and the profit-driven model, but rather had much more to do with the growing Black Lives Matter movement and the limited significance of private prisons in the United States's carceral landscape. The administration wasn't ready to take the same step with ICE because immigrant detention is predominantly run by private prisons.

Whereas 80 percent of immigrant detention beds are operated by private prison companies, as of 2023, private prisons only make up 7 percent of the overall prison and jail system in the United States.[2] Immigrant rights activists have naturally highlighted the influence of private prisons when exposing the problems with the deportation machine. While private prison–divestment campaigns, in truth, have been less impactful, state-level private prison bans have halted detention expansion, and there is no question that an end to private prisons would significantly reduce the detention system. However, immigrant rights activists' understandable emphasis on the impact of private prisons has created an unfortunate division between the broader antiprison movement and the immigrant rights movement. The importance of BOP phasing out private prisons should not be downplayed, but if the fight ends at getting rid of private prisons, we will have failed.

Private prisons may not be a key driver of mass incarceration; however, the economy in which prisons exist remains a central reason for keeping so many people locked up. As discussed in part I, the rise in mass incarceration happened as a result of the war on crime and punitive legislative reforms, but it also happened because prisons, jails, and detention centers became potential sources of revenue for communities across the country. Jobs were created and counties generated money for their dwindling local budgets. One study found that legislators were more supportive of private prisons if one existed in the area they represented.[3] It wasn't just the private prison lobby driving that growth, but the desire of politicians to protect the local economies of their constituents. Beyond private prisons themselves, various companies managing a variety of prison-related functions (food, guards, transportation, commissary, phones, health care) thrived as the prison industrial complex grew.

While much attention has been given to the role of the private prison industry, the reality is that funding for mass incarceration comes from the state. For immigrant detention, the appropriation of federal tax dollars to maintain and expand the system is determined annually through the congressional budget process. When examining the economics of detention, it soon becomes clear that the key drivers of expansion were not only harsher immigration laws but also the budget of DHS, which has increased considerably every year since its inception.

In 2017, as the Trump administration's war on immigrants raged, a new campaign emerged that fundamentally shifted the movement's approach to fighting the deportation machine. Three years before #DefundThePolice became a rallying cry during the 2020 racial justice uprisings, the Defund Hate campaign was launched to cut the budgets of ICE and Customs and Border Protection, the two agencies that carry out mass deportations and detention. As the movement came to better understand the appropriations process, the demand to defund began gaining steam. The attention on the budget provided a new and worthy focus, breaking from the constant push for CIR.

In this chapter, I will "follow the money" and reflect on the campaigns and strategies that have tried to address money in the system. I first explain the political economy of detention. (Yes, private prisons are part of the problem, but there is more to it than that.) I reflect on campaigns to divest from private prisons and their limitations, as well as what led to the private prison phaseout by the Federal Bureau of Prisons. Last, I share the origins and strategy of the Defund Hate campaign, which emerged in one of our most dire political moments as a movement. In focusing on the budget, Defund Hate changed our understanding of immigration enforcement and found a way to push an abolitionist agenda in DC.

The Political Economy of Immigrant Detention

Scrutinizing the economics of detention reveals the perverse incentives that have driven the growth of immigrant incarceration over the last forty years. The birth of the current immigrant detention system in the 1980s happened while large government was perceived as a problem and neoliberalism's market-centered political ideology was on the rise. Subcontracting ended up being the preferred method of securing detention beds. As a result, ICE today only owns and operates five immigrant detention centers: in Arizona (Florence), Florida (Krome), New York (Batavia), and Texas (El Paso and Port Isabel).[4] Even at those facilities, many of the services, such as food provision, guards, and transportation, are outsourced to private companies. All the remaining immigrant detention centers are jails operated by local governments or private prisons.

There are three types of ICE detention centers: those that ICE owns and operates, referred to as service processing centers; private prisons with direct contracts with ICE, called contract detention facilities (CDF); and county jails that rent out bed space to ICE through intergovernmental service agreements (IGSA). While IGSAs are technically arrangements between ICE and a local government, sometimes those arrangements involve counties playing intermediary between ICE and a private prison company. ICE prefers IGSAs because they are the easiest to secure and don't require a public bidding process, as direct contracts with private prison companies do. ICE also often piggybacks on US Marshals Service jail contracts, most of which are intergovernmental agreements with local jails (though some are also CDFs). The USMS jail system, which includes over 1,200 agreements with state and local governments, has been referred to as an "invisible giant" that is often "overlooked . . . because they do not run their own prison system."[5] Through this model of subcontracting, immigrant detention grew into a sprawling detention archipelago across the United States, allowing ICE to detain immigrants in every region of the country.

For organizers fighting detention expansion, understanding the contracting models is an essential part of our strategy. Knowing who the players are, who has decision-making power, and when and how contracts are secured helps us figure out how best to intervene.

The typology also reveals who financially benefits from immigrant detention. On average, ICE pays $148 to subcontractors per day to detain one person.[6] Private prison companies profit, as do local governments. ICE contracts have became a lucrative source of revenue for localities for the income they have brought in and the jobs they have created. As of 2019, 75 percent of immigrant detention capacity was dependent on IGSA contracts, where ICE was working with county and city governments to detain immigrants.[7] While private prisons were also involved in many of those contracts, local governments still had a stake in the contract. These types of arrangements have created a symbiotic relationship between ICE and local governments that have made IGSAs the bedrock of the immigrant detention system.

The Dilley Family Detention Center in south Texas is one infamous example. When ICE was ramping up its family detention capacity in 2014, it added a rider onto an IGSA contract with the city of Eloy in Arizona—located 900 miles from Dilley. Eloy operated as the intermediary between ICE and CoreCivic (formerly CCA), which runs the Eloy Detention Center. Eloy became the middleman for Dilley, even though the facility was in another state. Through this arrangement, the city of Eloy, a small town with a population of fifteen thousand, pocketed $1.5 million over four years thanks to Dilley's inclusion in the IGSA. Eventually, Eloy backed out of the contract when it was sued for $40 million by the mother of a toddler who died after being detained at Dilley. As we got wind of the news, we reached out to our members in Texas to see if there was a way we could intervene, but within days, ICE had already signed an IGSA with the city of Dilley to keep using the detention contract.

⁓

In addition to the contracting model, quotas in both the annual budget and detention contracts have created incentives to fill detention beds. In 2009, when senator Robert Byrd inserted the mandate to maintain 33,400 detention beds, there wasn't much uproar about it.

Then, in 2013 (as mentioned in chapter 2), after ICE released 2,000 immigrants from detention prior to mandatory federal spending cuts, the detention bed mandate emerged as a major point of contention. When this happened, we started to grow more concerned about the role of the quota language in the budget and how it was changing the detention system. DWN launched the End the Quota campaign in response.

We weren't exactly sure how the quota was operating. It was a tool the Republicans used to call out Democrats, but we needed to know if ICE was filling beds when they were empty to meet the required number. We wanted evidence and started working with the Center for Constitutional Rights, which filed a Freedom of Information Act request on our behalf, to figure it out. While we hoped to learn how the detention bed mandate operated, we discovered an additional, completely different way that quotas function in immigrant detention. We learned that, since at least 2003, ICE has been incorporating language in their contracts that essentially functions as local lock-up quotas. They are called "guaranteed minimums," and they stipulate that ICE pays contractors for a certain number of beds, regardless of whether or not they are filled. The contracts also include something called tiered pricing that gives ICE a discount for the number of beds filled beyond the guaranteed minimum.

Take the Northwest Detention Center as an example. NWDC, a GEO Group–run facility in Tacoma, Washington, has a capacity of 1,575 beds, and the current guaranteed minimum is 1,181. If ICE exceeds the minimum number of people detained, GEO gives the agency a discount to detain up to an additional 394 people per day. These types of models incentivize ICE to round up more people.[8] ICE is already not only paying for some beds regardless of how many people are locked up but also saving money if it detains more immigrants, since tiered pricing operates as a coupon.

Guaranteed minimums mostly exist in contracts with private prison companies, but they also show up in contracts with the five

ICE-owned facilities because many of the services are subcontracted out, and those contractors want assurances that they would get paid. Twenty-nine contracts had guaranteed minimums by the end of Obama's tenure. While Trump was in office, that number went up to forty-three, accounting for nearly 29,000 detention beds.[9] In 2017, Congress finally removed the nationwide quota language from the appropriations bill, but the facility-specific guaranteed minimums remain. During the pandemic, when the detention system was at a twenty-year low, companies were still getting paid, even with the reduced numbers. ICE defended the practice, saying that guaranteed minimums helped it maintain available bed space to allow for social distancing during the pandemic and in anticipation of any "surges" at the border.

Divestment Campaigns and Movement Tensions

Even though private prison companies operate only a small portion of the prison and jail system in the United States, activists often focus on them because of their profit-driven motives, perceiving private prisons as particularly evil. Campaigns to divest public entities (such as universities, pension funds, and banks) from private prisons have been a prominent strategy in the fight against mass incarceration. While well intentioned, these campaigns often center the corporations as targets and inadvertently end up minimizing the fundamental role that federal, state, and local governments play in creating and sustaining the prison industrial complex.

In the early 2000s, after massive protests confronted the World Trade Organization in Seattle, anticorporate campaigns gained traction on college campuses across the United States. One of these efforts, the Not With Our Money! campaign, targeted Sodexho Marriott (now Sodexo, Inc.), a campus food service provider whose parent company was a major shareholder in the CCA (known today as CoreCivic). As an undergrad at the University of Texas at Austin, I joined the effort on campus, and later went on to codirect the campaign after graduation.

After six universities ended contracts with Sodexho due to the campaign, the company divested from CCA, although it remained involved in private prison contracts in Europe and Australia.[10] While the campaign hurt CCA's reputation, it didn't have much impact on the company's bottom line. After this win, Not With Our Money! shifted to targeting Lehman Brothers, a major financier of the private prison industry. Lehman had bailed out CCA when it was on the verge of bankruptcy in the early 2000s and floated more than $100 million in bonds to Wackenhut (now the GEO Group).[11] University divestment from Lehman Brothers, which issued bonds to universities, could have been a much bigger blow to the private prison industry. However, and unsurprisingly, trying to explain higher education bond underwriting to the students whose support we sought proved to be a challenge, and the campaign failed to gain momentum. Lehman Brothers eventually went bankrupt during the 2008 financial crash due to its role in the subprime mortgage crisis, but other banks were still financing CCA and GEO, and its downfall had little impact on the private prison industry.

One foresight the previous organizers of the Not With Our Money! campaign had was to move the headquarters from New York to Texas, where my campaign codirector Bob Libal and I were based. Texas was ground zero for the private prison industry, with companies building jails on speculation and jumping on the post-9/11 boom. As we were organizing against private prisons nationally, we learned of the US Marshals Service's plan to solicit private companies to build the superjail in Laredo, referenced in chapter 3. In our efforts to stop the construction of the jail, we rallied around the fact that it would be privately operated. Here a focus on private prisons felt more useful—not because a state-run prison would have been better, but as a tactic to halt expansion. We knew the limits of the privatization argument and deployed it strategically in the superjail fight, given the absence of a broader understanding of the harms of incarceration in south Texas at the time.

At the national level, however, some criminal justice advocates were so fundamentally opposed to prison privatization that they were willing to create alliances with pro-incarceration unions to stop their growth. This naturally created rifts within the movement. Advocates often collaborated with public-sector unions that represented prison guards, like the American Federation of State, County, and Municipal Employees. Frustrations erupted when antiprivatization advocates invited the California Correctional Peace Officers Association (CCPOA) to strategy sessions. The union is notorious for the significant role it played in the prison boom in California. CCPOA spent millions lobbying to increase incarceration, supporting the 1994 three-strikes ballot initiative.[12] Their inclusion in the advocacy meetings against private prisons was a step too far for those organizing against prisons in California, and the divisions within the movement grew.

Some advocates believed that private prisons needed to be stopped before they became the norm, while others recognized that they were only a small part of the larger prison industrial complex. Abolitionist scholars and activists have repeatedly debunked several myths that nonetheless continue to drive the focus on private prisons. Anti–private prison activists often claim that the profit-driven nature of private prisons incentivizes them to reduce costs, creating worse conditions of confinement. Yet this perspective ignores the fact that government-run prisons and jails are equally driven by market forces and often cut costs to generate revenue amid deficits in municipal or state budgets. Another cause for alarm is the role private prison companies play in lobbying for harsher sentencing laws. Yet legislators from both parties and public prison guard unions (such as CCPOA) have been equally active and forceful advocates in expanding incarceration.

In 2015, Ruth Wilson Gilmore critiqued the focus on private prisons within the antiprison movement: "The long-standing campaign against private prisons is based on the fictitious claim that revenues raked in from outsourced contracts explain the origin and growth of mass incarceration."[13] One reason private prisons have become so prominent in the story of mass incarceration is because people would much rather blame evil corporations than their own government for the problems with the world. Gilmore's intervention challenged the movement to pay attention to the root of the issue: the federal, state, and local governments that built the PIC.

Since the Not With Our Money! campaign, there have been numerous campaigns focused on divestment from private prisons. In 2015, a successful student-led campaign pushed Columbia University to divest its shares from CCA and G4S, the world's largest private security firm. In 2017, Make the Road and other national organizations launched the Corporate Backers of Hate campaign. Two years later, six banks severed ties with private prison companies. While these wins should be celebrated for raising consciousness about the issue, there is little evidence of a direct or even indirect correlation between private prison–divestment campaigns and decarceration.

The Corporate Backers of Hate campaign was successful at getting a group of financial entities to drop private prison companies, but other banks will always be willing to step into their place as long as the government continues to contract with them. Maybe the terms won't be as profitable. The credit banks provide to the private prison companies may become a little more expensive, but it will still be issued as long as the federal government keeps paying the contractors. Focusing on private prisons as uniquely immoral clouds the issue by presupposing that government-run prisons are better and by ignoring that the main reason private prison companies exist is because the government is aligned with their agenda.

Divestment can be a useful tactic in certain contexts, but when it comes to mass incarceration, private prison–divestment campaigns have not resulted in a reduction in the number of people caged. Shifting our target to the government and its use of private prisons for immigrant detention can, however, be an effective strategy. Within the immigrant justice movement, campaigns to ban private prisons at the state level have successfully halted detention expansion (explained in chapter 6). Similarly, recent class action litigation that challenges the practice of private prison companies paying detained immigrants a dollar a day for their labor, essentially using immigrants to keep detention centers running, has been more effective at "starving the beast" (and cutting into private prison companys' bottom lines) than divestment campaigns. These efforts are important in making detention less lucrative for the industry while also improving the conditions for people currently detained. Targeting private prisons as a tactic for disrupting the government's overall carceral agenda can be worthwhile, so long as it is not understood as the core framework for what's wrong with the system.

The Federal Phaseout of Private Prisons

Prior to Biden issuing the executive order on private prisons, the Obama administration had reached the same decision. In August 2016, deputy attorney general Sally Yates announced that the BOP would phase out the use of private prisons. The announcement came as a surprise to many of us working on the issue. I had spent months before mapping out a plan for DWN to address the Justice Department's shadow system of Criminal Alien Requirement, or CAR, facilities—that is, private prisons that exclusively held a growing number of noncitizens in the federal system (explained in chapter 3). At the time of the announcement, 13 of the 122 BOP prisons were CAR facilities and had the capacity to hold 22,000 people.[14]

In the months leading up to the announcement, multiple media investigations revealed the severe conditions in CAR prisons and the high number of deaths due to negligence. And then, weeks before the Yates memo came out, DOJ's Office of the Inspector General released a scathing report regarding the health and safety concerns in CAR prisons. From a liberal perspective, government accountability worked like it was supposed to. The media exposed the harms of DOJ's private prisons, so the government evaluated itself and then determined that the use of these prisons was no longer tenable. But, however tempting such a perspective might be, it would be a mistake to think this was a result of the government righting the ship in response to media pressure and internal investigations. Fully considering the political conditions and the broader context leading up to the decision, a different—and more accurate—story emerges.

On January 31, 2009, shortly after Obama came into office, a riot broke out at the GEO Group–run Reeves County Correctional Center in Texas. This was the second protest by immigrants incarcerated at Reeves in two months. The first one took place after Jesus Manuel Galindo, a thirty-two-year-old Mexican immigrant, died in solitary confinement after his calls for medical care were ignored; the second protest happened because the prison continued to use solitary confinement as a response to medical requests.[15] In 2012, immigrants held at the Adams County Correctional Center in Mississippi, operated by CCA, rioted in response to the service of expired food and lack of medical care at the prison. The protesters took control over the facility, and a prison guard was killed during the standoff.[16] In 2015, a year before the Yates decision, 2,000 of the 3,000 people incarcerated at the privately operated Willacy County Correctional Center in Raymondville, Texas, organized and seized control of the prison and dismantled parts of the structure. The prison, nicknamed Ritmo (in reference to Gitmo, the extrajudicial detention center in Guantánamo Bay), was made of ten large Kevlar tents, some of which were burned down during the uprising.[17] In each of these instances, a significant portion of the immigrants incarcerated at these prisons were serving multiyear sentences for unlawful reentry.

In that same period, the Black Lives Matter movement had been gaining steam. After multiple uprisings in Ferguson, Baltimore, and elsewhere and an increase in BLM protests across the country, Obama felt pressure to respond. The BOP had already quietly not renewed contracts at some of these prisons, including at Willacy, but announcing an end to the use of private prisons would be perceived as a bold move. The BOP, unlike ICE, mostly operated its own prisons and preferred maintaining them to contracting with private prison companies. Ending BOP's private contracts would mainly mean shutting down the CAR prisons. While the end of CAR prisons was significant, the impact on BOP overall was less so.

After the Yates announcement, DHS conducted its own review of private prisons. Predictably, ICE had become so dependent on private prisons that it was impossible for DHS to imagine a phaseout. The DHS report stated: "Fiscal considerations, combined with the need for realistic capacity to handle sudden increases in detention, indicate that DHS's use of private for-profit detention will continue. . . . Congress should provide to ICE the additional monetary and personnel resources needed to provide for a more robust, effective, and coordinated inspection regime."[18]

Under Trump, Jeff Sessions rescinded the Yates memo and CAR prisons remained open. But upon taking office, Biden immediately reissued the order to phase out private prisons as part of his racial equity plan, which was unquestionably influenced by the George Floyd protests in 2020. A lot went into creating the conditions for the DOJ to phase out private prisons. But one thing is clear: uprisings and rebellions within prison walls and on the streets were critical factors in the decision.

Biden's hesitance to phase out ICE's private prisons makes clear that the federal government's decision to end their use by DOJ was never about decarceration or even treating private prisons—and their profit-driven model—as misaligned with American values. Instead, the primary consideration was whether the department could continue its carceral agenda without private prisons. The answer, for the DOJ, is yes. By contrast, ICE's dependence on private prisons helps explain why Biden did not include them in his announcement; at this point, the bipartisan deportation agenda requires locking up immigrants to facilitate their deportation, and private prisons (often subcontracted through local governments) are the primary source of bed space for this objective.

Since signing the executive order on private prisons, the Biden administration has converted shuttered CAR prisons into immigrant detention centers. On March 31, 2021, the Moshannon Valley Correctional Center in central Pennsylvania, operated by the GEO Group, closed. A few months later, Clearfield County, where the prison was located, came to an agreement with ICE to convert Moshannon into an immigrant detention center. It opened in November of that year. In 2022, it "generated an estimated $33.5 million to the Clearfield County area, including over $650,000 in local sales and property taxes."[19] Moshannon was the clearest evidence of Biden's hypocrisy on the private prison issue when it came to ICE.

Biden's DOJ has also supported litigation to block state-level private prison bans from going into effect in California and New Jersey. The government said that closure of the Elizabeth Detention Center run by CoreCivic in New Jersey "would seriously impair immigration operations in the region and cause irreparable harm to the United States," and that if more states passed private prison bans, it would have "a near-catastrophic impact" on ICE's mission.[20] While Biden claimed there should be "no private detention," his administration quietly defended the ability to keep contracting with them for immigrant detention.

Defund Hate

During the Trump presidency, the lessons we had already learned about the importance of federal funding for expanding detention and deportations became very important. Upon launching his presidential campaign in 2015, Trump declared emphatically, "I will build a great great wall, on our southern border, and I will have Mexico pay for that wall. Mark my words." Once he was in office, he tried to get

Congress to fund the wall, often throwing tantrums, one of which resulted in the longest government shutdown in United States history. In March 2017, Trump made his first request for several billion dollars in supplemental funding for the border wall, which also included money for 1,500 additional ICE and border patrol agents and 21,000 more detention beds. Similar to the post-9/11 moment, the mechanisms of carceral immigration enforcement were already in place, but additional funding meant DHS could apply them to a greater extent, resulting in more detentions and deportations. During Trump's first two years in office, there was a Republican trifecta, meaning both the House and Senate had Republican majorities, and the opportunities to pressure Democrats to take a stand were limited. The one place where there was some leverage was the federal budget; Trump and Congress needed Democrats to get it passed.[21]

In response to the initial supplemental funding request, several organizations came together to launch a short-term campaign to stop the funding. They included American Friends Service Committee, Church World Service, Detention Watch Network, National Immigrant Justice Center, Southern Border Communities Coalition, and United We Dream. While some funding went through, Trump did not get all the money he wanted because of the efforts of the campaign, which included collecting 290,000 petition signatures. Soon it became clear that Trump and DHS would continue to use the appropriations process as a way to ramp up detention and deportations. This led the group of organizations to launch the Defund Hate campaign in July 2017 to cut the amount of money appropriated to ICE and CBP.

DWN and United We Dream would go on to coanchor the campaign, bringing complementary expertise to the fight. While United We Dream's main focus had been fighting for affirmative relief to extend DACA and other ways for undocumented youth to secure status, the group had also been coordinating with racial justice organizations, highlighting the connections between police violence and

ICE and border patrol abuse in immigrant communities. DWN had previously launched the End the Quota campaign, and the demand to defund aligned with the organization's commitment to abolition. At the outset, many establishment organizations disagreed with our strategy. Some even attacked the campaign when Defund Hate launched, arguing that DHS needed adequate funding to treat people well, and told us that the effort would backfire. For years, Democrats in Congress often saw additional funding for immigrant detention as a good thing, since in their minds, it could be used for improving conditions. With Trump in office, it was an opportunity to shift their thinking.

Because of our work against the detention bed quota, there was some understanding among the groups involved in the campaign about the budget. However, movement literacy on appropriations was limited; it required a lot of training to bring people up to speed on the complicated process. But under Trump, people were scared, giving the demand to defund political salience. Many were eager to figure out how the budget process worked in order to throw a wrench in his plans. By March 2018, after numerous petitions, congressional visits, public education efforts, and protests, more than a hundred members of Congress were on the record calling for cuts in funding. The campaign had successfully stopped an additional $3.3 billion in funding for ICE and CBP. In the absence of anything else moving in Congress on the issue, Defund Hate became a way to both hold Democrats to account and move an abolitionist agenda in DC.

Through the process, the Defund Hate coalition figured out that ICE was routinely overspending its allocated budget on enforcement and detention. Before it ran out of money, ICE would transfer funds from other parts of DHS and merely notify Congress that they were doing so. Then ICE would use the inflated numbers as a starting point for the following year's spending negotiations. From 2016 to 2018, this strategy afforded ICE nearly $1 billion in additional funding. In August 2018, Defund Hate learned that ICE was trying to tack on another billion dollars to the fiscal year 2019 budget.

Meanwhile, through a Freedom of Information Act request and intel from a congressional staffer, Defund Hate learned that ICE had previously diverted $10 million from the Federal Emergency Management Agency (FEMA) for immigrant detention during the height of hurricane season. Defund Hate advocates disclosed the information to members of Congress, including Democratic Oregon senator Jeff Merkley. He then shared the FEMA story with Rachel Maddow at MSNBC, exposing ICE's underhanded tactics and blowing up the story. This episode combined with outrage over family separations earlier that year led many Democrats to come out against additional ICE funding in the budget negotiations.[22]

Defund Hate continued to be successful at preventing DHS from getting more money for ICE and CBP, blocking some $7 billion in additional funding. But because of ICE's trickery with the budget, including the aforementioned FEMA transfer as another hurricane headed toward Puerto Rico, immigrant detention was at an all-time high in the summer of 2019, with detention capacity at fifty-five thousand.[23] Then, in 2020, the campaign finally started seeing cuts for the first time. By this point, many mainstream organizations had come around, and more than fifty groups had joined the Defund Hate coalition, including MoveOn and SEIU. However, it was the impact of the pandemic in addition to the uprisings for Black lives and calls to defund the police that helped move the needle further. Immigrant rights advocates were more willing to demand an end to detention and call out ICE practices as akin to policing. Even the Migration Policy Institute, a moderate think tank that led the charge for CIR, made the connections in a blog post titled "As #DefundThePolice Movement Gains Steam, Immigration Enforcement Spending and Practices Attract Scrutiny."

These shifts, along with the groundwork the Defund Hate campaign had laid over the years, led Democratic representative Lucille Roybal-Allard, chair of the House Homeland Security Subcommittee for Appropriations, to introduce one of the largest cuts to immigrant detention ever proposed by the subcommittee. As written, the DHS spending bill for the fiscal year 2021 would have cut $1 billion from ICE's Enforcement and Removal Operations budget, phasing out family detention and reducing detention capacity to 22,000 beds— less than half of what had been funded at the time. And it stipulated that during the public health emergency capacity should be limited to ten thousand.[24] The bill would have also placed restrictions on ICE's ability to transfer money from other agencies. Unfortunately, other members of Congress did not show support for the level of cuts proposed in the House bill; however, the funding for detention that year was reduced to pre-Trump levels.

After Biden took office, Defund Hate continued its efforts for cuts in funding, though the framework of hate proved to be less effective without Trump in office. With Republicans and the media focused on the border, Biden hesitated to implement meaningful reforms and had essentially continued the status quo on immigration enforcement funding. But then, in his proposed budget for 2023, Biden reduced detention by 26 percent to twenty-five thousand beds. It was the largest cut a president had proposed to detention since the contemporary system's inception more than four decades prior. Defund Hate was critical to this development, but this shift was also greatly influenced by the increasing number of campaigns at the local and state levels to end detention. The grassroots strategy was key, as I explain in the next chapter.

With the announcement of Biden's budget request reducing immigrant detention capacity, advocates rightly pointed with alarm to the increase in funding for programs like ankle shackling and other forms of electronic monitoring, which have widened the net for immigrants under government surveillance. Yet it's important to see cuts to detention capacity as a victory because for years, both detention and e-carceration models have only increased. This time would have been no different but for the movement to end immigrant detention.

Unfortunately, by this point, many immigrant rights groups that had been involved in Defund Hate shifted their focus to the legalization fight. And without Trump in office, members of Congress no longer saw cutting ICE and CBP's budget as a priority. In the end, Congress passed a budget bill that kept detention numbers at a capacity of 34,000. Even if the quota is gone from the language of the appropriations bill, the number arbitrarily put into the budget in 2013 continues to have a hold on Congress. For several years now, Congress has funded detention at 34,000 beds despite detention numbers being consistently lower. It has almost become a neutral offering, set in stone by Robert Byrd through the detention bed mandate.

Despite this outcome, for most of Trump's presidency, Defund Hate mitigated the harm of the system and prevented it from reaching the extreme levels Trump had campaigned on, blocking some $15 billion in additional funding since it launched in 2017. Defund Hate also became an important counter to the focus on CIR, which had taken up so much of the energy and resources of the immigrant rights movement for nearly two decades. Through the campaign, anchored by two abolitionist organizations, DWN and United We Dream, defund became a popular demand for the immigrant rights movement.

Defund Hate helped expose the role of appropriations in the deportation machine. Sometimes our job as abolitionists is to ensure that things don't get worse, and during the Trump years, Defund Hate helped do that. It also functioned as a nonreformist reform to rally around. But it soon became clear that the framework of hate would only take us so far once Biden was in office. Abolitionist activist and writer Kay Whitlock notes that the "hate frame" often results in people believing that harm happens because of "irrational, personal prejudice" and "in this view, hate is not about structures, not about power hierarchies, not about institutional practice."[25] The focus on hate thus absolves the systems already in place. The term "hate" meant something because Trump was in office, and it was easy for people to see him as an aberration rather than a successor in a line of US presidents committed to increasing detention and deportations. Under Biden, the concept of hate doesn't get us very far because Biden is perceived as status quo, and therefore his immigration policies—even if some of them are the same as Trump's—are more acceptable. However, defund remains an important abolitionist demand and strategy that helps people see the extreme inequities in the federal budget on immigration, while also aligning with cross-movement efforts to defund the police, prisons, and the military.

Abolitionist Lessons

The popularity of the demand to defund the police in 2020 helped expose to a broader audience the role that money plays in maintaining and expanding carceral systems. The attention on the government and how it spends its money has been essential to addressing the exponential growth of the PIC and broadening our focus beyond private prisons. Nefarious actors are easier to shame and are often easier to expose than a massive state infrastructure rooted in racism and white supremacy carrying out a carceral and deportation agenda in partnership with whomever is willing. The closure of the BOP's private prisons is a good thing. But the problem with these prisons wasn't solely that they were private, but that they existed in the first place.

While an end to private prisons won't be the panacea some imagine for the abolition of the PIC, if DHS phases out the use of private prisons, it will likely mean that we have successfully made the case that mass detention in its present form should no longer exist. In the last several years, support for the abolition of immigrant detention has caught fire in the immigrant rights movement. As a result of relentless organizing, much of it involving people in detention facilities and their families and communities, several states have passed antidetention bills. Organizers in more than two dozen states have waged campaigns and scored many wins against county contracts with ICE. In the process, as described in the following chapter, the movement and some policymakers have embraced the abolition of immigrant detention. If the Biden administration or a future administration extends the phaseout of private prisons beyond DOJ to ICE facilities, it won't be because advocates and journalists made the case that private prisons are inherently evil. It will be because ordinary people—both those detained by ICE and in communities across the country—called for an end to detention altogether.

CHAPTER 6

Communities Not Cages

These are the victories that I live for, my purpose. Knowing that less people will be subjected to the ongoing conditions in Etowah is a prayer answered. I just hope they continue to spotlight similar facilities.
—Karim Golding, who was detained in the Etowah County Jail in Alabama from 2016 to 2021

The Etowah County Jail is an unremarkable if foreboding municipal building in downtown Gadsden, Alabama. Passersby may not notice the telltale signs of a jail: the gray and unadorned exterior, the tiny sliver of windows, or the barbed wire around the back of the building. But for twenty-four years, Etowah was one of the worst immigrant detention centers in the United States, and it came to symbolize everything wrong with the system. People detained there were routinely denied medical care or told to just drink water and take an ibuprofen for any ailment. They were also regularly served moldy and rotten food. An investigation in 2018 revealed that the sheriff had pocketed $750,000 allocated for food provision at the jail and had bought a beach house that cost a near-equivalent amount.[1] Most immigrants detained at Etowah were transferred from other states to await an appeal on their case. With no outdoor recreation

148

space, they would spend months or years in the jail without ever stepping foot outside.

Karim Golding, a Jamaican immigrant who had been living in the United States since he was nine years old, had already spent ten years in federal prison before he was transferred to Etowah for another four. At the onset of the pandemic, Golding and other detained immigrants staged protests over the negligent pandemic protocols in Etowah. In response, jail officials sent him to solitary confinement for two months. Protests inside and outside the jail were a common occurrence. Sometimes when activists protested outside the jail, people detained would post signs in the tiny windows across the building, saying, "Thank you," or simply, "We miss our kids."

To address the problems with immigrant detention, advocates often focus on improving the harsh conditions of confinement and increasing oversight of detention centers. Lawyers provide counsel to support individual cases and pursue impact litigation to minimize the time someone might spend in immigrant detention. Many highlight the remoteness of immigrant detention centers and the isolation it breeds. Advocates have argued that if detention centers were closer to major cities, the proximity to lawyers and other services could make the experience more humane. But during the Obama era, immigrant justice activists started to become disillusioned with the possibility of reform. Despite the countless reports, media investigations, hunger strikes, and protests exposing the cruelty of immigrant detention, conditions remained dire. People kept dying and the system kept expanding. Activists and advocates were less willing to accept the minimal changes achieved by working to make detention more humane, and demands for abolition proliferated. Obama and Trump's deportation regimes brought an increasing clarity and advanced the boldness of the demand. In turn, immigrant detention centers and the communities where they were located became key sites of resistance.

For over a decade, calling for closure of specific detention centers has been a central demand of the movement to end immigrant detention. Grassroots campaigns have employed two strategies against detention centers in communities across the country: (1) to prevent new contracts or stop the renewal of existing contracts and (2) to pass legislation at the state level to end the use of local jails or private prisons and phase out existing detention in the state. Since these efforts began, organizers and advocates along with people detained have successfully ended ICE detention contracts at over twenty local jails.

These strategies have been effective in some states with more friendly political environments, like California and Illinois. But in places like Alabama, where the Etowah County sheriff and local politicians are the jail's most vocal proponents, ending the contract required federal intervention. In 2015, a coalition of local and national organizations led by the Adelante Alabama Worker Center launched the Shut Down Etowah campaign. The campaign deployed various tactics, including filing mass habeas petitions to get people released, exposing the abuses and conditions inside Etowah, frequently protesting outside the facility, and pressuring DHS to end the contract through administrative advocacy. In April 2022, seven years after the campaign launched, DHS announced it would stop detaining immigrants at the Etowah County Jail.

Many shifting conditions help explain how we finally started winning campaigns to end detention contracts. After four years of Trump, the public was more aware of ICE's cruelty, and more local and state governments wanted to distance themselves from his xenophobic rhetoric. While few people were released due to the COVID-19 pandemic, limited interior enforcement actions and border closures resulted in fewer people being detained. Some counties were no longer making the same revenue from contracts because of the reduced population and, when pressed, were more open to ending ICE arrangements. And perhaps most critically, the George Floyd uprisings of the spring and summer of 2020 woke up the nation to the racist nature of these systems. As a result, many politicians and immigrant rights advocates were more willing to call for abolition of detention than ever before.

These conditions were critical, but local campaigns and the demand to shut facilities down were key to winning these "site fights." In this chapter, I share stories about some of the campaigns that have helped shift the national terrain. This is not an exhaustive history of the numerous antidetention campaigns; through these examples, I paint a picture of how communities fought back despite the obstacles they faced. These efforts often involved many players: people detained protesting on the inside, family members and organizers on the outside demanding their release and closure of the facility, attorneys supporting their cases or filing litigation, advocates pushing for state legislation or federal intervention, and researchers and journalists exposing all the harms of detention. For forty years, the trajectory of immigrant detention in the United States has been expansion: more money, more beds. But through these campaigns, the system shrank for the first time.

Beyond Reform: The Call to Shut Down

When I first joined the staff of DWN in March 2009 as an organizer, the member-led steering committee had put together a campaign plan for me to implement. The campaign would be focused on improving conditions and oversight of detention facilities, while also pushing for alternatives to detention and government-appointed counsel. Obama had just taken office and there was some hope that we could reform immigrant detention, but this particular campaign just felt to me like building nicer cages. Fortunately, there was room to shift. After discussions with DWN members and our executive director at the time, Andrea Black, we decided to focus on halting the expansion of the detention system, which had doubled since the organization was founded in 1997.

We were a small team with four on staff at the time, and our members were made up of a range of groups, including legal service providers, policy organizations, grassroots groups, and people formerly detained. DWN had never launched a campaign before, and there were a lot of lessons learned along the way. But even then, we knew that anchoring our demand to stop expansion with grassroots organizations would be essential. We launched the Dignity Not Detention campaign to prevent detention expansion in early 2010 in partnership with Puente in Arizona, Georgia Detention Watch in Georgia, and Grassroots Leadership in Texas.

But the detention system continued to grow. More people were being locked up than ever before—over four hundred thousand people each year under Obama. We were frustrated. Some staff and many grassroots organizers within the membership began to wonder whether the lack of clarity about our vision was hurting our ability to win. DWN's policy demand was "detention as a last resort," but this framing only furthered the idea that some people deserve to be detained. We began to discuss with the membership the possibility of calling for detention abolition.

At one conference in Austin in 2011, with 200 members attending, we had participants stand in different parts of the room based on their position on abolition versus improving the conditions of immigrant detention. It immediately became contentious. Some members became uncomfortable with the exercise and felt attacked for their work to make detention more humane. Others were energized and said the discussions helped them question the system itself and wondered if it was worth even engaging with ICE anymore. We continued to discuss whether to embrace abolition as an organization and reached out to Critical Resistance for guidance about how to bring members along.

Leading up to the 2012 election, we knew we had to do something bolder to get Obama to act in the final year of his first term. At a DWN strategy meeting in DC, members proposed focusing on a set of key detention centers, documenting conditions and calling for closure. Abraham Paulos of Families for Freedom came up with the name,

Expose and Close. A group of members, ranging from organizers to advocates to legal service providers to academics, came together to coordinate Expose and Close. We chose which facilities to prioritize and arranged who would take the lead on visiting each detention center, writing up a report, and organizing locally. Deciding on the list of facilities was a challenge, to say the least. They were all bad, but we aimed to highlight those jails that exemplified the problems with detention: the abysmal living conditions, the remoteness, the lack of medical care, the terrible food, the limited access to the outdoors, and the retaliation and abuse immigrants faced when protesting their incarceration. After we decided on the list, members visited facilities that summer to interview people detained and wrote reports in the fall. In the weeks leading up to the release, after a bit of pressure from funders, the communications outfit America's Voice joined the effort to amplify our demand.

Expose and Close launched shortly after the 2012 election with reports on each of the ten jails, with representative (eventually governor) Jared Polis of Colorado joining the press call. With help from America's Voice, journalists picked up the story. It turns out, the media loves a list. Many news articles focused on these jails being the ten worst, but we kept making the point that they just revealed the problems with the system as a whole. A few weeks later, over 300 organizations signed on to our call to close these ten detention centers.

The campaign helped clarify DWN's purpose: weeks after Expose and Close launched, the organization officially adopted a detention abolition vision. The Obama administration failed to act on our demands, but a decade later six of the ten jails on the list are no longer ICE detention centers, including the Etowah County Jail in Alabama and the Irwin County Detention Center in Georgia.

In the years that followed, we continued our efforts to shut down detention centers, but we tried other strategies as well: calling for an end to the detention bed quota and defunding ICE and CBP, exposing sham inspections and negligent deaths in the system, organizing people's tribunals at detention centers, and putting "ICE on Trial." But in

2018, we came back to this question of nationally coordinated efforts for shutdown. In the height of the family separation moment under Trump, due to the rising detention numbers, the administration began using Federal Bureau of Prisons facilities for ICE detention. Immigrants were detained at five BOP prisons in Arizona, California, Oregon, Texas, and Washington State. At the same time, ICE issued requests for proposals for a massive expansion of family detention at military bases, including the capacity to detain an additional 15,500 immigrants.

In response to the proposed expansion by Trump, DWN launched the Communities Not Cages campaign in October 2018 to halt detention expansion, shut down existing detention centers, and stop the proliferation of ICE's agenda into the Department of Justice and Department of Defense. The campaign initially focused on stopping the use of the five BOP prisons and supporting coordination between organizers and lawyers to ensure releases. By November 2018, BOP ended the practice of detaining immigrants in ICE custody, but ICE was still expanding immigrant detention across the country.

Like the NDLON-coordinated Not1More Deportation campaign, Communities Not Cages was an organic demand and strategy. It wasn't about DWN; it was about local communities learning from each other and advancing their campaigns. We were there to help coordinate, connect members, strategize, and provide resources and amplification. In late 2019, we came together at a convening of a hundred members and partners in Birmingham, Alabama, where organizers had been leading the Shut Down Etowah campaign. We hosted workshops on a variety of tactics and strategies: providing state legislative advocacy, supporting hunger strikers, deciphering detention contracts, filing public records requests, messaging against detention, and so on. Organizers took these lessons back to their communities to further fortify their efforts for shutdown.

The following year, as the call to #FreeThemAll grew (see the prologue) and the George Floyd uprisings took place, we were also amid scenario planning around the 2020 election. Learning from the Expose and Close effort and the attention it received, we decided to once again demand the closure of a set of detention centers as part of the campaign. This time, we called it First Ten to Communities Not Cages, identifying ten detention centers for Biden to shut down in his first year in office as a road map for ending detention for good.

An End to Family Detention

While most people in immigrant detention are single adults, the detention of family units has elicited considerable outrage, and for good reason. Facilities that detained families were often referred to as baby jails, and children in ICE custody experienced deep psychological trauma. Due to malnutrition and the stress of incarceration, children often lost weight while inside. With ICE as the authority, family relationships become confused. Some activists have perceived campaigns against family detention as more sympathetic and therefore as low-hanging fruit, but ending the practice was no easy feat. Efforts against family detention proved to be important building blocks toward the broader call to end all immigrant detention.[2]

During the height of Reagan's detention expansion project in the mid-1980s, the INS decided to stop releasing unaccompanied migrant children to anyone but a parent or guardian. For Jenny Flores, a fifteen-year-old girl from El Salvador, this posed a problem since her mother, with whom she was attempting to reunite in Los Angeles, was also undocumented. Her mother feared they would both be deported back to a war zone if she came to get her. While Flores's aunt and uncle had legal status and were willing to take her in, INS refused to release her to them. The INS contracted with a private company, Behavioral Systems Southwest, to begin detaining children at the Mardi Gras Motel in Pasadena.

The conditions were abysmal. After two months at the detention center, Flores had an "intermittent preoccupation with death, anorexia, and depression," according to a doctor's examination. At other detention centers, minors were routinely strip-searched upon arrival, a process that included invasive body cavity searches.[3] Attorneys filed a class action lawsuit on behalf of Flores and other children detained by INS that went on for years. It eventually led to a 1997 settlement with the federal government that would set out restrictions on child detention. These restrictions evolved over time, but the settlement allowed children to be released to relatives other than their parents, required certain conditions for children in custody, including state licensing of facilities, and encouraged prompt release. The Flores settlement later became one of the key tools used to end the practice of family detention.

The first immigrant family detention center, with parents being detained alongside their children, opened in 2001. The government converted a former nursing home turned youth jail in Leesport, Pennsylvania, into the Berks County Family Residential Center. The facility detained asylum-seeking families for a few weeks until their screening interviews had been completed. It was a small facility and could accommodate fewer than a hundred people.

In 2005, as the federal government was cracking down on immigration after 9/11, it started separating families arriving at the border, sending parents to detention and kids into the custody of the Office of Refugee Resettlement. Humanitarian organizations, including the Women's Refugee Commission, raised concerns about the separations. In response, DHS contracted with Corrections Corporation of America to convert one of the company's shuttered medium-security prisons north of Austin, Texas, into a family detention center as a "solution" to the family separations that were taking place. The T. Don Hutto Detention Center opened in May 2006 and had the capacity to detain five hundred people. Its opening sparked one of the first major shutdown campaigns to emerge as the movement started fighting back against mass immigrant detention.[4]

In September 2006, a group of us—organizers, advocates, and academics—met at the ACLU of Texas office in Austin to figure out what to do about Hutto. The group, including my colleague Bob Libal, continued to meet, and eventually formed Texans United for Families (TUFF), a coalition that included residents of Taylor, where Hutto is located. TUFF took a multipronged approach to the campaign to shut down Hutto that involved four tiers: litigation, grassroots organizing, media engagement, and legislative advocacy.

Vanita Gupta of the ACLU (who became the associate attorney general under Biden) and University of Texas Law School professor Barbara Hines took the lead on litigation. Once Hines toured Hutto, she discovered that many of the families were spending months there and that the facility had done very few updates from its previous iteration as a medium-security prison. Most of the children detained at Hutto were under the age of twelve, and those older than six were routinely separated from their parents within the facility. The younger kids would be held with their mothers in a cell with a toilet and a crib. All children were required to wear prison uniforms, with babies clothed in prison onesies.[5] Guards often threatened separation if children misbehaved. Hines, Gupta, and partners sued DHS over the conditions of confinement. In 2007, they settled the case after winning some conditions improvements and periodic review, but family detention continued. Gupta and Hines had extensive discussions with TUFF to figure out their next move.

Women's Refugee Commission documented abuses in the facility and kept the pressure on the agency in DC. But grassroots power was also essential. TUFF's grassroots organizing efforts involved regular vigils outside the detention center and building a base in Taylor. After getting wind of an ICE plan to open three new family detention centers, TUFF took the call to end family detention nationwide. In 2009, as Obama took office, TUFF organized "100 events in the first 100 days" to stop the expansions, during which organizers collected fifty-five thousand petition signatures, organized toy and book drives, and stepped up their outreach and media efforts to call attention to the issue.[6] The campaign hosted screenings of two documentary films about family detention, *Hutto: America's Family Prison* and *The Least of These*, which had debuted at the South by Southwest film festival in Austin. The documentaries included interviews with families formerly detained at Hutto and images from inside the jail—children and teens inside and cells with cribs. Hutto had become the most notorious detention center in the country.

Later that year, TUFF finally secured a major victory when the Obama administration ended family detention at Hutto, and children were no longer detained there. It was a rare positive reform under Obama on the issue of detention. But Hutto remained open for women, and the Berks facility in Pennsylvania continued to detain families.

Almost five years after the end of family detention at Hutto, Obama brought back mass family detention, converting the Karnes Residential Center and opening a new 2,400-bed family detention center in Dilley, Texas (explained in chapter 2). It was devastating blow to antidetention activists. Both facilities were farther from Austin than Hutto, making it more difficult for immigrants to access lawyers or other forms of support and obscuring family detention from the public. Conditions at the detention centers were dire, and both national and local organizations pushed for ICE to reverse the practice. In Pennsylvania, where Berks was located, news broke of a guard sexually assaulting a nineteen-year-old immigrant woman who had been detained at the facility with her three-year-old son. The incident was the impetus for local groups to launch the Shut Down Berks campaign in 2015.

Media covered the harms of family detention, organizers protested, and lawyers filed litigation. In 2015, US District Court judge Dolly Gee of California ruled that the Flores settlement applies to both unaccompanied and accompanied minors, which includes children in family detention. After the announcement, TUFF members converged in Austin at a local swimming hole, Barton Springs, to read the *New York Times* coverage of the decision and celebrate. The decision limited the amount of time a child could spend in family detention to twenty days, but the Obama administration was convinced that incarcerating families would help deter future migration and appealed the decision. Berks, Dilley, and Karnes continued to detain families through the end of his tenure as president.

The incarceration of more than 120,000 Japanese Americans during World War II remains the largest family detention project in US history. In the 1940s, adults and children of Japanese descent were rounded up and incarcerated in camps across the western United States. They were considered enemies of the state because of their ethnic origin. Satsuki Ina was born in one of these camps. After the war and before they were freed, Ina and her family were relocated to the Crystal City Internment Camp in south Texas, about halfway between the Dilley family detention center and the US-Mexico border.

In 2016, Ina, who is a trained psychotherapist, visited the Karnes Family Residential Center after Carl Takei, an ACLU attorney whose grandparents were incarcerated during World War II, encouraged her to go to evaluate the children for trauma. Ina recounts the visit: "It was like fractured pieces trying to converge—their experience today, my history—being in this place where I had been as a child."[7]

Later, in 2019, as Ina and others were planning a pilgrimage to Crystal City to remember and to heal from the generational trauma, she reached out to Bob Libal at Grassroots Leadership. He suggested they stop at Dilley after their pilgrimage to protest family detention. Around the same time Ina and other Japanese American activists founded the organization Tsuru for Solidarity to support the fight against immigrant detention.

Tsuru, the Japanese word for crane, represents transformation, healing, and nonviolence in Japanese culture. Before the protest, Tsuru issued a call for people across the country to send ten thousand origami cranes with "messages of solidarity, hope, and love" that they would then hang on the fences around Dilley. Dozens of boxes started arriving at the Grassroots Leadership office in Austin; they received thirty thousand cranes within two and half weeks. People incarcerated at the San Quentin State Prison in California were among those who sent origami cranes. The day of the protest, taiko drums boomed outside of Dilley as survivors stood along the fence, holding signs with images of themselves as children in the camps and the words "Not OK in 1942, not OK now."[8]

After the protest, Tsuru members and other survivors traveled to the border to meet with the Laredo Immigrant Alliance, a group that was supporting women and children recently released from detention. Through translators, the survivors formed a circle with the women and shared their stories of being incarcerated during World War II. Mike Ishii, a cofounder of Tsuru whose mother was incarcerated at a camp in Idaho, summarized some of what the survivors shared: "We understand what you have gone through because it happened to us. We came back for you. When we were rounded up, nobody protested, nobody came to the fences. We are here and we will fight for you. . . . You will survive. If we did, you will." One of the mothers eventually opened up about her experience: "I was in Karnes for a year, and they took my daughter away, and it was unbearable. But you were in there for four years it must have been worse for you."[9]

The Trump administration continued to challenge the Flores settlement in order to hold immigrant families indefinitely. In 2019, judge Dolly Gee ruled against the administration, calling its proposal "Kafkaesque."[10] Then, early in the pandemic, Judge Gee ordered the administration to release all children who had been in custody for more than twenty days.

Like many of the local campaigns against detention, 2020 was a pivotal year for the fight to end family detention. Groups that had been fighting for years against the practice—Shut Down Berks, Grassroots Leadership, RAICES, Tsuru for Solidarity, and DWN—started coordinating to get families released as COVID-19 spread through the detention system. Many of the families in Berks were from Haiti, and the organizations started working with Guerline Jozef, executive director of the Haitian Bridge Alliance, to strengthen the campaign. Together the group formed the Family Liberation Abolitionist Network (FLAN). At the end of 2020, the Trump administration tried to deport families quickly back to Haiti, but the FLAN groups and advocates in DC came together to get the House Judiciary Committee to encourage DHS to grant families reconsideration of their asylum claims. After a successful telephone campaign, including a viral TikTok that resulted in ten thousand calls to members of Congress, most reconsiderations were granted, and some deportation flights to Haiti were stopped on the tarmac to remove people whose cases were being reconsidered.

DWN included the three family detention centers among the First Ten list for the Biden administration to close in its first year. The administration stopped detaining children at Berks, but kept detaining women, following the trajectory of Hutto. Dilley and Karnes remained open and continued to detain families. To make them seem more palatable, the administration rebranded them as "reception centers" and said that families would only be held for short periods, in compliance with the Flores settlement. In response, FLAN members lambasted the Biden administration. Satsuki Ina wrote in an op-ed for *Time* about the rebranding attempt:

> No matter what it's called, a cage is still a cage. I know this firsthand; in 1945, the U.S. government published a propaganda film about the Crystal City internment camp where I was held, touting the flower gardens, medical staffing, and daily milk deliveries to this family prison. The film cited these as signs of the "normal living conditions" inside the fence. But—despite these superficial niceties—I knew that I lived in a prison, and that the job of the armed guards in the watchtowers was to prevent my escape.[11]

The groups kept a steady drumbeat, pressuring the Biden administration to end the practice. Through appropriations, they pushed to defund family detention, and members of Congress introduced the

Freedom for Families Act. It took almost a year, but in December 2021, the US government stopped detaining immigrant families at Dilley and Karnes, more than twenty years after it first started the practice at Berks.

In Pennsylvania, the Shut Down Berks coalition continued their efforts to close the facility; family detention had galvanized the community in opposition, but the group had taken on a detention abolition stance. In the eight years that the coalition existed, a wide variety of Pennsylvania groups came together. They bridged legal services, amplified the demands of detained immigrants, and advocated at the state and federal levels for closure of the facility. In November 2022, the coalition declared victory when ICE announced it was ending the contract at Berks. Jasmine Rivera, who helped coordinate the coalition, celebrated the resistance of the people detained: "It's a special victory to those who were incarcerated—the mothers who did the work strikes and hunger strikes; the fathers, mothers, women, who have made their voices heard and demanded that this not happen to anyone else."[12]

While the campaign against family detention has been perceived by some activists as a more sympathetic and therefore acceptable cause, it was an important laboratory for developing abolitionist strategies and tactics. The choice to focus on specific facilities, the call for shutdown, and the multipronged campaigns incorporating organizing, legal, and advocacy tactics proved to be the most effective strategy and one that has been replicated in localities across the country. In early 2023, rumors emerged that the Biden administration may bring back family detention, but the immediate backlash to the news staved off family detention's return, at least as of this writing.

California Leads the Way

Perhaps it is not surprising that the state with the largest foreign-born population in the nation has fought the hardest to protect immigrants from detention and deportation. But just thirty years ago, as California was going through an economic recession, it became a hotbed of state-level anti-immigrant initiatives, culminating in the passage of Proposition 187 (see chapter 1). A lot has changed since then. Through the tireless work of immigrant communities and their allies, the state of California has become relatively proimmigrant. In recent years, much attention has been given to harsh state legislation in Florida and Texas passed to punish immigrants, but in places like California, state-level strategies have been essential to protecting immigrants and pushing the federal government to change. The focus on state-level campaigns in California has made state legislation, including for limiting immigrant detention, a key site of advocacy for the immigrant justice movement nationwide.[13]

Several local campaigns emerged during the Obama years to end detention contracts throughout California. In Orange County, known for its conservative politics and willingness to work with ICE, the undocumented-led group Familia: Trans Queer Liberation Movement launched a multiyear campaign against detention at the Santa Ana city jail, which had the first dedicated unit for queer and transgender immigrants in the country. In 2016, after numerous direct actions, including activist hunger strikes and a shutdown of a city intersection, the Santa Ana city council announced its plans to phase out the ICE contract by 2020. The decision triggered ICE to end the contract earlier in 2017. The Orange County sheriff, claiming it was purely a business decision, later ended ICE contracts at two additional jails that local groups had waged campaigns against (one of which was included on the Expose and Close list).

In northern California, after a seven-year campaign, the sheriff of Contra Costa County ended the ICE contract at a county jail in Richmond (near Oakland), which had detained on average 200 immigrants a day. The campaign, led by the Interfaith Movement for Human Integrity and Freedom for Immigrants (FFI), involved monthly vigils and coordination with people detained. The campaign brought in health professionals, labor unions, and community members, who provided bond money for people to be released and housing for those in need, and helped make the case for closure. FFI regularly visited immigrants detained at the jail, supporting their deportation defense campaigns and amplifying their testimonials to argue against the contract. In 2018, after a series of actions, including a 4,000-person demonstration at the detention center during the height of the family separation crisis, the sheriff grew so frustrated with the protests that he fenced off the entire jail. The sheriff's office cited the costs associated with policing the protests against ICE as among the reasons for terminating the contract.[14] After the end of the contract, local attorneys noticed a reduction in ICE enforcement activity in northern California. Activists involved in the fight noted that the victory "contributed to the idea that detaining immigrants is immoral and unnecessary" and revealed that "less bed space makes it harder to house, detain, and deport people."[15]

In other parts of the state, communities struggled to make the case for closure, in large part due to California's enduring carceral economy, which had made many cash-strapped communities dependent on prisons, jails, and detention centers. The rural community of Adelanto, California, about ninety miles northeast of Los Angeles, is one such location. The city was hit by the downturn of the defense industry after the end of the Cold War, when the local George Air Force Base was decommissioned in 1992. As the prison boom of the 1990s took place in California and across the United States, Adelanto, the self-proclaimed "City of Unlimited Possibilities," jumped on the bandwagon and began building up its prison capacity. The area is now home to several facilities—including a federal prison, a county jail, and two private prisons—that formerly incarcerated people for the state of California, but have since been converted into immigrant detention centers. Together the capacity to incarcerate people in or near Adelanto, which nears ten thousand, makes up almost a third of the city's total population.[16]

The GEO Group began detaining immigrants at the Adelanto ICE Processing Center, one of the converted state prisons, in 2011. Immigrant rights groups started holding regular vigils outside the facility soon after it opened. The contract was an intergovernmental service agreement, with the city of Adelanto operating as the middleman between ICE and the GEO Group. GEO has expanded the detention center, making it one of the largest in the country, with a capacity to detain nearly 2,000 people. As a result, San Bernardino County, where Adelanto is located, became the county with highest ICE community arrests in the country. More beds meant more space to hold immigrants. The facility is notorious for its poor medical care, and hunger strikes protesting the conditions are frequent. At least seven people have died while detained there. The Adelanto detention center and its conditions became a catalyst for pushing for state-level interventions, changing the approach to antidetention advocacy in California and nationwide.

Many groups throughout California have coordinated to support immigrants who have frequently protested their conditions of confinement while detained at Adelanto. A hunger strike at the detention center caught the attention of state senator Ricardo Lara. He reached out to the Immigrant Legal Resource Center (ILRC), a California-based legal advocacy organization, and started to consider legislation to curb detention in California. Immigrant justice organizations, including immigrant youth who had been organizing to free people from detention, came together to form the Dignity Not Detention coalition to help pass legislation. Several other organizations have joined over the years, including the Inland Coalition for Immigrant Justice, which launched the Shut Down Adelanto campaign.

The coalition secured what they hoped was their first victory in 2016, with the passage of a bill to prevent local governments from operating as intermediaries between ICE and private companies like GEO. However, governor Jerry Brown vetoed the bill, urging DHS to take action for a more "permanent solution."[17] The Dignity Not Detention coalition did not give up, and the following year they helped pass two bills that created a moratorium on detention expansion for both private companies and local governments. Grisel Ruiz, an attorney at ILRC, said that the increased attention and investment in advocacy after Trump was elected helped build the groundswell of support needed to get permanent legislation against detention. As Ruiz explains, "Politically it was easier because the narrative around the good immigrant versus bad immigrant didn't come up in the same way."[18] The shift from Obama to Trump changed the discourse. But the evolving terrain on criminal legal system reforms amid Black Lives Matter protests, both in California and nationally, also played a role. Efforts to decarcerate California prisons had been gaining steam; as a result, many formerly incarcerated immigrant leaders were freed and joined statewide campaigns against detention and deportation. Some immigrants were transferred to ICE custody upon their release from state prison, like Ny Nourn, a Cambodian refugee and survivor of domestic abuse who had a felony conviction for a murder perpetrated by her abuser. Stories like Nourn's helped expose the problems with encouraging ICE to focus on "dangerous criminals." Organizers and advocates gained a better understanding of how the system worked, learning from those formerly incarcerated, and were able to challenge the good immigrant versus bad immigrant narrative more effectively through storytelling, highlighting individual cases. As a result, the Obama narrative of "felons, not families" did not have the same traction, and politicians were willing to go further to support all immigrants. The governor did not veto the antidetention bills this time.

The GEO Group went on the offensive after the bills passed. The company started kicking the local governments out of their role as middlemen to secure direct contracts with the federal government and circumvent the new state laws. ICE aided GEO by entering into emergency contracts that bypassed the public procurement process that is normally required. The Dignity Not Detention coalition began working to pass a private prison ban that would phase out these contracts once they expired as a strategy for reducing immigrant detention infrastructure in the state. Due to the speed with which GEO

obtained the direct contract with ICE, Adelanto's contract was slated
to end in 2019, after just one year.

The Dignity Not Detention coalition's efforts led to the passage of
California's AB 32 in October 2019. As a result of the law, Adelanto and
several other private detention centers in California would have been
shut down within a few years. But ICE and GEO colluded once again to
bypass the state law. The ban was to go into effect in January 2020. In
the short time between AB 32's passage in October and when it became
law, ICE accelerated the process and entered into fifteen-year contracts
at the remaining private detention centers in California. It was a devastating outcome for immigrant communities in California and the Dignity Not Detention coalition that had fought so hard to end detention
in the state. The federal government and GEO would go on to sue the
state of California over the private prison ban, a lawsuit that the Biden
administration also pursued once in office. As explained in chapter
5, for the Democrats, the issue was never really about private prisons,
but whether the government's carceral agenda could continue without
them. Biden phased out private prisons for DOJ while simultaneously
defending their use by another branch of the federal government.

While the effort to end detention in California via a state-level
private prison ban backfired, the strides that immigrant justice groups
made there laid the foundation for important wins across the country.
Learning from the efforts in California, organizers and advocates in
several states (Colorado, Illinois, Maryland, New Jersey, Oregon, and
Washington State) have been successful at passing legislation ending
detention contracts or preventing new expansion, and others are considering similar legislation.

The Midwest Versus ICE

In Obama's first term, as ICE was attempting to consolidate the system and shift toward immigrant-only private prisons, the Midwest
became a key location for expansion, given that most immigrants

detained in the region were held at county jails. What ICE didn't anticipate was that a dedicated group of organizers, advocates, faith leaders, and ordinary people would fight back at every proposed site, leading to one of the most effective games of whack-a-mole the movement had ever played. Fred Tsao, senior policy counsel at the Illinois Coalition for Immigrant and Refugee Rights (ICIRR), has been involved in these fights since the beginning. From his perspective, the central component to winning at all these proposed detention sites was the leadership of local community members. In eight campaigns to stop expansion, local organizers were able to succeed at every single site. A final struggle in Dwight, Illinois, ended when a state bill passed to block the expansion. The campaigns to prevent new detention centers also opened up space for ending contracts at the county jails used by ICE to detain immigrants. By the summer of 2022, Illinois had ended immigrant detention throughout the state. Efforts to stop expansion in Indiana, Michigan, Minnesota, and Wisconsin had succeeded as well. Thanks to the movement, ICE failed to get its Midwest detention center.[19]

The story of Illinois ending detention began in 2007 with two Catholic Sisters of Mercy, Sister JoAnn Persch and Sister Pat Murphy. Every Friday, they began standing vigil outside the Broadview Staging Center, where immigrants were transferred to await deportation, sometimes in snowy and frigid weather, in suburban Chicago. The Sisters also tried to get access to visit immigrants detained at the McHenry County Jail, located northwest of Chicago. As part of the federal government's post-9/11 expansion of county jails to hold people pretrial for the US Marshals Service and ICE, it bankrolled a $6.4 million expansion of the McHenry County Jail.[20] Both Broadview and McHenry denied the Sisters' requests to visit immigrants. They began working with Tsao at ICIRR to pass a bill mandating that jails holding people for ICE provide access for pastoral care programs for detained immigrants. In an effort to pass the bill, many faith leaders came together to form the Interfaith Community for Detained Immigrants (ICDI). The bill passed unanimously, with many Republicans supporting it in the name of religious freedom, and became law in 2009.[21] Even after the bill passed, McHenry County officials tried to resist access, but the Sisters were very persistent and the county eventually instated the visitation program.

Two years later, in 2011, ICE and CCA set their sights on expansion in Crete, Illinois, a small town with a population of 8,000, about forty miles from downtown Chicago. The local chapter of Pax Christi and other advocates working with ICDI to fight the proposed detention center began organizing petition drives, canvassing, and holding vigils in the main intersection of the village. ICIRR also started running a bill in the state legislature to ban private immigrant detention. The state had already banned private prisons in 1990, but the ban didn't extend to immigrant detention. In Chicago, community members were also organizing against the jail. On March 30, 2012, the Reverend José Landaverde led a forty-mile march from Little Village, a predominantly Latinx neighborhood in Chicago, to downtown Crete. Fifty activists joined him on the forty-eight-hour march with signs reading "Money for college, not detention" and "No more cages."[22]

Groups in Chicago and Crete continued to organize and were planning a big town hall with elected officials and ICE that May. ICE, however, got wind of the opposition to the detention center. Amid mass mobilizations planned against the upcoming NATO summit in the city, fearing a bigger protest, it withdrew from the town hall. The organizers then canceled the event: Tsao and others had to tell the seventy cars of supporters who had shown up to go home. The bill to ban private detention was still moving in the state legislature, but when it came to a vote, it fell short by one because the "yes" button malfunctioned for one of its supporters. By the time the revote was up, lobbyists for CCA had peeled off votes for the bill, which failed. But the long months of organizing had paid off. Eventually, the Crete village board decided the ICE detention center was more trouble than it was worth and voted to withdraw from the expansion deal.

After Crete, a new detention center was proposed practically every year, and at every location a new crop of local leaders began working with ICIRR and ICDI to block its construction. In 2012, in Joliet, Illinois, CCA again tried to secure a new contract for detention, but it was an election year, and organizers successfully campaigned for a new city council member, knocking out an incumbent who was the main proponent of the new detention center. CCA was defeated in Illinois, but the battle in the Midwest was far from over.

In 2013, the GEO Group decided to try their hand at expansion in northwest Indiana, just outside Chicago. In Hobart, Indiana, the GEO Group bought property for a new jail, but, after community members and local Unitarian and Methodist churches got wind of the plan, they lobbied the mayor against it, and GEO eventually sold the lot. In 2014, GEO tried again in Gary, Indiana. The fight went on for a couple years, but finally ended in 2016 after dozens of people testified at a five-hour-long hearing that ended with the city common council voting unanimously against the proposal. That same year, back in Illinois, another private prison company, MTC, tried to expand private detention in rural Pembroke Township, sixty-five miles south of Chicago. After four previous wins, local residents were hopeful that they could block the proposal—and joining together with Chicago-based organizations, they did. After that, a sheriff in Winnebago County, Illinois, also considered detaining immigrants for ICE but backed down amid community pressure. And then CoreCivic tried its hand again, in Elkhart County, Indiana, but local academics at Goshen College, Latinx community leaders, and other allies persuaded the county board to reject the proposal. In Newton County, Indiana, Tsao recalled that a father and son "got all up in arms" and mobilized their neighbors to fight and beat GEO.

Then, after an incredible eight wins under their belt, came the fight in Dwight, a small Illinois town about eighty miles southwest of Chicago. At this point, it felt like the groups in Illinois and Indiana were unstoppable. But, as Tsao puts it, Dwight became the "exception that proved the rule." Local leadership was essential to winning; in Dwight, they simply didn't have it. Many had joined the fight along the way, including Organized Communities Against Deportations, a Chicago group that had been waging campaigns against deportations and the use of gang databases for immigration enforcement; progressive leaders from various communities in central Illinois; and the Chicago-based National Immigrant Justice Center, which brought a national perspective to the fight. DWN staff based in Chicago also provided support. But in Dwight, which for many years had hosted a state women's prison, the local community was more open to a new detention facility, and opponents were less willing to speak publicly or organize.

Immigration Centers of America (ICA), a small private prison company that only operated one other immigrant detention center, in Virginia, courted the mayor of Dwight. By the time the plans became public in 2019, they already had draft agreements—all they needed was a vote by the village board. ICA had promised Dwight a dollar a day for each person detained, and the potential revenue was a major draw for the mayor and the town. At one point, ICIRR and others tried to organize a town hall with a local church in Dwight, but under community pressure the church canceled the event at the last minute, and the organizers had to turn people away. In March 2019, the village board held a special meeting at the high school gymnasium. The bleachers were full of people from Chicago, Bloomington, Peoria, and the University of Illinois at Urbana-Champaign, all opposing the jail. But ultimately it was the mayor who prevailed, and the village board voted 5–2 in favor of the new detention center. Fred Tsao pointed out that "even getting two votes against the jail was a victory given the reception we got in Dwight."

But all was not yet lost. Soon after the vote, ICIRR renewed its efforts to pass the ban against private immigrant detention in Illinois. With a new governor, JB Pritzker, ready to push back against the Trump administration, the bill became law in June 2019, and the detention center in Dwight was blocked.

Private detention was dead in Illinois. But there were still three county jails in use by ICE: McHenry County Jail; Kankakee County Jail, south of Chicago; and Tri-County Detention Center at the southern tip of the state, about six hours from Chicago. Mark Fleming, a senior litigator at the National Immigrant Justice Center, opined that the use of these jails may be in violation of a recent state law barring county jails from holding immigrants until ICE could take them into custody. ICIRR began developing the Illinois Way Forward Act, working to expand sanctuary policies in Illinois to include a ban on intergovernmental service agreements between county jails and ICE. With a Democratic supermajority in the state legislature and Pritzker in office, the bill passed, ending all three of the county jail contracts. McHenry and Kankakee counties attempted to block the legislation, but Fleming and the other advocates, anticipating such a challenge, built in language to ensure the law would be protected from potential litigation. Their lawsuit failed, and by July 2022 Illinois no longer detained immigrants for ICE.

These site fights and detention closures were a resounding victory that carried crucial lessons about the importance of strong local organizers working in tandem with city- and state-level advocates as well as with elected officials. Fred Tsao would go on to advise DWN members across the country who were waging campaigns against detention expansion.

Hudson and the Fight to End Detention in New Jersey

While in ICE custody, immigrants are often transferred from one detention center to another, sometimes two or more times. Advocates have raised concerns about transfers because they can disrupt immigration cases and make it harder for immigrants to access services and stay connected to family. ICE argues that transfers occur due to capacity constraints, but the shuffling of immigrants between detention centers is also a perverse tactic that ICE uses to disorient immigrants while in detention. As a remedy, some advocates have proposed situating detention centers close to metropolitan areas to prevent transfers and have thus opposed ending contracts at certain facilities near big cities. But abolitionists disagree, arguing that detention centers should close regardless of their location. Lending weight to their position, a recent study found that the greater the capacity for detention in a given area, the higher the rate of ICE arrests. The same holds for higher overall jail and prison capacity in an area: the more capacity, the more ICE makes arrests.[23] The debate over transfers and the geography of detention continues to be a contentious subject within the movement. These tensions came to a head in the fight to end detention in New Jersey.[24]

For many years, most immigrants arrested by ICE in New York City were sent to jails in New Jersey while they awaited their court dates. One of these facilities, the Hudson County Jail, had the same issues as other county jails: limited outdoor recreation, terrible food, lack of clean clothing, filthy living conditions, abuse by prison guards, and multiple deaths. For these reasons, DWN members in New York City, Families for Freedom, Human Rights First, and some local attorneys pushed to include Hudson on the Expose and Close list of the ten immigrant detention centers to shut down in 2012. That fall, as we were planning the release of reports, I soon realized that we had failed to do our due diligence. DWN members in New Jersey were not on board. They believed that detention closures could lead to transfers, and many groups had built their nonprofit programs around supporting access to counsel and visitation for immigrants detained in New Jersey jails. We talked it through; in the end, New Jersey groups remained divided. Some of them signed on to Expose and Close and others didn't.

Six years later, in 2018, a similar episode played out, but both the nonprofit infrastructure and rage against ICE had grown considerably in that time, making the tensions within the movement around detention closure even more pronounced. With Trump in office, "blue states" were appalled by ICE's treatment of immigrants. Many localities were eager to distance themselves from the administration. In response, Hudson County ended its 287(g) agreement in March 2018, but then in July, during an unscheduled vote, it renewed its ICE contract to detain immigrants at the jail. As the call to abolish ICE went mainstream that summer, activists turned up the pressure on local officials. Remarkably, in September of that year, Hudson County officials reversed their decision and planned to stop detaining immigrants before the contract was up at the end of 2020.

Prior to these developments, Robert Katzmann, an appeals court judge in New York, had been advocating for years to secure no-cost legal representation for New Yorkers in immigrant detention. Most immigrants who are locked up don't have access to lawyers, and being in detention makes it that much harder to secure counsel. Katzmann was finally successful when the New York City Council decided to fund representation for detained New Yorkers in 2013. It brought in a flood of money for legal service providers in New York and precipitated the launch of the New York Immigrant Family Unity Project (NYIFUP), which included the Bronx Defenders, the Legal Aid Society of New York, and Brooklyn Defender Services, specifically. Upon hearing the news about the termination of the Hudson contract, the NYIFUP groups sent a letter to county officials:

> We respectfully implore you to postpone the vote on a resolution phasing out the contract with [ICE].... To be clear, we strongly support the movement to abolish ICE and believe there is no place for the jailing of asylum-seekers, longtime community members, or anyone else based on birthplace in a just society.... That said, ending contracts for ICE detention in jails near large immigrant communities where attorneys are provided for free—while ICE continues to make arrests in these communities—will do far more harm than good and we question whether directly impacted people were engaged in this decision.... By ending the contract with ICE,

whether tomorrow or in 2020, the County would be harming
detained people and others arrested by ICE in the New York
City metropolitan area.[25]

From their perspective, it was more important to keep the contract so
that people wouldn't be transferred away, which would make it harder
for them to provide representation.

The NYIFUP statement divided the movement. Many organizations, including DWN members in New York and New Jersey, were
now hesitant to support the end of the Hudson contract because of
the NYIFUP stance on the issue. And the tensions spread across the
country. Organizers and lawyers were at odds, and there was confusion about whether to support closure campaigns as a result.

I was in New York City soon after the statement was released
and reached out to an NYIFUP attorney via email to see if we could
meet up to discuss their concerns. It was a few weeks before DWN
launched the Communities Not Cages campaign, and I was worried
that if advocates in New York City wouldn't affirm our calls to end
detention it could hurt the many campaigns we were supporting
across the country to shut down detention centers. In response to the
email, the NYIFUP attorney cc'd five additional attorneys to set up a
time for me to talk to all of them. The call was one of the lower points
of my many years doing this work. I asked a colleague to join me, and
we did our best to make the case for ending the contract. I explained
that we were working with groups across the country to shut down
detention centers and that building power against ICE in communities like New York City, where there are more resources and capacity,
would be essential to the national fight. The NYIFUP attorneys flatly
told us they didn't agree and that our strategy wouldn't work.

Some of the NYIFUP attorneys had become so convinced of
their argument that during one national conference call I joined about
the campaign for universal representation, an attorney claimed there
wasn't "enough detention" in New Jersey. Seemingly, she was making
this argument because transfers continued despite a recent increase

in the Hudson County Jail's ICE capacity. Scholar and activist James Kilgore has referred to this kind of thinking as "carceral humanism," in which, in the mind of some advocates and politicians, jails are seen as sites of social service provision. Kilgore points to instances where jail operators claim to offer mental health support by "providing opportunities and improved circumstances for those in custody," ignoring the trauma of being incarcerated.[26] In the case of Hudson, for attorneys with funding for legal representation, being near detention centers was necessary for providing counsel to immigrants and keeping their programs intact.

But not everyone at the NYIFUP organizations agreed with this assessment. Sophia Gurulé, an attorney at the Bronx Defenders, one of the NYIFUP providers, was supportive of the call for detention abolition. While providing legal support was important, she didn't think it should be an argument for keeping people detained in the horrible conditions at Hudson. She would later join others to both shift the NYIFUP position and advance the campaign to end the contract at the jail.

Meanwhile Tania Mattos, a Bolivian immigrant who came to the United States when she was four, had been witnessing the impact of ICE arrests in her community in Queens for years. She started organizing to support immigrant New Yorkers and connected with DWN. In 2018, she attended a DWN member conference in Denver where she participated in a workshop led by members of the California Dignity Not Detention coalition about their efforts to pass state legislation to curb detention. Mattos joined with other groups in New York, including Desis Rising Up and Moving, Black Alliance for Just Immigration, and Queer Detainee Empowerment Project. Together they decided to see if they could do something similar back on the East Coast. The initial set of groups planned "Abolish ICE" gatherings in 2019, but tensions around the Hudson contract were still fresh, and many established groups in the city were hesitant to engage with them. Mattos knew that because New Yorkers were detained in New

Jersey they needed to work with groups there, and she subsequently reached out to grassroots groups in New Jersey including local chapters of Movimiento Cosecha, Democratic Socialists of America, and Pax Christi, which were aligned with the demand to end detention.

In February 2020, the situation started to escalate when a family member of someone being targeted by ICE was shot in the face by an agent during an immigration raid in Brooklyn.[27] While the Trump administration complained that sanctuary policies in places like New York City prevented them from doing their job, ICE violently targeted immigrants living in the city through home raids and sent them to the Hudson County Jail. Raids were also being conducted in New Jersey, and with the onset of the pandemic organizers and advocates started mobilizing to get people released. In mid-March 2020, several hundred detained immigrants started hunger strikes at three of the ICE-contracted jails in New Jersey, which sparked NYIFUP groups to call for mass releases.[28] Never Again Action, a Jewish-led group of activists focused on immigrant justice, coordinated car rallies to support hunger strikers.[29] The "Abolish ICE" effort then expanded, and a set of disparate groups fighting immigration enforcement joined together to form Abolish ICE NY/NJ.

The Hudson contract continued to be a point of contention, and, with the pandemic and George Floyd uprisings, more people were on board for ending the contract than ever before. As everything went virtual, it became easier for people to attend public hearings regarding jail contracts. Activists learned that another vote regarding the Hudson contract was imminent. The groups started coordinating to make sure people were attending county meetings to track what was happening with the contract. In the meantime, some of the NYIFUP organizations were having internal unionization drives, and in the process of connecting with each other they learned that more NYIFUP staff were supportive of the plan to end the contract at Hudson. In November 2020, Hudson County commissioners were set to vote on the ICE contract once again. Amy Torres of the New Jersey Alliance for Immigrant

Justice said that everyone went into high gear once they knew the vote was happening: "We started driving calls to the county commissioners, organized Zoom trainings so people could join the hearing, pulled together letters of support, hosted a press conference, and pushed local mayors to make public statements against the contract."

More than 150 people joined what ended up being a marathon ten-hour public meeting that went well into the night. Not a single person spoke in support of the contract; the opposition was unanimous.[30] Beforehand NYIFUP had issued a statement, but took no position, explaining that "while transfers remain a concern, we also recognize that ending the contract with ICE may advance our goals of decarceration and freedom for the people we serve."[31] The staff unions of two of the NYIFUP groups, however, had come out against the contract. Gurulé represented her union during the virtual meeting and described the "disgusting" and "torture"-like conditions at the facility. She then spoke directly to the county officials: "If you vote to keep this contract, do not convince yourself that you are doing so in the best interests of the people detained by ICE at the Hudson County Jail. You will not be doing the right thing. You will not be the hero." Disregarding the hours of testimony from a hundred people against immigrant detention at Hudson, the commissioners voted to renew the ICE contract for another ten years. In their explanation, they cited the potential loss of revenue from the contract cancellation as well as the 2018 statement from NYIFUP, which convinced them they were helping people detained at Hudson.

Abolish ICE NY/NJ and other advocates did not let the Hudson decision deter them, and more groups joined the effort to end not only the Hudson contract but also the other ICE contracts in New Jersey. They started putting pressure on members of Congress to intervene. Both New Jersey senators, Cory Booker and Robert Menendez, issued statements against county jail partnerships with ICE. Menendez went on to call the revenue "blood money," which made state officials take notice.[32]

Amy Torres and other organizers started holding vigils outside the house of county executive Tom DeGise, who was in favor of the ICE contract. Torres said the vigils caught the attention of DeGise's neighbors: "They were sympathetic and ordering pizza for us and bringing us cookies."[33] But DeGise labeled them "left-wing extremists," filed a restraining order against them, and had the sheriff come out and detain several of them and charge them with contempt.[34] Conditions at one of the other jails, in Bergen County, worsened as the jail wardens started retaliating against immigrants detained. At an action in December 2020, organizers set up speakers to amplify the cries of detained immigrants via cell phone conversations to expose the harms taking place inside. In retaliation against the protest, the sheriff brutally confronted them during the action. Deputies used pepper spray and tackled some protesters. Nine people were arrested, eight of whom were New Yorkers.[35]

After these events, the organizers started to regroup to consider the most strategic way to end the contracts. Learning from the efforts in California, Illinois, and other states, groups started focusing on state legislation to place a moratorium on new detention contracts and renewals. Meanwhile, local officials in both Hudson County and Essex County, the site of another ICE jail in New Jersey, decided they were fed up with all the attention and announced they would stop detaining immigrants in the spring of 2021. The decision helped push state-level officials to pass the antidetention bill that July. New Jersey, which at times had five counties detaining immigrants, only had one remaining detention center.

Across the river, advocates started their own plan to pass antidetention state legislation in New York. At this point, the NYIFUP groups started to come around, and eventually did a one-eighty from their initial position.[36] Because the shift during the pandemic toward virtual meetings allowed lawyers to meet with clients and attend hearings from any location, they were still able to provide representation, even if people were transferred. Awareness had grown that having nearby bed space meant more people could be detained who otherwise would not have been targeted in the first place. Groups in New York started pushing for their own Dignity Not Detention bill to end contracts at the county jails north of the city, and upstate and NYIFUP groups signed on to the call.

The campaign to end the contract at Hudson and the other detention centers in New Jersey and New York provided many critical lessons for the movement. After Hudson County officials decided to renew the contract for an additional ten years, Abolish ICE NY/NJ and allied groups did not give up. To the contrary, they persevered and doubled down on the demand for closure. What seemed like a major loss turned into a victory less than one year later, when the same local officials decided to stop detaining immigrants for ICE. The groundswell of activity and clarity coming from a range of groups and stakeholders also helped reverse the NYIFUP position on the issue, demonstrating the power of movement building and sustained organizing.

Abolitionist Lessons

While many of the campaigns laid out in this chapter focus on more friendly political climates, these antidetention wins had impacts far beyond the locations in which they took place. The accumulating rejection of detention by states prevented ICE from implementing its plan to have large, dedicated immigrant detention centers in every region of the country. The salience of detention abolition forced the federal government's hand. In May 2021, DHS secretary Alejandro Mayorkas noted at a congressional hearing that there was an "overuse of detention," signaling a shifting view on the issue.[37] By December 2022, the Biden administration had ended contracts at five detention centers, citing concerns around conditions. Three of the five detention centers had been included on DWN's First Ten to Communities Not Cages list. Biden's 2023 budget request for detention would have reduced capacity to twenty-five thousand, half of what it had been during its height in 2019. The belief that detention was necessary had started to lose its hold on advocates and politicians alike.

Since DWN members began calling for detention closures back in 2012, local, state, and federal officials have ended contracts at over twenty detention centers in response to inside organizing and community pressure. Several ICE strongholds, like the McHenry County Jail in Illinois, which the federal government subsidized for expansion, and the Etowah County Jail, which Alabama politicians fought to maintain, no longer detain immigrants for ICE. Campaigns that seemed impossible to win a decade ago were finally succeeding. Combined with local efforts to stop ICE and police collaboration, immigrant arrests and deportations in the interior have fallen considerably. No less significantly, the annual average daily population in ICE detention remained below Obama-era levels during Biden's first three years in office. While some will attribute this reduction in detention to the pandemic era and the harsh border closures implemented by Trump and continued by Biden, the administration and local and state actors could have just kept the status quo, but they didn't. In late 2023, ICE detention returned to pre-pandemic levels, and Biden requested more funding for detention as the border panic consumed the political discourse on immigration. The about-face from the Biden administration shows that the fight to end detention will be a constant struggle. But the reduction in the system during these years and the end of contracts at numerous facilities were important movement victories that would not have been possible without the demand for abolition.

PART III

Making Abolition

CHAPTER 7

Abolitionist Approaches
to System Change

*Many remedies proposed for the all-purpose use of pris-
ons to solve social, political, and economic problems get
caught in the logic of the system itself, such that reform
strengthens, rather than loosens, prison's hold. In a sense,
the professionalization of activism has made many committed people so specialized and entrapped by funding
streams that they have become effectively deskilled when
it comes to thinking and doing what matters most.*
— Ruth Wilson Gilmore, *Golden Gulag*

When we are faced with significant challenges and unsure what to do, we often turn to our existing system for solutions. When Donald Trump was elected president, it was one of those moments. How would we stop him from unleashing his wrath on immigrant communities? Many turned to the American Civil Liberties Union. Days after the 2016 election, the ACLU took out a full-page ad in the *New York Times* proclaiming that the organization "will be vigilant every day" of Trump's tenure and preening, "Many of our country's most cherished rights are a result of ACLU litigation."[1] The

ad went on to list landmark cases such as those that affirmed our right
to use contraception and legalized same-sex marriage.

A little over two months later, Trump signed what became known
as the Muslim Ban, an executive order that banned people from
traveling to the United States from seven predominantly Muslim
countries in the Middle East and Africa for ninety days, indefinitely
suspended refugee arrivals from Syria, and prohibited other refugee
entry for 120 days. Protests erupted across the country at airports and
ports of entry, and a robust network of family members, organizers,
lawyers, and ordinary people mobilized opposition to the ban and
legal support for individuals who had been detained. Within days, the
ACLU received $24 million in donations, more than six times what it
raised in a typical year.[2] Over the next year and half, multiple versions
of the ban went to court, and the Trump administration kept adjust-
ing it slightly to meet the court's stipulations. In the end, litigation
couldn't stop the ban, and a somewhat restrained version of the executive order, the Muslim Ban 3.0, was upheld by the Supreme Court.
Noting the limitations of the litigation efforts, ACLU attorney Omar
Jadwat lamented, "The court failed today, and so the public is needed
more than ever."[3] Trump later added six countries to the list of those
banned. The ban remained in effect until Biden rescinded it upon taking office in 2021.

The court's decision that parts of the ban were constitutional, is
perhaps less surprising today. The Supreme Court has moved even
farther to the right in recent years. After it overturned *Roe v. Wade*
in 2022, its rightward nature and its repudiation of our civil liberties had achieved widespread public awareness. The ACLU showed
hubris in emphasizing its role in landmark court decisions; in reality, those court decisions were greatly influenced by the political and
social conditions of the time. Howard Zinn made this point many
years ago: "It would be naive to depend on the Supreme Court to
defend the rights of poor people, women, people of color, dissenters
of all kinds. Those rights only come alive when citizens organize, pro-

test, demonstrate, strike, boycott, rebel, and violate the law in order to uphold justice."[4] He points out that even *Roe v. Wade* in 1973 came about after states across the country had made abortion legal due to "grassroots agitation."

As discussed in chapter 3, when a Nevada judge ruled in 2021 that unlawful reentry prosecutions of migrants were unconstitutional due to the racist nature in which they became law, the decision came amid a broader racial reckoning in US society and public outrage over Trump's anti-immigrant agenda. The decision without a doubt was influenced by the political moment in which the case was heard. Despite the narrowness by which lawyers must argue their cases, the law and legal institutions do not exist in a vacuum, as Zinn so clearly understood. The decision to strike down reentry prosecutions failed to stick after the Biden administration defended the racist law and the Ninth Circuit reversed the lower court's ruling, revealing the limitations of centering legal strategies for creating change.

Legal interventions have aided in mitigating the harm caused by the immigration system, which remains a critical element of our work. But, as evidenced in previous chapters, the moments when we have finally been able to move the needle were results of deep organizing and movement building. As abolitionist legal scholar Derecka Purnell argues, citing the response to the Muslim Ban as a prime example, in recent years, more and more people are outsourcing the resistance to lawyers. She concludes, "Do we need a legal strategy? Of course. But we need mass resistance by everyday people. We need to go to the libraries where people are banning books to say, 'Absolutely not. We're not going to allow this.' We need strategic, disruptive, direct action."[5]

My intention is not to diminish the role of lawyers in the movement. To the contrary, lawyers, including ACLU attorneys and staff, were critical actors in the campaigns laid out in part II of this book. Partnerships between organizers and lawyers have led to some of our most innovative strategies and have helped throw a wrench in ICE's agenda. Many of the lawyers involved in these campaigns saw legal tactics as a supplemental tool to grassroots power and mobilization. Moving toward abolition of immigrant incarceration and the prison industrial complex requires us to think beyond our current system. Now an adage in our movements for social change, Audre Lorde's famous quote is one that should remain at the forefront of our minds as we consider abolitionist approaches to system change: "The master's tools will never dismantle the master's house. They may allow us to temporarily beat him at his own game, but they will never enable us to bring about genuine change."[6]

As the demand for abolition asserts, creating a more humane world will require us to not just tear down our current systems but also build a society in which everyone is valued and able to thrive. It is in these conditions that we will finally achieve racial and migrant justice. In the meantime, we can organize to make life better for immigrants and those seeking to migrate by limiting the reach of the prison industrial complex and chipping away at its structure. In this chapter, I provide some offerings for how abolition might guide us as the system continuously adapts. It's not just about imagining abolition, but making abolition. I've learned over time that we have to be nimble in our approach and assessment. Our strategies and tactics will change, but with abolition as a lens, we will be ready to tackle the evolving conditions.

—

The early months of the Biden administration provided an important testing ground for determining how far our calls for abolition would go. In the months leading up to the change in administration, immigrant rights groups offered policy proposals for how to reform the system, including an end to detention and stopping the criminalization of immigrants. After four years of Trump, it was hard to know what to expect, but January 20, 2021, was one of the most hopeful moments I can remember in doing this work. In a sweeping memo from acting secretary of homeland security David Pekoske, the Biden administration laid out a set of interior enforcement priorities that limited the power of ICE agents and included a hundred-day pause on deportations. The moratorium on deportations would not exclude people with past criminal convictions. The following day, Biden introduced a legalization bill that did not include criminal bars for those wanting to adjust their immigration status. Finally, all our calls against criminalization were being heard.

But then a few things happened in quick succession. First, Democrats in Congress introducing Biden's immigration bill were not happy with the lack of criminal bars and insisted on incorporating them into the final language of the bill. Biden was effectively to the left of Democrats in Congress on immigration. Then the state of Texas filed a lawsuit challenging both the deportation moratorium and new interior enforcement priorities memo. The Biden administration did little to fight for the deportation moratorium. It was never fully implemented and was soon dropped as a core demand by the well-resourced parts of the immigrant rights movement, which became more focused on the legalization fight in Congress.

In the aftermath of these developments, some groups began to retreat from their earlier positions on defunding ICE and CBP, instead proposing things like mass case management programs, risk assessment tools, and other reformist reforms that would do little to reduce detention and deportations. With Republican fearmongering around the border, some advocates argued that CBP needed more money to manage the large number of people arriving. It was frustrating but unsurprising. Under Trump, advocates were willing to go further because of his outwardly racist and vile rhetoric; with Biden, now that there was an opportunity for reforms, abolitionist demands were perceived as extreme or out of touch. Sometimes our job as abolitionists is to stop the reformist reforms that maintain the status quo. This was especially true under Obama, and later applied under Biden. We had to figure out how to hold an abolitionist line in a sea of reform.

—

As the call for abolition has become more popular, many people have come to interpret the demand in its most literal sense. This tendency often leads to two responses: (1) to perceive any reform as not radical enough, or (2) to see abolition as too extreme, often leading to the perennial question, "What about the murderers and rapists?" Both of these perspectives miss the point of abolition. For those worried that abolitionists don't care about harm or safety, Black feminist organizers Mariame Kaba and Andrea Ritchie implore them to consider the billions spent on systems that have "failed to prevent endemic rates of violence in our communities," and also that policing and prisons themselves are "sites of significant rape, battery, murder, and child abuse."[7] It is because abolitionists want to reduce harm and are committed to accountability that we call for the end of the prison industrial complex.

For people who believe that anything short of dismantling the entire system immediately is not abolition, organizer and scholar Rachel Herzing reminds us that abolition isn't "some kind of pure vision that doesn't require strategy or incremental moves."[8] No singular step will accomplish abolition. As both a lens and theory of change, abolition helps us determine what steps might chip away at the system and which ones maintain or strengthen it. Nonreformist reforms provide a strategy for how to move forward, even if they aren't the end goal. Our commitment to abolition shouldn't immobilize us to act because then our claim of being an abolitionist doesn't actually mean much. Abolition calls us to do something, not just critique the system.

In organizing, questions about how to prioritize our time and limited resources are always at the forefront. As calls to abolish and reform police and prisons emerged during the Black Lives Matter protests, Critical Resistance created a chart with questions and responses to provide guidance around policy proposals that are "reformist reforms which continue or expand the reach of policing, and abolitionist steps that work to chip away and reduce its overall impact." For example, many proposals for police accountability call for the requirement that cops use body cameras (which DHS also announced it would implement in 2023), but the chart explains that body cameras are reformist, in part because they "provide the police with another tool, increasing surveillance and increasing police budgets to acquire more gadgets." Rather, the chart advocates for prioritizing "spending on community health, education, [and] affordable housing" as a way to provide "resources that actually create well-being."[9]

Anticipating questions about which policy proposals to support and which ones to oppose as Biden took office, I asked DWN's advocacy director, Setareh Ghandehari, to create a similar chart for detention abolition in consultation with DWN members and partners. Following the work of Critical Resistance, we developed a series of questions to help guide us in determining which steps might be abolitionist and which were reformist.[10] They included the following:

- Does this step reduce the scale of detention and surveillance?
- Does this step chip away at the current system without creating new harms or helping some people at the expense of others?
- Does this step provide relief to people who will be or are currently detained or under surveillance?

In asking these questions, we set out to look at some of the current strategies advocates were proposing, which included reducing funding for ICE and CBP, shutting down detention centers, ending the use of private prisons, providing access to counsel for people in detention, and expanding alternatives to detention and opt-in, community-based services for supporting immigrants in proceedings.

A common question for many concerned about the broader prison industrial complex is whether private prison bans are abolitionist. From DWN's perspective, Ghandehari notes, "Yes, 80 percent of people in ICE detention are in facilities owned or operated by private prison companies," but it is only abolitionist "as long as capacity is not replaced by federally or locally operated facilities." In the context of private prisons, as I laid out in chapter 5, while ending their use would greatly reduce immigrant detention, demanding abolition of the whole system will likely be our best bet for getting rid of private prisons. However, because of Democrats' hypocrisy on the issue, calling attention to the unique relationship between the federal government and private prison companies specifically for immigration enforcement could provide some leverage as we make our case for detention abolition. It's important, though, to avoid arguments around private prisons being worse than other government-owned and -operated prisons and jails.

The epigraph to this chapter from Ruth Wilson Gilmore contends that the nature of the nonprofit system often prevents us from doing what matters most. Without realizing it, many advocates recommend reforms that reinforce the system they are trying to dismantle. Another consideration on the DWN chart addressed the many organizations that have called for the right to an attorney for detained immigrants. Ghandehari explains that, based on the questions, while more representation "may lead to releases for some people, tying representation to detention legitimizes the detention system and does not reduce its scale." In this case, it's also worth noting that incarceration in the United States ballooned after the landmark 1963 Supreme Court decision *Gideon v. Wainwright* that gave us a right to an attorney in criminal court. Legal representation in and of itself won't result in decarceration.

As explained in chapter 6, in the case of the Hudson County Jail in New Jersey, tying representation to detention resulted in attorneys advocating to keep a detention center open. Their core argument centered on the possibility of people being transferred to more remote locations, something advocates have little control over. Transfers remain a concern, but rather than responding with keeping detention centers open in urban centers, a better use of our time would be to focus our energy and resources on ensuring just closures, where organizers and lawyers work together for people to be released prior to the end of the contract, and supporting community organizing in the South and Southwest, where most detention is now concentrated. Likewise, while lawyers can help mitigate the harm of the system and support individuals seeking relief, some immigrants have argued that the process should be less burdensome; that they should not need to rely on lawyers to navigate the system. In a survey of nearly eighty thousand members of the Asylum Seeker Advocacy Project (ASAP), respondents did not prioritize the demand that every immigrant should have a lawyer. One ASAP member from Colombia wrote, "We should be able to file each document required in the process without a lawyer."[11] Individual legal defense remains an important part of the work, but advocating for shifts in policy that promote the agency of immigrants will be essential to undoing the harms of immigration enforcement.

Let's consider some concrete abolitionist steps to ending detention. In part II, I shared three key strategies that have reduced detention and deportation. First, ending collaborations between local law enforcement and ICE, such as 287(g) programs, ICE detainers, and database sharing, has limited ICE's access to prisons and jails. These strategies have helped reduce formal deportations from where they were in the Obama era. Some groups have also started pushing states to prevent transfers to ICE for people released from a prison or jail. Oregon's Sanctuary Promise Act, one of the most progressive sanctuary laws in the country, prohibits information from being "shared by state or local law enforcement to assist in detaining . . . any individual for immigration purposes."[12] In places like California where ICE and police collaboration is limited, transfers from the criminal legal system are the main pipeline into the detention system for immigrants already in the United States.

Calls to defund detention and terminate detention contracts remain core strategies. Shutting down detention centers and throwing a wrench in ICE's dragnet limits its ability to deport people. This strategy works in part because the agency has broad discretion over who gets detained and who doesn't. And because ICE runs the whole system, from arrest to detention to deportation, the detention system's capacity directly impacts the number of people who can be deported once they are in the country.

Many advocates have questioned the method of shutting down immigrant detention centers in order to dismantle the system, arguing that if a detention center shuts down in one location, another one will simply be opened somewhere else. This is why the call to both shut down facilities and defund ICE is so critical. It's not just about ending one contract or a series of contracts. Winning local campaigns helps us make the case for ending immigrant incarceration altogether, and it saps the legitimacy of ICE and the deportation agenda. These campaigns are connected to communities and real people whose lives have been upended by the system, and they help reveal how unnecessary detention is. The call to defund subsequently ensures that we shrink the detention system, not just keep playing a game of whack-a-mole. While some transfers are bound to happen (and happen for a variety of reasons beyond the geography of detention), it's important to remember that it's easier to build these systems up than to dismantle them. Dismantling won't be a perfect process. Getting rid of systems that cause harm will likely cause some harm (including job losses), but that is not a reason for keeping detention centers open indefinitely.

While these abolitionist steps are key to reducing ICE's reach, organizers should remain careful about how they are employed and consider the messaging used to advocate for them. In the immigrant rights movement, campaigns to reduce ICE-police collaboration are potentially abolitionist steps, but they have often reinforced support for law enforcement and the criminal legal system, which hurts both immigrants and other communities of color. For example, sanctuary campaigns have often led with the idea that collaborations with ICE prevent trust in law enforcement, even going so far as calling legislation "TRUST Acts," or laws to help build trust between immigrants and police. Many of these efforts also include carveouts for certain crimes, which keep some immigrants in the pipeline for detention and deportation. Winning on these issues will often result in some compromises, but advocating for all immigrants can help disrupt the criminalization narratives driving mass incarceration and bridge the divide between the migrant justice and racial justice movements.

Because immigration is largely controlled by the executive branch, administrative strategies like pressuring the White House and DHS remain critical. The immigration enforcement system was built by both Republicans and Democrats, but given the growing divide between the two parties, especially on the issue of immigration, putting pressure on a Republican president will have minimal results. But with Democratic administrations, if we don't keep up the pressure, it will open space for them to move further to the right on immigration. And if we are able to build more power on the issue, it could lead to victories. Both DACA and the federal litigation against Arizona's SB 1070 were results of numerous campaigns involving boycotts, civil disobedience, and mass mobilizations that forced the Obama administration to finally take action.

As for federal legislative strategies, beyond calling to defund DHS, it can be hard to envision changes to the immigration enforcement system, given the state of Congress. But it's still worth advocating for abolitionist language in marker bills that could be included in future omnibus legislation. This is currently our best hope for a more permanent end to immigrant detention. The New Way Forward Act, for example, would repeal many of the harsh provisions of past immigration laws, including ending mandatory detention and criminal prosecutions for border crossing. If passed, it would drastically reduce the number of people detained and deported each year and allow people who have been deported an opportunity to return home to their families and communities.

Despite the many roadblocks to transformative change, in recent years deportations of immigrants already living in the United States have remained considerably lower than during the Obama years. Some of this can be explained by limited enforcement actions due to the pandemic and the emphasis on border enforcement, but much of it is a result of local- and state-level campaigns to stop ICE-police collaborations and curb immigrant detention.[13] From California to Illinois to New Jersey, states with some of the largest immigrant populations in the country blocked ICE from engaging in rampant deportations. While immigrants continue to be targeted every day for detention and deportation, the scale has reduced thanks to the immigrant justice movement.

It's important to remember that abolition is about sustained organizing and movement building. It's about doing the work, not just making a demand. Yes, the demand is important—it helps clarify where we're going and opens up space for us to make our case to reduce the harm caused by the prison industrial complex. But our ability to create change is dependent on the power that we have. It requires building a base, identifying targets, developing strategies, waging campaigns, deploying various tactics, and harnessing our power when there are openings. That is the work. That is abolition.

CHAPTER 8

Beyond "Abolish ICE"

In these trying circumstances, the black revolution is much more than a struggle for the rights of Negroes. It is forcing America to face all its interrelated flaws—racism, poverty, militarism, and materialism. It is exposing the evils that are rooted deeply in the whole structure of our society. It reveals systemic rather than superficial flaws and suggests that radical reconstruction of society itself is the real issue to be faced.

—Martin Luther King Jr.,
"A Testament of Hope," 1969

In October 2022, I returned to south Texas eighteen years after I first started traveling there to organize against the Laredo superjail. This time it was to join a Grassroots Leadership delegation to observe how governor Greg Abbott was implementing Operation Lone Star, a statewide initiative focused on prosecuting migrants arriving at the border. As with Arizona's "show me your papers" law, through Operation Lone Star Abbott seized authority over immigration through the state criminal legal system to racially profile and prosecute migrants. Billions of dollars have been poured into the effort, which includes a range of tactics: deploying Texas National Guard troops, enlisting law enforcement agencies from across the state to travel to border towns to arrest migrants, changing state law to create harsher penalties, hiring retired judges to rule on the cases, and converting state prisons into facilities just for migrants. Through Operation Lone Star, thousands of migrants have been prosecuted for enhanced crimes of trespassing and smuggling under a bogus declaration of statewide disaster.

During the delegation, as we made our way through Uvalde, Kinney County, Dilley, Eagle Pass, and across the US-Mexico border to Piedras Negras, we saw the impact of Operation Lone Star everywhere. Law enforcement was omnipresent, convened on the area from localities hours away in other parts of the state: a Galveston County constable vehicle in the parking lot at the Kinney County courthouse, San Angelo fire trucks at the Val Verde County Detention Center, and so on. We witnessed the Texas National Guard detaining a migrant under the international bridge in Eagle Pass while they awaited the arrival of border agents. We observed a virtual hearing for two people: one a migrant from Honduras charged with trespassing, the other a US citizen and new father whose bond was set at four hundred thousand dollars for "smuggling" two migrants. Under the guise of border security, small communities across south Texas were becoming police states right before our eyes.

Equally concerning was how Operation Lone Star was creating its own carceral economy, one on which many poor, small south Texas towns were becoming dependent. We learned that Kinney County had been padding its annual budget through forfeited bond money from individuals who had been arrested through Lone Star and then deported. Grassroots organizers observed that in Del Rio, local motels started to upgrade their rooms to accommodate law enforcement officers from across the state who wanted nicer lodging. As we crossed the border to Piedras Negras, the woman taking our fee to cross the bridge, an Eagle Pass resident, saw our shirts that read "End Operation Lone Star" and responded, "We're a poor town. I hope they don't end Operation Lone Star." Lone Star, like Operation Streamline before it, was becoming more than just a tool for prosecuting migrants; it was another example of the insidious nature of the prison industrial complex and its exponential growth.

The moral panic around the border now drives most policy decisions on immigration. In our work for migrant justice, it is critical that we challenge the right-wing fearmongering about the border in order to create safer conditions for people wanting to migrate. The immigrant rights struggle is inherently an intersectional struggle. People migrate for a variety of reasons. Global inequality as a result of capitalism and US empire has created unstable, impoverished, and often violent conditions across the world. Climate catastrophe has only exacerbated these conditions. As more migrants seek safety, the tools the federal government uses to deter migration, including prisons, police, and the military, will continue to be lifted up as necessary for preventing the "surge" or "flood" or whatever the disaster metaphor of the day is.

The intersectional nature of the immigrant rights struggle should not be seen as a challenge but as an opportunity to bridge issues and connect the dots to imagine another world in which everyone can thrive. The Martin Luther King Jr. quote starting out this chapter illuminates how the civil rights and Black liberation struggle of the 1960s unearthed the systemic flaws that have continued to exacerbate the social inequities of the United States. As Mariame Kaba poses, reflecting on the uprisings for Black lives in 2020: "What would the country look like if it had billions of extra dollars to spend on housing, food, and education for all? This change in society wouldn't happen immediately, but the protests show that many people are ready to embrace a different vision of safety and justice."[1] More than anything, the idea of immigration evokes concerns about the lack of resources and jobs. But what if we lived with a commitment to abundance instead of scarcity? What if the money the government spent on the carceral state and war machine were to be diverted toward helping people and creating healthier communities here and abroad?

The nonprofit system often boxes us in and prevents us from bridging across struggles and movements. I recall one funder describing how philanthropy considered different issues: "Criminal justice was the Black issue, immigration the Latino issue, and national security the Arab, Muslim, and South Asian issue." It was a glib view and, sadly, is often how our movements are perceived. It's also a recipe for disempowerment. But there are opportunities to challenge the pigeonholes and work together toward the true meaning of abolition. It's time to push beyond the siloed nature of our work and demand a different vision for our future.

The summer of 2018 was a turning point for the national discourse on immigration. As the Trump administration's family separation policy made headlines, the call to abolish ICE went mainstream. It was a disorienting moment for many of us who had been working against detention and deportation in the years before Trump took office. Suddenly, "Abolish ICE" became a litmus test for progressive Democrats and their stance on immigration. Most media pointed to Data for Progress founder Sean McElwee, who had popularized the hashtag #AbolishICE on Twitter, as the catalyst for the movement, as if he were the first person to ever consider the notion. But this narrative disregarded the power of immigrant communities that had been challenging ICE's tactics long before Trump came into office.

While the call to abolish ICE galvanized the immigrant rights movement and Democrats to engage with the issue in new ways, there were a couple of points of confusion. First, the family separations and Trump's border militarization agenda had more to do with CBP and various other agencies than with ICE, per se. Second, many politicians emphasized that ICE as an agency had only existed for fifteen years at that point and implied that going back to the previous model of immigration enforcement would somehow be better.

In the hubbub of the moment, journalists started asking politicians what would happen if ICE were to be abolished. Democrats in the House, including Wisconsin representative Mark Pocan and

Washington representative Pramila Jayapal, introduced legislation to eliminate ICE, pointing out that the Trump administration was "grossly misusing" the agency and that ICE was "broken beyond repair."[2] The bill was essentially a messaging bill with no real proposal for transforming immigration enforcement. The bill's main provision involved "establishment of a commission to administer transition of functions," thus reaffirming the need for immigration enforcement.[3] Ultimately, the Democrats' issue was Trump's handling of ICE rather than a core problem with the agency itself. When Republicans "called their bluff," threatening to bring the bill to a vote, Jayapal balked at the suggestion: "We'll all vote no on it, because we're all clear that it's not a serious attempt to do anything."[4] The whole episode revealed how fleeting Democrats' support for abolishing ICE was.

I often look back at the summer of 2018 as a missed opportunity for the immigrant justice movement to advance a vision for immigration that didn't include detention and deportation. But the moment helped strengthen many of the campaigns and strategies that limited ICE's reach. That summer, Latinx organization Mijente released the Free Our Future platform, which exposed the relationship between the border prosecutions and interior immigration enforcement, both complicating and clarifying what the demand to abolish ICE should mean. The platform called for ending Operation Streamline and defunding border patrol in addition to disbanding ICE as an agency.[5] The "Abolish ICE" moment was also when DWN developed the Communities Not Cages campaign, and many more people and organizations joined the fight to end immigrant detention.

Others began to outline what a post-ICE future could look like. In a paper titled "Abolish ICE . . . and Then What?" law professor Peter Markowitz calls for a shift from the enforcement paradigm, which would "cure the inhumanity and brutality that characterize immigration enforcement under ICE—most notably by eliminating immigration detention and mass deportation." He proposes "a new system . . . [that promotes] compliance with immigration law."[6] Central to his argument is the fact that despite the creation of ICE, the United States has more—not fewer—undocumented immigrants than it did before 9/11 (increasing from seven million to twelve million at the height), revealing how the system hasn't worked as intended.

While the proposal is well intentioned, it, like many liberal reform proposals, focuses on the stated goal of immigration enforcement: to ensure compliance with immigration law. In doing so, it ignores the economic, political, and racial implications of why our immigration enforcement system operates as it does. Immigration control has much more to do with maintaining a flow of cheap, subminimum-wage labor (undocumented immigrant workers) and keeping out those whom the government perceives as unproductive (migrants seeking asylum, especially those who are Black). As we determine a vision for the future that promotes migrant justice, understanding how the fight against detention and deportation is part and parcel of other struggles for racial and economic justice will be essential to advancing the cause.

—

After years of witnessing a continuous expansion of the detention system, it was thrilling to finally start winning campaigns and seeing places like the Etowah County Jail in Alabama no longer used for immigrant detention. About a year after Etowah stopped detaining immigrants, I met up with Karim Golding in Brooklyn. He had been detained at Etowah for over four years and organized for his own release and on behalf of other immigrants detained at the jail. We debated various strategies for abolition. I brought up the Etowah win and all it had taken to get to it, including his organizing on the inside. But Golding hesitated to call it a complete victory. "People are still locked up there," he said. I agreed but argued that ending the ICE contract was still worth celebrating. He relented, "It's like the battle versus the war." We won this battle, but there was still so much left to do.

The truth is, despite the many wins discussed in chapter 6, these jails did not shut down. Most of them remain open even with the end of the ICE contracts. Many former ICE jails still have underlying federal contracts with the US Marshals Service, which means that immigrants who are detained pretrial or serving a sentence for unlawful entry or unlawful reentry continue to be detained in these facilities. They are often detained alongside people who are jailed because of their inability to pay a bond or who have been flagged by a probation or parole officer to remain in custody until trial. After the ICE contracts ended, I couldn't help but think about all the people who will continue to be locked up at the county jails under the same terrible conditions that immigrants experienced while detained for ICE.

At any given time in the United States, more than four hundred thousand people are in pretrial detention, meaning they are jailed while they wait for their day in court. Reflecting broader social inequities, Black people make up 43 percent of the pretrial detention population.[7] Immigrant detention and pretrial detention for people charged with but not necessarily convicted of a crime have a lot in common. Both groups are imprisoned because of the fear that the individual might abscond or commit a future crime if not incarcerated. Most county jails are meant for short-term stays, but sometimes people are incarcerated for months or even longer because of their inability to post bail or because they are awaiting deportation. The deplorable conditions in local jails breed extreme despair. People are constantly dying in them, with suicide as the leading cause.[8]

The commonalities between immigrant detention and pretrial detention (which often use the same jails) provide a potential site of convergence for the migrant justice and prison abolition movements. Despite the broader consciousness around the crisis of mass incarceration, more than a hundred localities across the United States are considering opening new jails or expanding existing ones.[9] Private companies conducting jail assessments often convince communities that expansion is needed, arguing that a new jail is the only way to address conditions or overcrowding. But in reality many alternatives to jail expansion could create better material conditions for those caught up in the system. Local groups have deployed several strategies for reducing pretrial populations, including implementing bail reform, ending federal contracts at local jails, and stopping expansion plans. Economic reforms that invest in the public good and provide universal child care, family leave, social housing, and other efforts to build up social safety nets can also help limit someone's vulnerability to arrest.

Supporting people prosecuted for migration-related offenses can also be a way for migrant justice activists to organize against the prison and jail system. In Austin, for example, Grassroots Leadership began showing up at court hearings and connecting with family members of people who had been prosecuted for unlawful reentry. As organizers learned more about the trends and how migrants were being swept up into the criminal legal system, they discovered that the Austin Police Department had been recommending migrants for prosecution. It revealed how local police were collaborating not only with ICE but also with the US Marshals Service and federal prosecutors to arrest migrants.

In addition to police departments, local sheriffs have an oversized role in immigration enforcement. Joe Arpaio, former sheriff of Maricopa County, Arizona, and perhaps the most prominent anti-immigrant sheriff in recent memory, was perceived as extreme in his approach, but many sheriffs share similar views. A Marshall Project survey of 449 sheriffs found that nearly 90 percent agreed or strongly agreed with the need to increase federal spending on "tightening border security and preventing illegal immigration."[10] Because the federal government relies on local governments to carry out enforcement actions, unseating draconian sheriffs can have a considerable impact on reducing pretrial detention and jail populations, for immigrants and nonimmigrants alike.

——

Efforts to decarcerate prisons, jails, and detention centers have gained traction in recent years. It has been an exciting development in places like Louisiana, which was labeled the prison capital of the world due to its incarceration rate. In 2017, the state legislature passed criminal justice reforms aimed at reducing the prison population by 10 percent over ten years. In the years that followed, the state prison population decreased. However, the consequent loss of jobs and revenue because of the thousands of empty prison beds left many communities reeling. ICE decided to swoop in. Over the course of a year, ICE contracted with seven additional facilities in the state, expanding its capacity there by roughly 6,000 beds. While criminal justice advocates intended to reduce the rate of incarceration in Louisiana, they hadn't anticipated that those beds would then be used by ICE. When asked about the immigrant detention expansion, law professor Andrea Armstrong, who had worked on the reforms, replied: "We didn't think about that population. And perhaps we should have."[11]

The story of Louisiana's criminal justice reforms is not unique. Often decarceration efforts focus on a specific population but fail to consider that another could take its place. In California, after criminal justice reforms shuttered some state-contracted private prisons, three were converted into ICE detention centers. In New Jersey, when ICE contracts ended at multiple county jails, the counties scrambled to find other sources of revenue, which included partnering with a neighboring county to incarcerate people in criminal custody.[12]

As these stories illustrate, a major obstacle to dismantling the prison industrial complex is the economy that has been created to sustain and expand it. The carceral economy is embedded not only in rural areas that have seen prison building as a source of jobs and revenue but also in municipal, state, and federal infrastructure that has generated profit for the prison contractors. In the climate justice movement, organizers have proposed a just transition from extractive economies, such as the oil and gas industry. Abolitionist organizers have drawn inspiration from this framework and propose a similar shift away from the oppressive systems of policing, prisons, and surveillance. A just transition aims to support a regenerative economy that restores community stewardship and emphasizes sustainable practices and the prioritization of human dignity.[13] As Ruth Wilson Gilmore contends, abolition "is about presence, not absence. It's about building life-affirming institutions."[14]

The aftermath of Louisiana's sentencing reforms is a cautionary tale of the unintended consequences if we continue to stay siloed. We must think and strategize more holistically; because interaction with the criminal legal system remains a driver of immigration arrests, sentencing reform at the state level can help ensure that immigration consequences of certain crimes are less severe. Similarly, it's important to strategize across movements to permanently close jails and prisons. Repurposing or decommissioning these structures will ensure that jails and prisons are not used by other law enforcement agencies. Around the country, successful decarceration efforts have resulted in communities repurposing former prisons and jails into alternative forms of economic development: a movie and TV studio in Staten Island, New York; a whiskey distillery in Morgan County, Tennessee; a nonprofit office space in Dallas, Texas.[15]

One critical place for cross-movement alignment is calling attention to how the state spends its money. In 2019, the Poor People's Campaign, which is rooted in civil rights–era demands, released a moral budget, arguing that "the abundance of our society will grow even greater when we stop investing in maintaining injustice to benefit the few, and turn instead to policies based on the needs of the many."[16] It could be so simple, yet the federal government continues to build up institutions of repression. As the demand to defund has gained steam, many groups have proposed alternative budget proposals to move away from extreme spending on police, prisons, jails, and the military. The invest/divest framework is not new, but it has more salience in light of the growing call for abolition and provides a mechanism by which to weaken the prison industrial complex.

In 2021, the Defund Hate campaign released a transformative budget called Beyond the Enforcement Paradigm. The budget encouraged divestment from immigrant detention and border patrol and encouraged investments in voluntary, community-based resettlement services and a rights-respecting approach to the border. As

Biden took office and arguments about the need for additional CBP funding emerged in response to Haitians arriving at the border, the transformative budget offered a counter to this kind of thinking. Upon its release, Patrice Lawrence, codirector of the UndocuBlack Network, commented that "the disparate treatment of Black migrants in particular is a matter of choice and priority."[17]

The call to defund ICE and CBP provided a new entry point for engaging with groups focused on demilitarization and abolition. Much of this book has focused on the limited racial justice analysis in the mainstream immigrant rights movement. But the immigrant rights movement has also failed to meaningfully address the root causes of migration, and often reinforces pro-military agendas. A notable example is the emphasis on legalizing immigrants who serve in the military in legislation such as the DREAM Act. The need to be pro-American in order to secure legalization erases the history of US militarism that has resulted in increased migration from Central America, the Middle East, and beyond.

Through Defund Hate, immigrant justice groups were able to break from this paradigm at the federal level and began collaborating with organizations such as Muslims for Just Futures, a group that advocates abolishing the war on terror, and the National Priorities Project (NPP), which provides analysis of federal budget spending. Given that roughly half of discretionary federal government spending goes to the military, NPP highlights the disparities between this spending and that for other public services and the need to reprioritize. For example, NPP points out that in 2023 "the average taxpayer paid $298 to the top five military contractors, and just $19 for mental health and substance abuse programs." On immigration, "The average taxpayer paid $70 for deportations and border control, versus just $19 for refugee assistance."[18]

Local and statewide groups have also been pushing an invest/divest approach. The Dignity Not Detention coalition in California has partnered with numerous organizations, including Californians

United for a Responsible Budget, a coalition working to reduce incarceration in the state, to introduce the Budget 2 Save Lives.[19] The budget analysis highlights a range of issues, from public safety to immigration to health, housing, and education. In June 2023, the group secured a victory when California passed a budget initiative called HEAL (Healthy Economies Adapting to Last) in which the state "dedicate[d] 5 million dollars to incentivize California localities to divest from immigration detention by providing them funding to invest in new industries and jobs."[20]

The backlash since 2020 to the demand to defund has caused some advocates to retreat from the position, but a focus on the federal, state, and local budgets remains crucial to chip away at the prison industrial complex and build up social infrastructure to support people who are vulnerable to incarceration and deportation.

—

The carceral landscape in the United States can at times feel hidden. In 2020, when air travel was still considered risky due to the pandemic, I wanted to see my parents, so I drove with my partner to Houston that December. Coming back, as we made our way through west Texas and the borderlands, the carceral landscape began to emerge all around us. A particularly extreme stretch included passing by the Cibola, Otero, Sierra Blanca, and Tornillo detention centers.

The weather was not ideal; snowstorms almost left us stranded in Texas and Utah. But after passing through a storm on our way from Utah to Idaho, we stopped at the Minidoka National Historic Site. During World War II, 13,000 Japanese Americans were incarcerated at the Minidoka War Relocation Center. It was the seventh-largest city in Idaho at the time. As we arrived in Minidoka, the clouds started to part, and the sun shone down on the site, illuminating the golden grass that surrounded the reconstructed buildings and watchtower. I tried to imagine what life at Minidoka was like as I walked around and read the words of survivors on plaques across the site. For a moment, I wondered what it would be like if all those detention centers we had passed by earlier became like Minidoka one day. Remnants of a violent history. Reminders of what we should never do again.

In July 2023, I returned to Minidoka. This time it was to join a pilgrimage organized for Japanese American survivors of World War II incarceration and their descendants. I didn't know what to expect, imagining a serious and somber gathering, but the first night, when I arrived in Twin Falls to join the group dinner, it wasn't anything like that. The venue was bustling with multigenerational families: survivors and descendants with their children and grandchildren and great grandchildren reuniting and remembering together. The next morning, Japanese American poet Brandon Shimoda gave the keynote in which he reflected on the question, "What kind of ancestors do we want to be?" It was a question many activists and Indigenous community members had posed over the years. In this case, Shimoda was referencing a moment during the George Floyd uprisings in 2020 when a Japanese American activist called on Asian Americans to confront the anti-Blackness within the community and to "be the kind of ancestors who were loud and disobedient and stood on the side of justice."[21] The question stayed with me after the pilgrimage. What kind of ancestors do we want to be? What is the world we want to leave behind? How do we start making that world now?

When I started conceiving of this book in 2021, I was hyperfocused on the current conditions. Biden had just taken office. It was a year after the uprisings for Black lives, but there was also a backlash to movements to defund the police and a border panic. Immigrant rights advocates had started retreating on positions they had taken just months earlier. I was frustrated and planned to channel my frustrations into this book (how original!). But in the process of writing and spending time looking back at how we got here and how much has changed from the time I started organizing against prison and detention expansion more than twenty years ago now, I was struck by how far we had come and started to feel hopeful. When I finished writing part II of the book, realizing how many stories didn't make it in, I was blown away by the movement work over the years. While I, like many, often look to the horizon and dream of a more just future for our communities, the truth is that we have already begun making abolition every day.

ACKNOWLEDGMENTS

When I set out to write this book, I treated the project as any organizer would and thought to myself: Who can help me do this? It turns out, a great number of people were not only willing but eager to support me in this endeavor. This book would not be what it is without their insights, expertise, feedback, and encouragement. Though if there are any inaccuracies or errors, they are mine alone.

Anthony Arnove reached out in 2021 about the possibility of working on a book for Haymarket. A few people had suggested it over the years, but at that moment it didn't seem as absurd a prospect. Anthony's feedback and recommendations after reading my first few chapters were invaluable and gave me a road map for how to approach the rest of the book. I am especially grateful to my editor at Haymarket, Maria Isabelle Carlos, who shepherded this process along, and whose enthusiasm for the project and warmth helped make the experience enjoyable despite how overwhelming it could feel.

The concept for this book emerged from a piece I wrote for the *Forge*, published in March 2021. I want to thank Cristina Jiménez Moreta, the guest editor of the issue, for asking me to contribute and supporting my vision for the essay. In addition, portions of chapter 5 were adapted from the *Inquest* article "Beyond Private Prisons," originally published on March 3, 2022, and the beginning of chapter 8 was adapted from a piece published on *Truthout*.

I benefited greatly from being accepted into the inaugural Changemaker Authors Cohort, a project of Narrative Initiative and the Unicorn Authors Club. Writing a book can be a very solitary experience, which is quite foreign to my usual way of operating. Being in the cohort made me feel like I wasn't alone in this and gave me the tools to be a better writer. I can't imagine having gotten to this point without Minal Hajratwala's generous coaching and Jhani Randhawa's steady encouragement over the year I was in the cohort. The writing space that has continued after, with sujatha baliga, Ellen Bravo, Hans Lindahl, and Beth Howard, helped me get through the final stages of editing the manuscript.

I was fortunate enough to spend two magical weeks at the Mesa Refuge writing residency in Point Reyes, California. Being able to think and write somewhere so beautiful, where so many writers had passed through over the years, was both humbling and motivating.

Leah Montange came in to support this project at a later stage, for which I am eternally grateful. What a gift to have her insights and synthesis as I tried to make sense of the changes to the system and the movement. Her adept editing and understanding of this history and these issues are unparalleled.

The analysis and arguments in this book were honed over many years of engagement with people and organizations that have advanced my understanding of abolition and the prison industrial complex. Though not an exhaustive list, I'd like to extend my gratitude to the following for their lessons early on: Judith Greene, Ruth Wilson Gilmore, Craig Gilmore, Xochitl Bervera, MayVa Lor, Kevin Pranis, Tracy Huling, Kung Li Sun, Nicole Porter, Michelle Fei, Paromita Shah, and the staff and members of Families for Freedom.

My heartfelt thanks to those who allowed me to interview them and helped fill out the stories and analysis in parts II and III of the book: Amy Torres, Fred Tsao, Chris Newman, Sophia Gurulé, Tania Mattos, Grisel Ruiz, David Bennion, Jacinta Gonzalez, Mike Ishii, and Greisa Martínez Rosas. These conversations were critical to making sure the book told a more complete story, even if it was hard to capture all that went into these inspiring campaigns and efforts.

My dear and brilliant friend Amna Akbar, who graciously wrote the foreword for this book, was the only person to read the whole first draft other than my editor. She gently pushed me to think more broadly than my soapbox about the lack of analysis on prisons and policing in the immigrant rights movement. I can't thank her enough for her thoughtfulness and care in her reading and in our friendship, which I cherish deeply. During the writing process, Angélica Cházaro became a sort of anchor for me, checking in regularly, discussing the arguments of the book, and reviewing pieces. I would be doubting myself, and then Angélica would call, and I'd be ready to keep going. Her own writing and thinking on these issues were also essential resources. My forever comrade, Bob Libal, who shows up periodically in this book, has been a constant in this work since we met during our freshman year of college. His enthusiasm for the project from the get-go and willingness to talk through pieces, help jog my memory, and his review of chapters made me feel more confident in my retelling. I knew when I started this process that I'd be reaching out to Andy Hsiao for advice, but I didn't realize what an advantage it would be. Andy was ready to answer any random question I had about publishing; he reviewed my book proposal and helped problem solve in moments when I wasn't sure how to proceed, including helping me come up with a title when my original one was taken.

Many other friends and comrades reviewed chapters or sections, talked through arguments, provided moral support and advice, or helped in some other aspect of the book. Many thanks to: Elaina Ellis, Tania Shahani, Lena Graber, Chandan Reddy, Patrisia Macías-Rojas, Jenna Loyd, Jesse Franzblau, Sa'dia Rehman, Erin Shigaki, Greg Youmans, Anjali Kamat, Seth Freed Wessler, Frank Edwards, Heather Posten, Liz Ogbu, Claudia Muñoz, Svati Shah, Chris Vargas, Leyla Mei, Ruthie Epstein, Mon Mohapatra, Julian Liu, Tamara Nopper, and Fernando Lopez.

My family has always been supportive of my work. My mother, Surekha, whose empathy and compassion know no bounds, was excited about me writing a book from the beginning and sent me the most delicious care package of homemade Gujarati snacks in the final few weeks of drafting to help me get to the finish line. My father, Ashok, has taught me many lessons, but perhaps the most important one was that it's OK to follow your own path, giving me space to commit to this work. My sister, Sona, a prolific and opinionated reader, reviewed parts of the book and offered generative comments and encouragement. I am also grateful to Beth Anderson, Eric Paulus, Samir Shah, Susmita Shah, and our extended family for their support over the years. My niblings Nova and Aakash, both avid readers, give me hope for the future we are fighting for.

I would have been much more hesitant to take on this project if I hadn't had Charles Anderson by my side throughout the process. His love, support, insights, feedback, and humor kept me going when I was feeling unsure or overwhelmed. A social historian through and through, his commitment to telling the stories of people who have resisted injustice despite the odds was a constant guide for me. I am a better thinker, writer, and person because of him.

Ultimately, this project was possible because of the people and organizations that have made up Detention Watch Network over the years. By the time this book is released, I'll have been connected to DWN for nearly twenty years, with fifteen years on staff. It's impossible to name everyone, but I must start with Andrea Black, who has been there since the beginning and took a chance on me when she hired me back in 2009. Andrea shared stories about what it was like in those days after the 1996 laws passed and on the shifts in DWN over the years, filling in some of the gaps for me. Emily Tucker and Mary Small both shared their policy expertise, giving an additional perspective on the Obama and Trump eras. I am also grateful to Ana Carrion and Bárbara Suárez Galeano for their support and friendship.

Attempting to write a book while also being an executive director was a challenge, but the current board and staff have been encouraging throughout the process. I can't thank them enough for giving me space to work on this. Victoria Lopez and Liz Sweet, our board chairs during this period, anchored much of the discussion and parameters around me taking time off and were constantly championing this project. Aimee Nichols and Stacy Suh not only took on more responsibility but also reviewed chapters and shared their perspectives on parts of the movement I had less knowledge of. Getting to know them and learning from both of them has been one of the highlights of my time at DWN. Gabriela Viera was eager to help however she could, and her contributions and perspective were crucial. I'd also like to thank Setareh Ghandehari, Luis Suarez, and Hillary Li for reviewing pieces and Carly Pérez Fernández, Liz Castillo, Jolie Steinert, Marcela Hernandez, and Gabriela Marquez-Benitez for their support and insights.

And last, but certainly not least, I must thank the members of Detention Watch Network, who inspire me every day and without whom this book would not exist.

NOTES

Introduction

1. Adolfo Flores, "An ICE Detainee Complained of Pain for Weeks and Lost 17 Pounds. Then He Died," *BuzzFeed News*, June 30, 2022, https://www.buzzfeednews.com/article/adolfoflores/ice-detainee-death-repeated-complaints.
2. Gabriela Viera, "If You Build It, ICE Will Fill It," CERES Policy Research, Detention Watch Network, Immigrant Legal Resource Center, September 2022, https://www.detentionwatchnetwork.org/sites/default/files/If%20They%20Build%20It,%20ICE%20Will%20Fill%20IT_Report_2022.pdf.
3. Keeanga-Yamahtta Taylor, *From #BlackLivesMatter to Black Liberation* (Chicago: Haymarket Books, 2016), 3.
4. Quoted in Melissa Burch, "Critical Resistance South: A Report from the Southern Conference and Strategy Session in New Orleans, Louisiana, April 4th-6th, 2003," Critical Resistance, April 2003, https://www.freedomarchives.org/Documents/Finder/DOC510_scans/Critical_Resistance/510.critical.resistance.south.2003.pdf.

Chapter 1: The US Prison Boom and the Growth of Immigrant Detention

1. Naomi Murakawa, *The First Civil Right: How Liberals Built Prison America* (Oxford: Oxford University Press, 2014), 77.
2. Elizabeth Hinton, "Why We Should Reconsider the War on Crime," *Time*, March 20, 2015, https://time.com/3746059/war-on-crime-history.
3. Michelle Alexander, *The New Jim Crow: Mass Incarceration in the Age of Colorblindness* (New York: New Press, 2010), 2.
4. Douglas S. Massey, Karen A. Pren, "Unintended Consequences of US Immigration Policy: Explaining the Post-1965 Surge from Latin America," *Population and Development Review* 38, no. 1 (2012): 1–29, https://doi.org/10.1111/j.1728-4457.2012.00470.x.

5. Mai M. Ngai, *Impossible Subjects: Illegal Aliens and the Making of Modern America* (Princeton: Princeton University Press, 2004), 258.

6. Ngai, *Impossible Subjects*, 261.

7. Charles Kamasaki, *Immigration Reform: The Corpse That Will Not Die* (Simsbury, CT: Mandel Vilar Press, 2019), 48 (ebook).

8. Nicholas de Genova quoted in Ngai, *Impossible Subjects*, 261.

9. Ngai, *Impossible Subjects*, 262.

10. Ngai, *Impossible Subjects*, 262; Abby Budiman and Neil G. Ruiz, "Key Facts About Asian Americans, a Diverse and Growing Population," Pew Research Center, April 29, 2021, https://www.pewresearch.org/short-reads/2021/04/29/key-facts-about-asian-americans.

11. "Success Story of One Minority Group in the U.S." *U.S. News & World Report*, December 26, 1966, https://www.dartmouth.edu/~hist32/Hist33/US%20News%20&%20World%20Report.pdf.

12. Dan Baum, "Legalize It All: How to Win the War on Drugs" *Harper's*, April 2016, https://harpers.org/archive/2016/04/legalize-it-all.

13. Joe Hagan, "The Long Lawless Ride of Sheriff Joe Arpaio," *Rolling Stone*, August 2, 2012, https://www.rollingstone.com/culture/culture-news/the-long-lawless-ride-of-sheriff-joe-arpaio-231455.

14. Leo Ralph Chavez, *Covering Immigration: Popular Images and the Politics of the Nation* (Berkeley and Los Angeles: University of California Press, 2001).

15. "Prison Population Over Time," The Sentencing Project, https://www.sentencingproject.org/research.

16. Deborah Anker quoted in John Washington, *The Dispossessed: A Story of Asylum and the US-Mexican Border and Beyond* (New York: Verso, 2020), 174.

17. Carl Lindskoog, *Detain and Punish: Haitian Refugees and the Rise of the World's Largest Immigration Detention System* (Gainesville, FL: University of Florida Press, 2019), 33.

18. A. M. Stephens, "Making Migrants 'Criminal': The Mariel Boatlift, Miami, and U.S. Immigration Policy in the 1980s," *Anthurium* 17, no. 2 (2021): 4, http://doi.org/10.33596/anth.439; César Cuauhtémoc García Hernández, *Migrating to Prison: America's Obsession with Locking Up Immigrants* (New York: New Press, 2019), 61.

19. Nayan Shah, *Refusal to Eat: A Century of Prison Hunger Strikes* (Berkeley and Los Angeles: University of California Press, 2022), 266–69.

20. Kristina Shull, *Detention Empire: Reagan's War on Immigrants and the Seeds of Resistance* (Chapel Hill, NC: University of North Carolina Press, 2022), 153.

21. Jenna M. Loyd, "Carceral Citizenship in an Age of Global Apartheid," *Occasion* 8 (2011), https://arcade.stanford.edu/sites/default/files/article_pdfs/Occasion_v08_Loyd_final.pdf.

22. Danny Rivero, "Detention by Design," *WLRN News*, October 5, 2022, https://www.wlrn.org/podcast/detentionpod.

23. Shull, *Detention Empire*, 102.

24. Shull, *Detention Empire*, 145.

25. Frances Frank Marcus, "Prison for Aliens Opens in Louisiana," *New York Times*, April 9, 1986, https://www.nytimes.com/1986/04/09/us/prison-for-aliens-opens-in-louisiana.html.

26. Jenna M. Loyd and Alison Mountz, *Boats, Borders, and Bases: Race, the Cold War, and the Rise of Migration Detention in the United States* (Berkeley and Los Angeles: University of California Press, 2018), 101.

27. Shull, *Detention Empire*, 199.

28. Shull, *Detention Empire*, 199–200.

29. Shull, *Detention Empire*, 205.

30. Philip Mattera and Mafruza Khan, "Jail Breaks: Economic Development Subsidies Given to Private Prisons," Good Jobs First, October 2001, https://www.goodjobsfirst.org/wp-content/uploads/docs/pdf/jailbreaks.pdf.

31. "GEO Group History Timeline," GEO Group, https://www.geogroup.com/history_timeline.

32. David Stein, "The Untold Story: Joe Biden Pushed Ronald Reagan to Ramp Up Incarceration—Not the Other Way Around," *Intercept*, September 17, 2019, https://theintercept.com/2019/09/17/the-untold-story-joe-biden-pushed-ronald-reagan-to-ramp-up-incarceration-not-the-other-way-around.

33. Jack Norton and Jacob Kang-Brown, "If You Build It: How the Government Fuels Rural Jail Expansion," *In Our Backyards Stories*, Vera Institute of Justice, January 10, 2020, https://www.vera.org/in-our-backyards-stories/if-you-build-it.

34. Ronald J. Ostrow, "1984 Crime Control Act Leads to 32% Rise in Prisoners," *Los Angeles Times*, January 9, 1986, https://www.latimes.com/archives/la-xpm-1986-01-09-mn-14186-story.html.

35. Melanie Newport, *This Is My Jail: Local Politics and the Rise of Mass Incarceration* (Philadelphia: University of Pennsylvania Press, 2022), 170.

36. Loyd and Mountz, *Boats, Borders, and Bases*, 129.

37. Nicole Hemmer, *Partisans: The Conservative Revolutionaries Who Remade American Politics in the 1990s* (New York: Basic Books, 2022), 37.

38. Loyd and Mountz, *Boats, Borders, and Bases*, 132.

39. "The Criminal Alien Program (CAP): Immigration Enforcement in Prisons and Jails," American Immigration Council, August 1, 2013, https://www.americanimmigrationcouncil.org/research/criminal-alien-program-cap-immigration-enforcement-prisons-and-jails.

40. "US: 20 Years of Immigrant Abuses," Human Rights Watch, April 25, 2016, https://www.hrw.org/news/2016/04/25/us-20-years-immigrant-abuses.

41. Patrisia Macías-Rojas, *From Deportation to Prison: The Politics of Immi-*

gration Enforcement in Post-Civil Rights America (New York: New York University Press, 2016), 58.

42. Alina Das, *No Justice in the Shadows: How America Criminalizes Immigrants* (New York: Bold Type Books, 2020), 19.

43. María Cristina García, "National (In)Security and the Immigration Act of 1996," *Modern American History* 1, no. 2 (2018): 233–36, doi:10.1017/mah.2018.6.

44. "PDD-9-Alien Smuggling, 6/18/1993," Clinton Digital Library, https://clinton.presidentiallibraries.us/items/show/12740.

45. García, "National (In)security."

46. Logan Hullinger, "Decades after Golden Venture, York County Is an Immigration Detention Hub," *York Dispatch*, April 26, 2019, https://www.yorkdispatch.com/story/news/politics/2019/04/26/decades-after-golden-venture-york-county-immigration-detention-hub/3586202002.

47. "Comprehensive Annual Financial Report for the Year Ended December 31, 2007," County of York, Pennsylvania, 4, https://yorkcountypa.gov/ArchiveCenter/ViewFile/Item/78.

48. Celia W. Dugger, "Chinese Immigrants from Stranded Ship Are to Be Released," *New York Times*, February 15, 1997, https://www.nytimes.com/1997/02/15/nyregion/chinese-immigrants-from-stranded-ship-are-to-be-released.html.

49. "NAFTA'S Broken Promises 1994–2013: Outcomes of the North American Free Trade Agreement," Public Citizen, March 15, 2013, https://www.citizen.org/article/naftas-broken-promises-1994-2013-outcomes-of-the-north-american-free-trade-agreement.

50. Harsha Walia, *Border and Rule: Global Migration, Capitalism, and the Rise of Racist Nationalism* (Chicago: Haymarket Books, 2021), 51.

51. Tracy Huling, "Building a Prison Economy in Rural America," in *Invisible Punishment: The Collateral Consequences of Mass Imprisonment*, Marc Mauer and Meda Chesney-Lind, eds. (New York: New Press, 2002), 198.

52. Ruth Wilson Gilmore, *Golden Gulag: Prisons, Surplus, Crisis, and Opposition in Globalizing California* (Berkeley: University of California Press, 2011), 50.

53. Patrisia Macías-Rojas, "Immigration and the War on Crime: Law and Order Politics and the Illegal Immigration Reform and Immigrant Responsibility Act of 1996," *Journal on Migration and Human Security* 6, no. 1 (2018): 1–25, https://doi.org/10.1177/233150241800600101.

54. "Illegal Aliens. Ineligibility for Public Services. Verification and Reporting." California Proposition 187 (1994), https://repository.uclawsf.edu/ca_ballot_props/1104.

55. Patrick J. McDonnell and Dave Lesher, "Clinton, Feinstein Declare Opposition to Prop. 187," *Los Angeles Times*, October 22, 1994, https://

www.latimes.com/archives/la-xpm-1994-10-22-mn-53251-story.html.

56. Murakawa, *First Civil Right*, 130.

57. Lauren-Brooke Eisen, "The 1994 Crime Bill and Beyond: How Federal Funding Shapes the Criminal Justice System," Brennan Center for Justice, September 9, 2019, https://www.brennancenter.org/our-work/analysis-opinion/1994-crime-bill-and-beyond-how-federal-funding-shapes-criminal-justice.

58. Dara Lind, "The Disastrous, Forgotten 1996 Law That Created Today's Immigration Problem," *Vox*, April 28, 2016, https://www.vox.com/2016/4/28/11515132/iirira-clinton-immigration.

59. Melissa Cook, "Banished for Minor Crimes: The Aggravated Felony Provision of Immigration and Nationality Act as a Human Rights Violation," *Boston College Third World Law Journal* 23, no. 2 (2003): 305.

60. Jennifer A. Beall, "Are We Only Burning Witches? The Antiterrorism and Effective Death Penalty Act of 1996's Answer to Terrorism," *Indiana Law Journal* 73, no. 2 (Spring 1998), https://www.repository.law.indiana.edu/ilj/vol73/iss2/17.

61. "The Three- and Ten-Year Bars," American Immigration Council, October 28, 2016, https://www.americanimmigrationcouncil.org/research/three-and-ten-year-bars.

62. *Departments of Commerce, Justice, and State, the Judiciary, and Related Agencies Appropriations for 1998, "Hearings Before a Subcommittee of the Committee on Appropriations* 105th Cong. (1997) (statement of Doris Meissner, commissioner of Immigration and Naturalization Service, https://www.govinfo.gov/content/pkg/CHRG-105hhrg41832/html/CHRG-105hhrg41832.htm.

63. Emily Kassie, "Detained: How the United States Created the Largest Immigrant Detention System in the World," Marshall Project and *Guardian*, September 24,.2019, https://www.themarshallproject.org/2019/09/24/detained.

64. Deepa Kumar, *Islamophobia and the Politics of Empire* (Chicago: Haymarket Books, 2012), 142–43.

65. James Forman Jr., "Exporting Harshness: How the War on Crime Helped Make the War on Terror Possible," *Georgetown Law Faculty Publications and Other Works* (2009): 385, https://scholarship.law.georgetown.edu/facpub/385.

66. H.R. Rep 107-139 at 2 (2001). Office of the Federal Detention Trustee, Department of Justice, "Detention Needs Assessment and Baseline Report," 2001, https://www.motherjones.com/wp-content/uploads/2019/09/federal_detention_report_2002-1.pdf.

67. US Government Accountability Office, *Prisoner Operations: United States*

Marshals Service Could Better Estimate Cost Savings and Monitor Efforts to Increase Efficiencies, GAO-16-472 (Washington, DC: USGAO, 2016), 7, https://www.gao.gov/assets/gao-16-472.pdf; "Immigration Detention: Recent Trends and Scholarship," Center for Migration Studies, March 26, 2018, https://cmsny.org/publications/virtualbrief-detention.

68. Department of Homeland Security, Immigration and Customs Enforcement, *Endgame: Office of Detention and Removal Strategic Plan, 2002–2012: Detention and Removal Strategy for a Secure Homeland* (Washington, DC: Department of Homeland Security, 2003), ii, https://irp.fas.org/agency/dhs/endgame.pdf.

69. A. Naomi Paik, *Bans, Walls, Raids, Sanctuary: Understanding U.S. Immigration for the Twenty-First Century* (Berkeley and Los Angeles: University of California Press, 2020), 93–94.

70. Courtney Crowder and MacKenzie Elmer, "Postville Raid Anniversary: A Timeline of Events in One of America's Largest Illegal Immigration Campaigns," *Des Moines Register,* May 10, 2018, https://www.desmoinesregister.com/story/news/investigations/2018/05/10/postville-raid-anniversary-timeline-aaron-rubashkin-agriprocessors-postville-iowa-immigration-raid/588025002.

71. Fox Butterfield, "Privately Run Juvenile Prison in Louisiana Is Attacked for Abuse of 6 Inmates," *New York Times,* March 16, 2000, https://www.nytimes.com/2000/03/16/us/privately-run-juvenile-prison-in-louisiana-is-attacked-for-abuse-of-6-inmates.html.

72. Karen Carrillo, "Locking Away Profits: Capitalizing on Immigrant Detentions Has Turned Into a Booming Business for Lehman Brothers," *Colorlines,* 2002, https://www.thefreelibrary.com/Locking+away+profits%3a+-capitalizing+on+immigrant+detentions+has+turned...-a090794907.

73. Abigail F. Kolker, "The 287(g) Program: State and Local Immigration Enforcement," Congressional Research Service, August 12, 2021, https://crsreports.congress.gov/product/pdf/IF/IF11898.

74. Jessica Pishko, "The Power of Sheriffs: Explained," *Appeal,* January 4, 2019, https://theappeal.org/the-power-of-sheriffs-an-explainer.

75. Wade Goodwyn, "In Arizona, Program to Recruit Police to Help ICE Agents Gets Mixed Reviews," *Morning Edition,* March 9, 2017, https://www.npr.org/2017/03/09/519283560/in-arizona-program-to-recruit-police-to-help-ice-agents-gets-mixed-reviews.

76. "Defunct Louisiana Juvenile Private Prison Reactivated by GEO for Immigrants," *Prison Legal News,* June 15, 2008, https://www.prisonlegalnews.org/news/2008/jun/15/defunct-louisiana-juvenile-private-prison-reactivated-by-geo-for-immigrants.

Chapter 2: Obama, Criminalization, and the Limits of Reform

1. Julia Preston, "Obama to Push Immigration Bill as One Priority," *New York Times*, April 8, 2009, https://www.nytimes.com/2009/04/09/us/politics/09immig.html.

2. Dara Lind, "The Campaign Promise That's Still Haunting Obama," *Vox*, June 9, 2014, https://www.vox.com/2014/6/9/5793870/the-promise-haunting-obama-immigration-reform-promesa.

3. Nina Bernstein, "U.S. to Reform Policy on Detention for Immigrants," *New York Times*, August 5, 2009, https://www.nytimes.com/2009/08/06/us/politics/06detain.html.

4. Adam Goodman, *The Deportation Machine: America's Long History of Expelling Immigrants* (Princeton, NJ: Princeton University Press, 2020), 1. Previous presidents had higher levels of "returns" (e.g., people turned away at the border), but in this chapter, I focus on Obama's formal deportations (or removals), which carried legal consequences, including a potential prison sentence upon return to the United States. While formal deportations are more severe, in *The Deportation Machine*, Goodman explains that most deportations throughout US history have been through "voluntary departure" and "self-deportation." These may be less punitive, but they have in fact involved government coercion and force to scare people into leaving.

5. Alison Parker, "Locked Up Far Away: The Transfer of Immigrants to Remote Detention Centers in the United States," Human Rights Watch, December 2, 2009, https://www.hrw.org/report/2009/12/02/locked-far-away/transfer-immigrants-remote-detention-centers-united-states.

6. Bruce Rushton, "Dora's Darling," *Phoenix New Times*, June 3, 2004, https://www.phoenixnewtimes.com/news/doras-darlings-6396589.

7. Dora Schriro, *Immigration Detention Overview and Recommendations*, US Immigration and Customs Enforcement (Washington, DC, 2009), http://www.ice.gov/doclib/about/offices/odpp/pdf/ice-detention-rpt.pdf.

8. Schriro, *Immigration Detention Overview*, 13.

9. Two good resources for understanding how criminal justice reforms have failed are Kay Whitlock and Nancy A. Heitzeg, *Carceral Con: The Deceptive Terrain of Criminal Justice Reform* (Berkeley: University of California Press, 2021) and Maya Schenwar and Victoria Law, *Prison By Any Other Name: The Harmful Consequences of Popular Reforms* (New York: New Press, 2021).

10. Adam Clymer, "Robert C. Byrd, a Pillar of the Senate, Dies at 92," *New York Times*, June 28, 2010, https://www.nytimes.com/2010/06/29/us/politics/29byrd.html.

11. William Selway and Margaret Newkirk, "Congress Mandates Jail Beds for 34,000 Immigrants as Private Prisons Profit," *Bloomberg*, September

24, 2013, https://www.bloomberg.com/news/articles/2013-09-24/congress-fuels-private-jails-detaining-34-000-immigrants.

12. Anita Sinha, "Arbitrary Detention? The Immigration Detention Bed Quota," *Duke Journal of Constitutional Law & Public Policy* (2016): 77–121, https://scholarship.law.duke.edu/djclpp/vol12/iss2/3.

13. Maureen Chowdhury, "Because of Budget Cuts, U.S. Releases Hundreds of Illegal Immigrants," NPR, February 26, 2013, https://www.npr.org/sections/thetwo-way/2013/02/26/173002227/because-of-budget-cuts-u-s-releases-hundreds-of-illegal-immigrants.

14. Chowdhury, "Because of Budget Cuts."

15. Megan Jula and Daniel González, "Eloy Detention Center: Why So Many Suicides?" *AZ Central*, July 28, 2015, https://www.azcentral.com/story/news/arizona/investigations/2015/07/28/eloy-detention-center-immigrant-suicides/30760545.

16. *2011 Operations Manual ICE Performance-Based National Detention Standards*, US Immigration and Customs Enforcement, 2011, https://www.ice.gov/detain/detention-management/2011.

17. US Immigration and Customs Enforcement, "Request for Inter-Governmental Service Agreement (IGSA), Concept Proposal: Northeast, Statement of Objectives, Immigration Detention Reform," 2010 (on file with author).

18. Kirk Semple and Tim Easton, "Detention for Immigrants That Looks Less Like Prison," *New York Times*, March 13, 2012, https://www.nytimes.com/2012/03/14/us/model-immigration-detention-center-unveiled-in-texas.html.

19. Felicia Escobar, "New Karnes County Civil Detention Facility: Continuing Our Commitment to Immigration Detention Reform," *White House* (blog), March 26, 2012, https://obamawhitehouse.archives.gov/blog/2012/03/26/new-karnes-county-civil-detention-facility-continuing-our-commitment-immigration-det.

20. Caitlin Dickerson, "We Need to Take Away Children," *Atlantic*, August 7, 2022, https://www.theatlantic.com/magazine/archive/2022/09/trump-administration-family-separation-policy-immigration/670604.

21. Lauren-Brooke Eisen, "Private Prisons Are Poised for a Comeback Under Trump. Here's How to Reform Them," *Vox*, January 13, 2017, https://www.vox.com/the-big-idea/2017/1/13/14258350/private-prisons-reform-trump-incarceration; Bethany Carson and Eleana Diaz, "Payoff: How Congress Ensures Private Prison Profit with an Immigrant Detention Quota," Grassroots Leadership, April 2015, https://www.grassrootsleadership.org/publications.

22. Muzaffer Chishti, Sarah Pierce, and Jessica Bolter, "The Obama Record

on Deportations: Deporter in Chief or Not?" Migration Policy Institute, January 26, 2017, https://www.migrationpolicy.org/article/obama-record-deportations-deporter-chief-or-not.

23. Kevin Sieff, "Immigrant Detention Center in VA Would Be Mid-Atlantic's Largest," *Washington Post*, July 18, 2010, https://www.washingtonpost.com/wp-dyn/content/article/2010/07/17/AR2010071701416.html.

24. "Immigration Detention: Recent Trends and Scholarship," Center for Migration Studies, March 26, 2018, https://cmsny.org/publications/virtualbrief-detention.

25. "DHS's 'Secure Communities': No Rules for the Road," National Immigration Law Center, March 2011, https://www.nilc.org/issues/immigration-enforcement/scomm-no-rules-of-road-2011-03-0.

26. Aarti Kohli, Peter L. Markowitz, Lisa Chavez, *Secure Communities by the Numbers: An Analysis of Demographics and Due Process* (Berkeley: Warren Institute of Law and Policy, UC Berkeley, 2011), https://ssrn.com/abstract=3527648.

27. Conor Friedersdorf, "Police Have a Much Bigger Domestic-Abuse Problem Than the NFL Does," *Atlantic*, September 19, 2014, https://www.theatlantic.com/national/archive/2014/09/police-officers-who-hit-their-wives-or-girlfriends/380329.

28. "ICE Director Morton's Prosecutorial Discretion Memo Offered Hope, Yet to Be Realized," *America's Voice* (blog), April 17, 2012, https://americasvoice.org/blog/ice-director-mortons-prosecutorial-discretion-memo-offered-hope-yet-to-be-realized.

29. TRAC Reports, "ICE Prosecutorial Discretion Initiative: Latest Figures," Transactional Records Access Clearinghouse, April 19, 2012, https://trac.syr.edu/immigration/reports/278.

30. Dara Lind, "Immigration Prosecutors Were Told Not to Push for Deportation in Cases Like His. He Was Ordered Deported the Next Day," *ProPublica*, July 27, 2012, https://www.propublica.org/article/immigration-prosecutors-were-told-not-to-push-for-deportation-in-cases-like-his.

31. John Morton, "Exercise Prosecutorial Discretion Consistent with Civil Immigration Enforcement Priorities of the Agency for the Apprehension, Detention, and Removal of Aliens," memorandum, US Immigration and Customs Enforcement, June 17, 2011.

32. Judith A. Greene, Bethany Carson, and Andrea Black, *Indefensible: A Decade of Mass Incarceration of Migrants Prosecuted for Crossing the Border* (Austin, TX: Grassroots Leadership and Justice Strategies, 2016), 18, https://www.justicestrategies.org/sites/default/files/publications/indefensible_book_web.pdf.

33. Heitzeg and Whitlock, *Carceral Con*, 117.

34. Kate Evans and Robert Koulish, "Manipulating Risk: Immigration Detention through Automation," *Lewis & Clark Law Review* 24 (2020): 795, https://scholarship.law.duke.edu/faculty_scholarship/3994.

35. Evans and Koulish, "Manipulating Risk," 794.

36. Puck Lo, "From Data Criminalization to Prison Abolition," Community Justice Exchange, February 2022, https://abolishdatacrim.org/en.

37. Will Coley, "Let My People Stay," interview with Ravi Ragbir and Amy Gottlieb, *Indefensible*, podcast audio, 2017, https://www.immigrantdefenseproject.org/indefensible-episode-5.

38. Mary Small, "A Toxic Relationship: Private Prisons and U.S. Immigration Detention," Detention Watch Network, December 2016, https://www.detentionwatchnetwork.org/sites/default/files/reports/A%20Toxic%20Relationship_DWN.pdf.

39. Katharina Obser, "The Family Case Management Program: Why Case Management Can and Must Be Part of the US Approach to Immigration," Women's Refugee Commission, June 2019, https://www.womensrefugeecommission.org/wp-content/uploads/2020/04/The-Family-Case-Management-Program.pdf.

40. Small, "Toxic Relationship," 12.

41. Obser, "Family Case Management," 4.

42. "Budget Overview, Fiscal Year 2017, Congressional Justification" US Immigration and Customs Enforcement, US Department of Homeland Security, 149, https://www.dhs.gov/sites/default/files/publications/U.S.%20Immigration%20and%20Customs%20Enforcement.pdf.

43. TRAC Reports, *Immigrants Monitored by ICE's Alternatives to Detention Program Vary by Nationality, Gender, and State,* Transactional Records Access Clearinghouse, October 11, 2022, https://trac.syr.edu/reports/698.

44. Naomi Murakawa, *The First Civil Right: How Liberals Built Prison America* (Oxford: Oxford University Press, 2014), 3–4.

45. President William Jefferson Clinton, "State of the Union Address," US Capitol, January 23, 1996, https://clintonwhitehouse4.archives.gov/WH/New/other/sotu.html.

Chapter 3: Deterring the Crisis

1. Miriam Jordan, "Family Members Separated at Border May Each Get Up to $450,000," *New York Times*, October 28, 2021, https://www.nytimes.com/2021/10/28/us/politics/trump-family-separation-border.html.

2. Brittney Bringuez, et al., "'Part of My Heart Was Torn Away': What the U.S. Government Owes the Tortured Survivors of Family Separation," Physicians for Human Rights, April 19, 2022, https://phr.org/our-

work/resources/part-of-my-heart-was-torn-away.

3. "Departments of Justice and Homeland Security Release Data on
    Incarcerated Aliens," Office of Public Affairs, Department of Justice,
    October 16, 2020, https://www.justice.gov/opa/pr/departments-jus-
    tice-and-homeland-security-release-data-incarcerated-aliens.

4. Todd Miller, "A Lucrative Border-Industrial Complex Keeps the US
    Border in Constant 'Crisis,'" *Guardian*, April 19, 2021.

5. "The Cost of Immigrant Enforcement and Border Security," American
    Immigration Council, January 20, 2021, https://www.americanim-
    migrationcouncil.org/research/the-cost-of-immigration-enforce-
    ment-and-border-security.

6. Miller, "Lucrative Border-Industrial Complex."

7. Achille Mbembe, *Necropolitics* (Durham, NC: Duke University
    Press, 2019), 3.

8. Mai M. Ngai, *Impossible Subjects: Illegal Aliens and the Making of Modern
    America* (Princeton: Princeton University Press, 2004), 27.

9. Kelly Lytle Hernández, *Migra!: A History of the U.S. Border Patrol*
    (Berkeley and Los Angeles: University of California Press, 2010), 30.

10. Kelly Lytle Hernández, *City of Inmates: Conquest, Rebellion, and the Rise
    of Human Caging in Los Angeles, 1771–1965* (Chapel Hill, NC: Universi-
    ty of North Carolina Press, 2017), 134.

11. Hernández, *City of Inmates*, 137.

12. Isaac Stanley-Becker, "Who's Behind the Law Making Undocument-
    ed Immigrants Criminals? An 'Unrepentant White Supremacist,'"
    Washington Post, July 27, 2019, https://www.washingtonpost.com/
    nation/2019/06/27/julian-castro-beto-orourke-section-immigration-il-
    legal-coleman-livingstone-blease.

13. Kara Hartzler, "The Aggressively Racist History of America's Most-Pros-
    ecuted Federal Crimes: Immigration Offenses," *Balls and Strikes*, Decem-
    ber 5, 2022, https://ballsandstrikes.org/law-politics/illegal-entry-immi-
    gration-law-federal-crime.

14. Hartzler, "Aggressively Racist History."

15. Hernández, *City of Inmates*, 138.

16. Torrie Hester, "Can the Courts Decriminalize Immigration?"
    Public Books, August 4, 2021, https://www.publicbooks.org/
    can-the-courts-decriminalize-immigration/#fnref-44387-14; Jesse
    Franzblau, "A Legacy of Injustice: The U.S. Criminalization of Migration,"
    National Immigrant Justice Center, July 2020, https://immigrantjustice.
    org/research-items/report-legacy-injustice-us-criminalization-migration.

17. 8 U.S.C. §§ 1325 and 1326.

18. *Affidavit of Dr. S. Deborah Kang, Associate Professor, University of Virginia,*

United States of America v. Darwin Lopez Ramos, Case No. 2:18-cr-00112-AWA-DEM (E.D. Va. December 6, 2021), 1.

19. US Customs and Border Patrol, "Border Patrol Strategic Plan 1994 and Beyond: National Strategy," US Department of Homeland Security (digital library), July 1994.

20. Joseph Nevins and Mizue Aizeki, *Dying to Live: A Story of U.S. Immigration in an Age of Global Apartheid* (San Francisco: Open Media/City Lights Books, 2008).

21. TRAC Immigration, *Lead Charges for Criminal Immigration Prosecutions FY 1986–FY 2011*, Transactional Records Access Clearinghouse, 2011, https://trac.syr.edu/immigration/reports/251/include/imm_charges.html.

22. Caitlin Dickerson, "'We Need to Take Away Children,'" *Atlantic*, August 7, 2022, https://www.theatlantic.com/magazine/archive/2022/09/trump-administration-family-separation-policy-immigration/670604/.

23. Jeremy Slack, "In Harm's Way: Family Separation, Immigration Enforcement Programs and Security on the US–Mexico Border," *Journal on Migration and Human Security 3*, no. 2 (2015): 109–28.

24. Patrisia Macías-Rojas, *From Deportation to Prison: The Politics of Immigration Enforcement in Post-Civil Rights America* (New York: New York University Press, 2016), 91.

25. Judith A. Greene, Bethany Carson, and Andrea Black, *Indefensible: A Decade of Mass Incarceration of Migrants Prosecuted for Crossing the Border*, (Austin, TX: Grassroots Leadership and Justice Strategies, 2016), 45, https://www.justicestrategies.org/sites/default/files/publications/indefensible_book_web.pdf.

26. Eric Schlosser, "The Prison-Industrial Complex," *Atlantic*, December 1998, https://www.theatlantic.com/magazine/archive/1998/12/the-prison-industrial-complex/304669/.

27. "Private Prison News," *Grits for Breakfast*, September 22, 2008, https://gritsforbreakfast.blogspot.com/2008/09/private-prison-news.html.

28. Quoted in Todd Miller, *Border Patrol Nation: Dispatches from the Front Lines of Homeland Security* (San Francisco: City Lights, 2014), 235.

29. TRAC Immigration, *At Nearly 100,000, Immigration Prosecutions Reach All-time High in FY 2013*, Transactional Records Access Clearinghouse, 2013, https://trac.syr.edu/immigration/reports/336.

30. Seth Freed Wessler, "'This Man Will Almost Certainly Die,'" *Nation*, January 28, 2016, https://www.thenation.com/article/archive/privatized-immigrant-prison-deaths.

31. Wessler, "This Man."

32. Jesse Franzblau, "A Legacy of Injustice: The U.S. Criminalization of Migration," National Immigrant Justice Center, July 2020, https://immigrant-

justice.org/sites/default/files/uploaded-files/no-content-type/2020-07/
NIJC-Legacy-of-Injustice-report_2020-07-22_FINAL.pdf.

33. Slack, "In Harm's Way," 114.

34. Jonathan Simon, "A Summer Classic: Moral Panic over a Pier Shooting," *Berkeley Blog,* July 8, 2015, https://blogs.berkeley.edu/2015/07/08/a-summer-classic-moral-panic-over-a-pier-shooting.

35. Carla Marinucci and Heather Knight, "Feinstein Scalds S.F. for Freeing Man Accused of Pier Shooting," *SF Gate,* July 8, 2015, https://www.sfgate.com/bayarea/article/Feinstein-Immigrant-charged-in-killing-should-6371304.php.

36. Alina Das, "The Immigration Debate Still Has a Willie Horton Problem," *Slate,* May 26, 2021, https://slate.com/news-and-politics/2021/05/immigration-deportation-willie-horton.html.

37. Beth Schwartzapfel and Bill Keller, "Wille Horton Revisted," Marshall Project, May 13, 2015, https://www.themarshallproject.org/2015/05/13/willie-horton-revisited.

38. Erin Blakemore, "How the Willie Horton Ad Played on Racism and Fear," History, November 2, 2018, https://www.history.com/news/george-bush-willie-horton-racist-ad.

39. Peter Baker, "Bush Made Willie Horton an Issue in 1988, and the Racial Scars Are Still Fresh," *New York Times,* December 3, 2018, https://www.nytimes.com/2018/12/03/us/politics/bush-willie-horton.html.

40. Jesse Franzblau, "Landmark Decision Finds 'Illegal Reentry' Charges Are Racist in Origin, Discriminatory in Practice," National Immigrant Justice Center, August 26, 2021, https://immigrantjustice.org/staff/blog/landmark-decision-finds-illegal-reentry-charges-are-racist-origin-discriminatory.

41. Caitlin Dickerson, "Hundreds of Immigrant Children Have Been Taken from Parents at U.S. Border," *New York Times,* April 20, 2018, https://www.nytimes.com/2018/04/20/us/immigrant-children-separation-ice.html.

42. Dickerson, "'We Need to Take Away Children.'"

43. Lisa Rain, "Meet the Man the White House Has Honored for Deporting Illegal Immigrants," *Washington Post,* April 27, 2016, https://www.washingtonpost.com/news/powerpost/wp/2016/04/25/meet-the-man-the-white-house-has-honored-for-deporting-illegal-immigrants.

44. Franzblau, "Legacy of Injustice."

45. Rachel Zohn, "Recent ICE Raids Overload Mississippi Legal System," *U.S. News,* October 18, 2019, https://www.usnews.com/news/best-states/articles/2019-10-18/recent-ice-raids-by-us-immigration-and-customs-enforcement-overload-mississippi-legal-system.

46. Michelle Mark, "An Obscure Section of US Law Became a Flashpoint in the Democratic Debate and Sparked a Confrontation between

Julián Castro and Beto O'Rourke. Here's Why It's So Controversial," *Business Insider*, June 27, 2019, https://www.businessinsider.com/section-1325-julian-castro-beto-o-rourke-immigration-debate-2019-6.

47. Abby Livingston, "Julián Castro Spars with Democratic Front-Runner Joe Biden during Party's Second Presidential Debate," *Texas Tribune*, July 31, 2019, https://www.texastribune.org/2019/07/31/julian-castro-joe-biden-spar-immigration-during-democratic-debate.

48. *Karina Cisneros Preciado Opening Statement, U.S. Senate Permanent Committee on Investigations, Committee on Homeland Security and Governmental Affairs*, 117th Cong. (November 15, 2022), https://www.hsgac.senate.gov/wp-content/uploads/imo/media/doc/Cisneros%20Preciado%20Testimony1.pdf.

49. Leah Wang, "Both Sides of the Bars: How Mass Incarceration Punishes Families," Prison Policy Initiative, August 11, 2022, https://www.prisonpolicy.org/blog/2022/08/11/parental_incarceration.

50. Nazgol Ghandnoosh, Emma Stammen, and Kevin Muhitch, "Parents in Prison," The Sentencing Project, February 2021, https://www.sentencingproject.org/app/uploads/2022/09/Parents-in-Prison.pdf.

51. Seth Freed Wessler, *Shattered Families: The Perilous Intersection of Immigration Enforcement and the Child Welfare System*, Race Forward, 2011, https://www.raceforward.org/research/reports/shattered-families.

52. Dorothy Roberts, *Torn Apart: How the Child Welfare System Destroys Black Families—and How Abolition Can Build a Safer World* (New York: Basic Books, 2022), 23.

53. Hyunil Kim, Christopher Wildeman, Melissa Jonson-Reid, and Brett Drake, "Lifetime Prevalence of Investigating Child Maltreatment Among US Children," *American Journal of Public Health* 107, no. 2 (February 1, 2017): 274–80, https://doi.org/10.2105/AJPH.2016.303545.

54. Hina Naveed, et al., "'If I Wasn't Poor, I Wouldn't Be Unfit,'" The Family Separation Crisis in the US Child Welfare System," Human Rights Watch, November 17, 2022, https://www.hrw.org/report/2022/11/17/if-i-wasnt-poor-i-wouldnt-be-unfit/family-separation-crisis-us-child-welfare.

55. Jessica Leung, et al. "Notes from the Field: Mumps in Detention Facilities that House Detained Migrants — United States, September 2018–August 2019," *Morbidity and Mortality Weekly Report* 68, no. 34 (2019): 749–50; Caitlin Dickerson and Michael D. Shear, "Before Covid-19, Trump Aide Sought to Use Disease to Close Borders," *New York Times*, May 3, 2020, https://www.nytimes.com/2020/05/03/us/coronavirus-immigration-stephen-miller-public-health.html.

56. Brian Naylor and Tamara Keith, "Kamala Harris Tells Guatemalans Not

to Migrate to the United States," NPR, June 7, 2021, https://www.npr.org/2021/06/07/1004074139/harris-tells-guatemalans-not-to-migrate-to-the-united-states.

57. César Cuauhtémoc García Hernández, "Creating Crimmigration," *Brigham Young University Law Review* 2013, no. 6 (February 28, 2014) 1457–1515; Glenn R. Schmitt and Lindsey Jeralds, *Overview of Federal Criminal Cases, Fiscal Year 2021*, United States Sentencing Commission, April 2022, https://www.ussc.gov/research/data-reports/overview-federal-criminal-cases-fiscal-year-2021.

58. Julia Craven, "The Ugly History behind Those Border Agents Chasing Haitian Migrants on Horseback," *Slate*, September 25, 2021, https://slate.com/news-and-politics/2021/09/border-patrol-horseback-haitian-migrants-del-rio.html.

59. "Homeland Security Secretary Alejandro Mayorkas on Immigration," C-SPAN, April 30, 2021, https://www.c-span.org/video/?511376-1/homeland-security-secretary-alejandro-mayorkas-immigration.

60. Hartzler, "Aggressively Racist History."

61. Ellen M. Gilmer, "Mayorkas Eyes Increased Criminal Prosecutions at Southern Border," *Bloomberg Government*, May 17, 2022, https://about.bgov.com/news/mayorkas-eyes-increased-criminal-prosecutions-at-southern-border.

62. Juno Mac and Molly Smith, *Revolting Prostitutes: The Fight for Sex Workers' Rights* (London and New York: Verso, 2018), 57. While human trafficking largely takes place in other labor sectors, sex worker activists have had to become experts on the subject because of the moral panic created around sex trafficking.

63. Mac and Smith, *Revolting Prostitutes*, 62.

64. Ryan Devereaux, "Humanitarian Volunteer Scott Warren Reflects on the Borderlands and Two Years of Government Persecution," *Intercept*, November 23, 2019, https://theintercept.com/2019/11/23/scott-warren-verdict-immigration-border.

65. Stuart Hall, Chas Critcher, Tony Jefferson, John Clarke, and Brian Roberts, *Policing the Crisis: Mugging, the State, and Law and Order* (London: Palgrave, 1978). The book focuses on the targeting of young Black men over "mugging" in postwar Great Britain, but for purposes of my argument, I include "brown" in reference to the way moral panics have operated to scoop up more Latinx migrants specifically.

66. Jenna M. Loyd, "Race, Capitalist Crisis, and Abolitionist Organizing," in *Beyond Walls and Cages: Prisons, Borders, and Global Crisis*, ed. Jenna M. Loyd, Matt Mitchelson, Andrew Burridge (Athens, GA: University of Georgia Press, 2012), 43.

Chapter 4: From Legalization to Racial Justice

1. Ali Noorani, "Focusing U.S. Detention Costs," Reuters, March 4, 2013, https://www.reuters.com/article/idUS386213515620130304.
2. Marc R. Rosenblum, "US Immigration Policy since 9/11: Understanding the Stalemate over Comprehensive Immigration Reform," Migration Policy Institute, 2011, https://www.migrationpolicy.org/pubs/RMSG-post-9-11policy.pdf.
3. Gracie Mae Bradley and Luke de Noronha, *Against Borders: The Case for Abolition* (London and New York: Verso Books, 2022), 153.
4. *How Democracy Works Now: Twelve Stories*, story one, *The Game Is On*, directed and produced by Shari Robertson, Michael Camerini, Epidavros Project, 2001.
5. Andrew Willis Garcés, "Neidi Dominguez on 'Not Listening to DC' and Embracing Disagreement in the Fight to Win DACA," November 15, 2022, *Craft of Campaigns*, podcast audio, November 15, 2022, https://www.trainingforchange.org/craft-of-campaigns-s1e1.
6. Cristina Jiménez Moreta, "The Immigrant Youth Movement: Here to Dream and Here to Fight," in *Immigration Matters: Movements, Visions, and Strategies for a Progressive Future*, ed. Ruth Milkman, Deepak Bhargava, and Penny Lewis (New York: New Press, 2021), 111.
7. Katherine Cavanaugh, "Immigrant Rights Protests in Washington State, Spring 2006," Seattle Civil Rights & Labor History Project, https://depts.washington.edu/civilr/2006_immigrant_rights.htm.
8. Diana Welch, "Immigration Storm Reaches Hurricane Strength," *Austin Chronicle*, April 14, 2006, https://www.austinchronicle.com/news/2006-04-14/356705.
9. Angélica Cházaro, "Beyond Respectability: Dismantling the Harms of 'Illegality,'" *Harvard Journal on Legislation* 52, (2015), https://digitalcommons.law.uw.edu/faculty-articles/52.
10. "Sen. Menendez Dresses Down Immigration Activists in 2007," *Washington Post*, March 16, 2013, https://www.washingtonpost.com/video/politics/sen-menendez-dresses-down-immigration-activists-in-2007/2013/03/16/116bebea-8ccd-11e2-b63f-f53fb9f2fcb4_video.html.
11. Randal C. Archibold, "Challenges to a Sheriff, Both Popular and Reviled," *New York Times*, September 27, 2008, https://www.nytimes.com/2008/09/28/us/28sheriff.html.
12. Larry Rohter, "Musicians Differ in Responses to Arizona's New Immigration Law," *New York Times*, May 28, 2010, https://www.nytimes.com/2010/05/29/arts/music/29boycott.html.
13. "Arizona Immigration Law Sparks Huge Rallies," *CBC News*, May 1, 2010, https://www.cbc.ca/news/world/arizona-immigra-

tion-law-sparks-huge-rallies-1.967969.

14. Evan Wyloge, "Thousands Take to Phoenix to Protest Arizona's New Immigration Law," *Arizona Capitol Times*, May 29, 2010, https://azcapitoltimes.com/news/2010/05/29/thousands-take-to-phoenix-to-protest-arizonas-new-immigration-law.

15. Julianne Hing, "Report: SB 1070 Has Cost Arizona $141 Million," *Colorlines*, November 18, 2010, https://colorlines.com/article/report-sb-1070-has-cost-arizona-141-million.

16. Frank Sharry, "Arizona's Ugly Law, Congress' Urgent Challenge," *Milwaukee Journal Sentinel*, May 1, 2010, https://archive.jsonline.com/news/opinion/92557749.html.

17. Linda Greenhouse, "The Lower Floor," *New York Times Opinionator*, May 2, 2012, https://archive.nytimes.com/opinionator.blogs.nytimes.com/2012/05/02/the-lower-floor.

18. Marie Landau, "Out of the Shadows, Into the Spotlight," *In These Times*, July 5, 2010, https://inthesetimes.com/article/out-of-the-shadows-into-the-spotlight.

19. Tania Unzueta, "How I Stopped Believing in CIR and Learned to Love 'Piecemeal' Legislation," *Immigration Daily*, January 2, 2013, https://discuss.ilw.com/articles/articles/380798-article-how-i-stopped-believing-in-cir-and-learned-to-love-piecemeal-legislation-by-tania-unzueta.

20. Garcés, "Neidi Dominguez."

21. Claudia Muñoz and Michael P. Young, "Is Infiltrating Migrant Prisons the Most Effective Way to Challenge Detention Regimes? The Case of the National Immigrant Youth Alliance," working paper, Global Detention Project (November 2016), https://www.globaldetentionproject.org/wp-content/uploads/2016/11/Munoz-and-Young-GDP-Working-Paper-Nov-2016.pdf.

22. Barack Obama, "Remarks by the President on Immigration," (speech, Washington DC, June 15, 2012) White House, Office of the Press Secretary, https://obamawhitehouse.archives.gov/the-press-office/2012/06/15/remarks-president-immigration.

23. Garcés, "Neidi Dominguez."

24. Ana Gonzalez-Barrera, "Record Number of Deportations in 2012," Pew Research Center, January 24, 2014, https://www.pewresearch.org/short-reads/2014/01/24/record-number-of-deportations-in-2012; John F. Simanski and Lesley M. Sapp, "Immigration Enforcement Actions: 2012," Office of Immigration Statistics, Department of Homeland Security, December 2013, https://www.dhs.gov/sites/default/files/publications/Enforcement_Actions_2012.pdf.

25. Alliance for Citizenship talking points on file with author.

26. "A Guide to S.744: Understanding the 2013 Senate Immigration Bill," American Immigration Council, July 10, 2013, https://www.american-immigrationcouncil.org/research/guide-s744-understanding-2013-senate-immigration-bill.

27. Julia Preston, "Beside a Path to Citizenship, a New Path on Immigration," *New York Times*, April 16, 2013, https://www.nytimes.com/2013/04/17/us/senators-set-to-unveil-immigration-bill.html.

28. Richard Cowan and Thomas Ferraro, "Senate Backs Border Amendment to Immigration Bill," Reuters, June 26, 2013, https://www.reuters.com/article/us-usa-immigration/senate-backs-border-amendment-to-immigration-bill-idUSBRE95P0ZX20130626.

29. "Derechos Opposes Hoeven-Corker Amendment; New Immigration Bill is a Step Backward for Border Communities and Many Immigrant Families," Coalición de Derechos Humanos, https://derechoshumanosaz.net/derechos-opposes-hoeven-corker-amendment-new-immigration-bill-is-a-step-backward-for-border-communities-and-many-immigrant-families.

30. Ed O'Keefe, "Senate Approves Comprehensive Immigration Bill," *Washington Post*, June 27, 2013, https://www.washingtonpost.com/politics/senate-poised-to-approve-massive-immigration-bill/2013/06/27/87168096-df32-11e2-b2d4-ea6d8f477a01_story.html.

31. Daniel Denvir, *All-American Nativism: How the Bipartisan War on Immigrants Explains Politics as We Know It* (London and New York: Verso, 2020), 228.

32. Alan Gomez, "Some Liberal Groups Turn on Senate Immigration Plan," *USA Today*, June 27, 2013, https://www.usatoday.com/story/news/politics/2013/06/27/immigration-border-security-opposition/2459287.

33. Email on file with author.

34. Benjy Sarlin quoted in Denvir, *All-American Nativism*, 228.

35. Tania Unzueta, Maru Mora Villalpando, and Angélica Cházaro, "We Fell in Love in a Hopeless Place: A Grassroots History from #Not1More to Abolish ICE," *Medium*, https://medium.com/@LaTania/we-fell-in-love-in-a-hopeless-place-a-grassroots-history-from-not1more-to-abolish-ice-23089cf21711.

36. Ray Stoeve, "They Started by Blockading a Bus Full of Detainees—and Went on to Shake Up the Immigration Debate," *Yes! Magazine*, April 17, 2014, https://www.yesmagazine.org/social-justice/2014/04/17/hunger-strikes-lockdowns-and-border-actions-how-the-undocumented-are-shaking-up-the-immigration-debate.

37. TRAC Immigration, *ICE Apprehensions Half Levels of Five Years Ago*, Transactional Records Access Clearinghouse, June 12, 2018, https://

trac.syr.edu/immigration/reports/517/.

38. "Governor Signs 8 Laws Granting Rights to Immigrants," Fox 5 San Diego, October 7, 2013, https://fox5sandiego.com/news/worries-over-legal-rights-for-those-here-illegally.

39. Lisa Pickoff-White and Mina Kim, "California Is Sending Far Fewer Immigrants to Feds under New State Law," KQED, April 8, 2014, https://www.kqed.org/news/131900/california-is-sending-far-fewer-immigrants-to-feds-under-new-state-law.

40. Reid J. Epstein, "NCLR Head: Obama 'Deporter-in-Chief,'" Politico, March 4, 2014, https://www.politico.com/story/2014/03/national-council-of-la-raza-janet-murguia-barack-obama-deporter-in-chief-immigration-104217.

41. National Day Laborer Organizing Network Staff, "Ferguson: A Miscarriage of Justice and a Movement That Won't Give Up," NDLON, November 25, 2014, https://ndlon.org/franco-ferguson.

42. "Home Page," Freedom Side, https://freedomside.org.

43. Interview with Greisa Martínez Rosas on May 30, 2023.

44. "Our DNA," Mijente, https://mijente.net/our-dna.

45. "The Network," UndocuBlack, https://undocublack.org/asdasd.

46. John Gramlich, "How Border Apprehensions, ICE Arrests and Deportations Have Changed under Trump," Pew Research Center, March 2, 2020, https://www.pewresearch.org/short-reads/2020/03/02/how-border-apprehensions-ice-arrests-and-deportations-have-changed-under-trump.

47. Dianne Gallagher, Catherine E. Shoichet, and Madeline Holcombe, "680 Undocumented Workers Arrested in Record-Setting Immigration Sweep on the First Day of School," CNN, August 9, 2019, https://www.cnn.com/2019/08/08/us/mississippi-immigration-raids-children/index.html.

48. "U.S. Immigration and Customs and Enforcement Fiscal Year 2019; Enforcement and Removal Operations Report," US Immigration and Customs Enforcement, October 29, 2021, 17, https://www.ice.gov/sites/default/files/documents/Document/2019/eroReportFY2019.pdf.

49. Bradley and de Noronha, Against Borders, 153–54.

Chapter 5: Private Prisons and the Demand to Defund

1. Anita Kumar, "Biden Begins Selling His $4T Spending Plans," Politico, April 29, 2021, https://www.politico.com/news/2021/04/29/biden-4-trillion-spending-plan-485055.

2. Wendy Sawyer and Peter Wagner, "Mass Incarceration: The Whole Pie 2023," Prison Policy Initiative, March 14, 2023, https://www.prisonpolicy.org/reports/pie2023.html#myths.

3. Loren Collingwood, Jason L. Morin, and Stephen Omar El-Khatib, "Ex-

panding Carceral Markets: Detention Facilities, ICE Contracts, and the Financial Interests of Punitive Immigration Policy," *Race and Social Problems* (July 2018): 1–18, https://doi.org/10.1007/s12552-018-9241-5.

4. El Centro, another federal facility that has a long history of immigrant incarceration, closed in 2014, but the chance that the government could bring it back online remains.

5. "Custody and Detention," US Marshals Service, https://www.usmarshals.gov/what-we-do/prisoners/operation/custody-detention; César Cuauhtémoc García Hernández quoted in Seth Freed Wessler, "Inside the US Marshals' Secretive, Deadly Detention Empire," *Mother Jones*, November/December 2019, https://www.motherjones.com/crime-justice/2019/10/inside-the-us-marshals-secretive-deadly-detention-empire.

6. "U.S. Immigration and Customs Enforcement Budget Overview, FY 2023 Congressional Justification," Department of Homeland Security, Washington, DC, https://www.dhs.gov/sites/default/files/2022-03/U.S.%20Immigration%20and%20Customs%20Enforcement_Remediated.pdf.

7. "Cut the Contracts: It's Time to End ICE's Corrupt Detention Management System," National Immigrant Justice Center, March 16, 2021, https://immigrantjustice.org/research-items/policy-brief-cut-contracts-its-time-end-ices-corrupt-detention-management-system.

8. Dean J. Koepfler, "A Rare Look Inside Tacoma's Northwest Detention Center," *News Tribune*, September 9, 2012, https://www.invw.org/2012/09/09/a-rare-look-inside-tacoma-1309.

9. US Government Accountability Office, *Immigration Detention, Actions Needed to Improve Planning, Documentation, and Oversight of Detention Facility Contracts*, GAO 21-149 (Washington, DC: USGAO: 2021), 24 https://www.gao.gov/assets/gao-21-149.pdf.

10. Rebekah Wilce and Mary Bottari, "Outsourcing America: Sodexo Siphons Cash from Kids and Soldiers While Dishing up Subprime Food," *Huffington Post*, September 24, 2013, https://www.huffpost.com/entry/post_b_3982325.

11. Bob Libal, "Could the Fall of Lehman Brothers Signal Trouble for Private Prison Corporations?" *Prison Legal News*, November 15, 2008, https://www.prisonlegalnews.org/news/2008/nov/15/could-the-fall-of-lehman-brothers-signal-trouble-8232for-private-prison-corporations.

12. Victoria Law, *"Prisons Make Us Safer": And 20 Other Myths about Mass Incarceration* (Boston: Beacon Press, 2021), 35.

13. Ruth Wilson Gilmore, "The Worrying State of the Anti-Prison Movement," *Social Justice Journal*, February 23, 2015, http://www.socialjusticejournal.org/the-worrying-state-of-the-anti-prison-movement.

14. Matt Zapotosky and Chico Harlan, "Justice Department Says It Will End

Use of Private Prisons," *Washington Post*, August 18, 2016, https://www.washingtonpost.com/news/post-nation/wp/2016/08/18/justice-department-says-it-will-end-use-of-private-prisons.

15. Matt Clarke, "Denial of Medical Care Causes Two Riots at GEO Group Texas Prison," *Prison Legal News*, February 15, 2010, https://www.prisonlegalnews.org/news/2010/feb/15/denial-of-medical-care-causes-two-riots-at-geo-group-texas-prison.

16. Janosch Delcker, "Fatal Corrections: Inside the Deadly Mississippi Riot That Pushed the Justice Department to Rein In Private Prisons," *Intercept*, December 17, 2016, https://theintercept.com/2016/12/17/inside-the-deadly-mississippi-riot-that-pushed-the-justice-department-to-rein-in-private-prisons.

17. Seth Freed Wessler, "The True Story of a Texas Prison Riot," *Nation*, June 23, 2015, https://www.thenation.com/article/archive/the-true-story-of-a-texas-prison-riot.

18. Homeland Security Advisory Council, "Report of the Subcommittee on Privatized Immigration Detention Facilities," US Department of Homeland Security, December 1, 2016, https://www.dhs.gov/sites/default/files/publications/DHS%20HSAC%20PIDF%20Final%20Report.pdf.

19. Gant Team, "MVDEP Spotlight on Business: Moshannon Valley Processing Center," *GANTNews*, January 13, 2023, https://gantnews.com/2023/01/13/mvedp-spotlight-on-business-moshannon-valley-processing-center.

20. Isabela Dias, "A Judge Just Halted Efforts to End Immigration Detention in New Jersey," *Mother Jones*, August 30, 2023, https://www.motherjones.com/politics/2023/08/ice-corecivic-judge-halts-efforts-to-end-new-jersey-immigration-detention.

21. This section on Defund Hate draws from interviews with Gabriela Viera, Mary Small, and Greisa Martínez Rosas.

22. Eli Johnson, "We Stopped ICE from Getting an Extra Billion; Now Let's Defund It Totally," *Truthout*, October 15, 2018, https://truthout.org/articles/we-stopped-ice-getting-an-extra-billion-now-lets-defund-it-totally.

23. Claudia Grisales, "As Puerto Rico Braces for Storm, DHS, FEMA to Move $271 Million to Border Operations," NPR, August 27, 2019, https://www.npr.org/2019/08/27/754838143/as-puerto-rico-braces-for-storm-dhs-fema-to-move-271-million-to-border-operation.

24. "Chairwoman Roybal-Allard Statement at Subcommittee Markup of FY 2021 Homeland Security Funding Bill," https://web.archive.org/web/20200807134419/https:/appropriations.house.gov/news/statements/chairwoman-roybal-allard-statement-at-subcommittee-markup-of-fy-2021-homeland.

25. Lindsay Beyerstein, "Beyond the Hate Frame, an Interview with Kay Whitlock and Michael Bronski," Political Research Associates, July 27, 2015, https://politicalresearch.org/2015/07/27/beyond-the-hate-frame-an-interview-with-kay-whitlock-michael-bronski.

Chapter 6: Communities Not Cages

1. Connor Sheets, "Etowah Sheriff Pockets $750K in Jail Food Funds, Buys $740K Beach House," AL.com, March 13, 2018, https://www.al.com/news/birmingham/2018/03/etowah_sheriff_pocketed_over_7.html.
2. This section on the campaign against family detention draws on interviews with Bob Libal, David Bennion, Mike Ishii, and Liz Castillo.
3. Philip G. Schrag, *Baby Jails: The Fight to End the Incarceration of Refugee Children in America* (Berkeley and Los Angeles: University of California Press, 2020), 11–14.
4. Schrag, *Baby Jails*, 86–87.
5. Schrag, *Baby Jails*, 90–91.
6. Bob Libal, Lauren Martin, and Nicole Porter, "A Prison Is Not a Home," in *Beyond Walls and Cages: Prisons, Borders, and Global Crisis*, ed. Jenna M. Loyd, Matt Mitchelson, Andrew Burridge (Athens, GA: University of Georgia Press, 2012), 256–57.
7. Molly Hennessy-Fiske and Cindy Carcamo, "'What Happened in World War II Is Happening Again': Immigrant Detention Centers through the Eyes of a Therapist," *Los Angeles Times*, April 11, 2016, https://www.latimes.com/nation/la-na-internment-detention-20160411-story.html.
8. Norma Martinez, "'They Separated My Dad and My Oldest Brother'—Crystal City Camp Survivors Protest Family Separation," Texas Public Radio, April 5, 2019, https://www.tpr.org/border-immigration/2019-04-05/they-separated-my-dad-and-my-oldest-brother-crystal-city-camp-survivors-protest-family-separation.
9. Interview with Mike Ishii, January 30, 2023, and email correspondence, October 5, 2023.
10. Miriam Jordan, "Judge Blocks Trump Administration Plan to Detain Migrant Children," *New York Times*, September 27, 2019, https://www.nytimes.com/2019/09/27/us/migrant-children-flores-court.html.
11. Satsuki Ina, "A Cage Is Still a Cage: President Biden Must End U.S. Detention of Children and Families," *Time*, March 11, 2021, https://time.com/5945307/biden-end-detention-migrant-children.
12. John L. Micek, "A Controversial Pa. Prison for Migrants Is Closing. Three Things to Know," *Pennsylvania Capital-Star*, December 2, 2022, https://www.penncapital-star.com/civil-rights-social-justice/a-contro-

versial-pa-prison-for-migrants-is-closing-three-things-to-know-friday-morning-coffee.

13. This section on efforts to curb detention in California draws on interviews with Grisel Ruiz and Stacy Suh.

14. Aaron Davis, "Sheriff Bans Protests on Richmond Jail Grounds," *East Bay Times*, July 26, 2018, https://www.eastbaytimes.com/2018/07/26/sheriff-bans-protests-on-richmond-jail-grounds.

15. "Lessons from the ICE Detention Contract Termination in Contra Costa County, CA," Interfaith Movement for Human Integrity, December 2019, https://www.im4humanintegrity.org/2019/12/lessons-from-the-ice-detention-contract-termination-in-contra-costa-county-ca.

16. Christina Fialho, Victoria Mena, and Mary Small, "Abuse in Adelanto: An Investigation into a California Town's Immigration Jail," CIVIC (now Freedom for Immigrants) and Detention Watch Network, October 2015, https://www.detentionwatchnetwork.org/sites/default/files/reports/CIVIC%20DWN%20Adelanto%20Report.pdf.

17. Anthony Victoria, "Brown Signs TRUTH Act, Vetoes 'Dignity Not Detention,'" *IE Community News*, 2016, https://iecn.com/brown-signs-truth-act-vetoes-dignity-not-detention.

18. Interview with Grisel Ruiz on January 29, 2023.

19. This section on the Midwest resistance to immigrant detention draws on an interview with Fred Tsao on December 19, 2022.

20. "INS Offers to Pay $6 Million for Jail," *Chicago Tribune*, February 5, 2003, https://www.chicagotribune.com/news/ct-xpm-2003-02-05-0302050122-story.html; Chris Mai, Mikelina Belaineh, Ram Subramanian, and Jacob Kang-Brown, *Broken Ground: Why America Keeps Building More Jails and What It Can Do Instead* (New York: Vera Institute of Justice, 2019), https://www.safetyandjusticechallenge.org/wp-content/uploads/2019/11/MacArthur-Jail-Construction_layout_FINAL2_111519_reduced-file-size.pdf.

21. "How It All Started," Interfaith Community for Detained Immigrants, https://www.icdichicago.org/our-story.

22. "Detention Center Opponents Finish 48-Hour March to Crete," CBS Chicago, April 2, 2012, https://www.cbsnews.com/chicago/news/detention-center-opponents-finish-48-hour-march-to-crete.

23. Gabriela Viera, "If You Build It, ICE Will Fill It," CERES Policy Research, Detention Watch Network, Immigrant Legal Resource Center, September 2022, https://www.detentionwatchnetwork.org/sites/default/files/If%20They%20Build%20It,%20ICE%20Will%20Fill%20IT_Report_2022.pdf.

24. This section on the Hudson County Jail fight draws on interviews with Sophia Gurulé, Tania Mattos, and Amy Torres.

25. Andrea Sáenz, Sarah Deri Oshiro, Hasan Shafiqullah on behalf of New York Immigrant Family Unity Project to Thomas A. DeGise, Hudson County Executive, September 11, 2018, https://www.bronxdefenders. org/wp-content/uploads/2018/09/NYIFUP-Letter-to-County-Ex-ec-DeGise.pdf.

26. James Kilgore, "Repackaging Mass Incarceration," *CounterPunch*, June 6, 2014, https://www.counterpunch.org/2014/06/06/repackag-ing-mass-incarceration.

27. Claudia Irizarry Aponte, "Wounds Still Wide Open for Family of Erick Díaz-Cruz, Shot by ICE in Brooklyn," *City*, February 16, 2020, https:// www.thecity.nyc/immigration/2020/2/16/21210523/wounds-still-wide-open-for-family-of-erick-diaz-cruz-shot-by-ice-in-brooklyn.

28. The Legal Aid Society, Brooklyn Defender Services, and the Bronx Defenders, "Immigrant in NJ Detention Center Organize Hunger Strike; NYIFUP Condemns Egregious Conditions in Local ICE Jails Amid COVID-19 Pandemic," press release, March 18, 2020, https://legalaidnyc. org/wp-content/uploads/2020/03/03-18-20-Immigrants-in-NJ-Deten-tion-Center-Organize-Hunger-Strike-NYIFUP-Condemns-Egregious-Conditions-in-Local-ICE-Jails-Amid-COVID-19-Pandemic.pdf.

29. "ICE Detainees Hunger Strike in Essex County, New Jersey in Response to COVID-19," *Perilous Chronicle*, March 17, 2020, https://perilous-chronicle.com/2020/03/17/ice-detainees-hunger-strike-in-new-jersey-in-response-to-covid-19.

30. Matt Katz, "NJ Democrats Reverse Stance, Reject Residents' Pleas, and Vote to Continue Jailing NYC Immigrants," *Gothamist*, November 25, 2020, https://gothamist.com/news/nj-democrats-reverse-stance-reject-residents-pleas-and-vote-to-continue-jailing-nyc-immigrants.

31. "NYIFUP Statement about Hudson County's ICE Contract," New York Immigrant Family Unity Project, November 17, 2020, https://www.bronx-defenders.org/nyifup-statement-about-hudson-countys-contract-with-ice.

32. Joshua Rosario, "Booker and Menendez Come Out against County ICE Contracts, while Hudson County Officials Stand by Their Deal," *Jersey Journal*, December 5, 2020, https://www.nj.com/hudson/2020/12/booker-and-menendez-come-out-against-county-ice-contracts-while-hudson-county-officials-stand-by-their-deal.html.

33. Interview with Amy Torres on December 16, 2022.

34. Teri West, "4 Charged With Contempt after DeGise Wins Temporary Restraining Order against ICE Contract Protests," *Jersey Journal*, Decem-ber 9, 2020, https://www.nj.com/hudson/2020/12/4-charged-with-contempt-after-degise-wins-temporary-restraining-order-against-ice-contract-protests.html.

35. "Sheriff: 9 Arrested During NJ Protest over ICE Detainees," Associated Press, December 13, 2020, https://apnews.com/article/arrests-hackensack-immigration-496c5cd91079e7d6b81db6384a6c997f.

36. "NYIFUP Urges Enactment of the Dignity Not Detention Act in New York State," New York Immigrant Family Unity Project, May 20, 2021, https://legalaidnyc.org/wp-content/uploads/2021/05/05-20-21-NYIFUP-Urges-Enactment-of-the-Dignity-Not-Detention-Act-in-New-York-State-1.pdf.

37. Rebecca Beitsch, "Biden Official Defends Trump-Era Immigration Policy," *Hill*, May 26, 2021, https://thehill.com/policy/national-security/555551-mayorkas-defends-trump-era-covid-policy-immigration-enforcement.

Chapter 7: Abolitionist Approaches to System Change

1. American Civil Liberties Union, "Dear President-Elect Trump" *New York Times*, November 11, 2016, https://www.aclu.org/documents/aclu-letter-president-elect-trump-published-new-york-times.

2. Zamira Rahim, "The ACLU Was Given $24 Million over the Weekend," *Time*, January 30, 2017, https://time.com/4653189/aclu-muslim-ban-donald-trump.

3. "Timeline of Muslim Ban," ACLU Washington, https://www.aclu-wa.org/pages/timeline-muslim-ban.

4. Howard Zinn, "Don't Despair about the Supreme Court," *Progressive*, October 21, 2005, https://progressive.org/op-eds/howard-zinn-despair-supreme-court.

5. Derecka Purnell, Olúfẹ́mi O. Táíwò, and Keeanga-Yamahtta Taylor, "After the Uprising, What Is to Be Done?" *Hammer & Hope*, Winter 2023, https://hammerandhope.org/article/issue-1-article-5.

6. Audre Lorde, "The Master's Tools Will Never Dismantle the Master's House," in *This Bridge Called My Back: Writings by Radical Women of Color*, ed. Cherríe Moraga and Gloria Anzaldúa (New York: Kitchen Table Press, 1983), 95.

7. Mariame Kaba and Andrea J. Ritchie, *No More Police: A Case for Abolition* (New York: New Press, 2022), 101.

8. Kaba and Ritchie, *No More Police*, 131.

9. "Reformist Reforms vs. Abolitionist Steps in Policing," Critical Resistance, May 14, 2020, https://criticalresistance.org/resources/reformist-reforms-vs-abolitionist-steps-in-policing.

10. Setareh Ghandehari, "Ending Immigration Detention: Abolitionist Steps vs. Reformist Reforms," Detention Watch Network, October 2021, https://www.detentionwatchnetwork.org/sites/default/files/Abolition-

ist%20Steps%20vs%20Reformist%20Reforms_DWN_2022.pdf.

11. "5 Ways to Change the Asylum Process," Asylum Seeker Advocacy Project, September 7, 2022, https://help.asylumadvocacy.org/5-ways-to-change-the-asylum-process.

12. "Sanctuary Promise," Oregon Department of Justice, https://www.doj.state.or.us/oregon-department-of-justice/civil-rights/sanctuary-promise.

13. David K. Hausman, "Sanctuary Policies Reduce Deportations Without Increasing Crime," *Proceedings of the National Academy of Sciences* 117, no. 44 (October 19, 2020), https://www.pnas.org/doi/10.1073/pnas.2014673117.

Chapter 8: Beyond "Abolish ICE"

1. Mariame Kaba, "Yes, We Mean Literally Abolish the Police," *New York Times*, June 12, 2020, https://www.nytimes.com/2020/06/12/opinion/sunday/floyd-abolish-defund-police.html.

2. Mark Pocan, "We Must Abolish ICE," CNN, July 2, 2018, https://www.cnn.com/2018/07/02/opinions/we-must-abolish-ice-pocan/index.html.

3. "Establishing a Humane Immigration Enforcement System Act," H.R. 6361, 115th Cong. (2018).

4. Justin Akers Chacón, *The Border Crossed Us: The Case for Opening the US–Mexico Border* (Chicago: Haymarket Books, 2021), 230; Ella Nilsen and Tara Golshan, "Democrats Aren't Ready to Actually Vote for an 'Abolish ICE' Bill," *Vox*, July 13, 2018, https://www.vox.com/2018/7/13/17568170/house-democrats-abolish-ice-bill-jayapal-pocan-immigration-congress.

5. "Free Our Future: An Immigration Policy Platform for Beyond the Trump Era," Mijente, June 2018, https://mijente.net/wp-content/uploads/2018/06/Mijente-Immigration-Policy-Platform_0628.pdf.

6. Peter Markowitz, "Abolish ICE . . . and Then What?" in *Immigration Matters: Movements, Visions, and Strategies for a Progressive Future*, ed. Ruth Milkman, Deepak Bhargava, and Penny Lewis (New York: New Press, 2011), 206.

7. Wendy Sawyer and Peter Wagner, "Mass Incarceration: The Whole Pie 2023," Prison Policy Initiative, March 14, 2023, https://www.prisonpolicy.org/reports/pie2023.html#myths.

8. Leah Wang, "Rise in Jail Deaths Is Especially Troubling as Jail Populations Become More Rural and More Female," Prison Policy Initiative, June 23, 2021, https://www.prisonpolicy.org/blog/2021/06/23/jail_mortality.

9. Mon Mohapatra, email to author, May 30, 2023.

10. Maurice Chammah, "We Surveyed U.S. Sheriffs. See Their Views on

Power, Race and Immigration," Marshall Project, October 18, 2022, https://www.themarshallproject.org/2022/10/18/we-surveyed-u-s-sheriffs-see-their-views-on-power-race-and-immigration.

11. Noah Lanard, "Louisiana Decided to Curb Mass Incarceration. Then ICE Showed Up," *Mother Jones*, May 1, 2019, https://www.motherjones.com/politics/2019/05/louisiana-decided-to-curb-mass-incarceration-then-ice-showed-up.

12. Setareh Ghandehari, Lena Graber, et al., *Carceral Carousel*, Detention Watch Network and Immigrant Legal Resource Center, May 23, 2023, https://www.ilrc.org/resources/carceral-carousel.

13. "Just Transition: A Framework for Change," Climate Justice Alliance, https://climatejusticealliance.org/just-transition.

14. Ruth Wilson Gilmore, "Making and Unmaking Mass Incarceration," keynote conversation with James Kilgore and Mariame Kaba, University of Mississippi, December 5, 2019, Oxford, MS, https://mumiconference.com/transcripts.

15. Nicole Porter, "Repurposing Correctional Facilities to Strengthen Communities," The Sentencing Project, 2022, https://www.sentencing-project.org/app/uploads/2022/10/Repurposing-Correctional-Facilities-to-Strengthen-Communities.pdf.

16. Poor People's Campaign, "Poor People's Moral Budget," June 15, 2020, https://www.poorpeoplescampaign.org/resource/poor-peoples-moral-budget.

17. "Defund Hate Coalition Releases Transformative Budget Proposal for U.S. Immigration," Defund Hate, April 20, 2021, https://defundhate-now.org/2021/04/20/defund-hate-coalition-releases-transformative-budget-proposal-for-u-s-immigration.

18. "Tax Day 2023," National Priorities Project, April 17, 2023, https://www.nationalpriorities.org/analysis/2023/tax-day-2023.

19. "Advocacy Efforts & Legislation, A Budget to Save Lives," Californians United for a Responsible Budget, https://curbprisonspending.org/advocacy/campaigns-legislation.

20. "Healthy Economies Adapting to Last (HEAL) Community FAQ," Immigrant Legal Resource Center, September 7, 2023, https://www.ilrc.org/resources/HEAL-faq.

21. "Asian American Anti-Blackness Is Real—And So Is Our Responsibility to End It," Densho, May 28, 2020, https://densho.org/catalyst/asian-american-anti-blackness-is-real-and-so-is-our-responsibility-to-end-it.

Index

9/11
  2016 election compared to,
    119, 141
  anti-immigrant backlash follow-
    ing, 2, 17, 19, 35, 37–41, 102,
    156, 168, 202
  immigrant rights movement
    following, 100–4
  Islamophobia and, 6, 38
  prison boom following, 6, 10, 40,
    134, 168
287(g), 36, 40, 56, 103, 193
  Hudson County and, 174
  Maricopa County and, 41, 106
  Not1More campaign, 115

Abbott, Greg, 197
Abolish ICE NY/NJ, 177–78, 180
Adams County Correctional
  Center, 121, 138
Adelante Alabama Worker Center,
  150
Adelanto ICE Processing Center,
  164–65, 167
Affordable Care Act, 112
Afghanistan, 38
Africa, 20, 186
Alabama, xi, 63, 103, 148, 150, 153,
  181, 202
Alexander, Michelle, 20
Alien Criminal Apprehension

Program and Institutional
  Removal Program, 30
Alliance for Citizenship, 112–16
American Civil Liberties Union
  (ACLU), 41, 156–57, 159,
  185–87
American Constitution Society, 63
American Federation of State,
  County, and Municipal
  Employees, 135
American Friends Service
  Committee, 63, 141
America's Voice, 108, 112, 153
Anti-Drug Abuse Act, 29–30, 74
Antiterrorism and Effective Death
  Penalty Act, 35–36
Applied Research Center, 86
Appropriations Subcommittee on
  Homeland Security, 51
Arizona, 19, 23, 41, 48, 103, 106–9,
  130, 204
  BOP prisons in, 154
  CIR and, 108
  Dignity Not Detention
    campaign, 152
  Eloy Detention Center, 52
  No More Deaths in, 91
  Not1More campaign in, 115
  Operation Streamline in, 78
  SB 1070, 107–9, 195, 197
Armstrong, Andrea, 205

Arpaio, Joe, 23, 41, 103, 106–7, 204

Artesia, New Mexico, 55

Arulanantham, Ahilan, 89

Ashcroft, John, 38

Asia, 20

Asylum Seeker Advocacy
    Project, 193

Atlanta, 126

Atlantic, 84

Atwater, Lee, 82

Aurora Processing Center, 27

Austin, 75, 104, 133, 156, 158–59,
    204

Austin Police Department, 204

Australia, 134

Baltimore, 59, 64, 99, 138

Barahona, Nilson, 126

Batavia Detention Center, 37

Batavia, New York, 130

Behavioral Systems Southwest, 155

Bergen County, 179

Berks County Family Residential
    Center, 156, 158–62

Berlin Wall, 28

Beyond the Enforcement
    Paradigm, 206

Biden administration, 65, 123, 146,
    181, 188–89, 209
    border militarization by, 88, 123,
        207
    CAP and, 56
    family detention and, 161–62
    First Ten to Communities Not
        Cages, 161
    Gupta in, 157
    private prisons and, 167
    reformist reforms and, 189, 191
    Section 1326 and, 89, 187
    Texas and, 189
    Title 42 and, 88–90

Biden, Joe, xvii, 27, 34, 87–90, 181
    CIR and, 122
    criminalization and, 85
    Defund Hate and, 144–46
    Muslim Ban and, 186
    private prisons and, 80, 126–27,
        137, 139–40
    Republican Party and, 88

BI Incorporated, 63

Birmingham, Alabama, 154

Bixby, Fred, 72

Black Alliance for Just Immigration,
    114, 176

Black, Andrea, 105, 151

Black Lives Matter, 11, 58, 99, 127,
    143, 166, 199, 209
    Obama and, 118–19, 138
    reformist reforms and, 190

Black Youth Project 100, 119

Blease, Coleman Livingston, 73

Bloomington, Indiana, 171

Booker, Cory, 178

Border Protection, Anti-terrorism,
    and Illegal Immigration Con-
    trol Act, 104

Border Security, Economic Op-
    portunity, and Immigration
    Modernization Act, 113

Bracero Program, 21

Bradley, Gracie Mae, 124

Broadview Staging Center, 168

Bronx Defenders, 174, 176

Brooklyn, 177, 202

Brooklyn Defender Services, 174

Broward Detention Center, 110, 127

Brown, Jerry, 117, 165

Brown, Michael, 118

Budget 2 Save Lives, 208

Buffalo, New York, 37

Build Back Better, 123

Bureau of Justice Statistics, 86

Bureau of Prisons. *See* Federal
  Bureau of Prisons
Bush administration, 39–41, 57,
  78–79, 103
Bush, George H. W., 82
Bush, George W., 37, 45, 101, 107, 121
Byrd, Robert, 50–51, 131, 145

California, 33–34, 72, 77, 81, 121,
  150, 158, 193, 207–8
  AB 32, 167
  BOP prisons in, 154
  Critical Resistance in, 7
  detention protest campaigns in,
    xi, 162–67, 176, 179, 196, 207
  Operation Intercept in, 23
  prison boom in, 135
  private prisons and, 140, 205
  Proposition 184, 33–34
  Proposition 187, 34, 163
  Reagan and, 82
  San Quentin State Prison in, 160
  TRUST Act, 117, 120, 194
California Correctional Peace Offi-
  cers Association, 135
California Immigrant Youth Net-
  work, 104
Californians United for a Responsi-
  ble Budget, 207
Castro, Fidel, 25
Castro, Julián, 85
Center for American Progress, 108
Center for Community Change,
  101, 105, 112
Center for Constitutional Rights,
  107, 132
Central America, 26, 88, 207
Cházaro, Angélica, 105
Chicago, 5, 53, 64, 104, 109, 168–71
Chinese Exclusion Act of 1882, 21
Church World Service, 141

Cibola detention center, 208
Citizenship and Immigration
  Services, 39
Clearfield County, 140
Clinton administration, 30–31, 33,
  75, 78
Clinton, Bill, 17, 31–34
  AEDPA and, 35–36
  criminalization and, 45
  State of the Union address, 67, 90
Coalition for Humane Immigrant
  Rights of Los Angeles, 103
Cold War, 17, 19, 24–25, 28, 33, 164
Colombia, 193
Colorado, 153, 167
Columbia University, 136
Communities Not Cages campaign,
  154, 175, 201
Community Education Centers, 53
Comprehensive Crime Control Act
  of 1984, 28
Congress, 3, 7, 26, 27, 41, 86, 161,
  180, 189
  "abolish ICE" and, 178
  AEDPA and, 35, 74
  Anti-Drug Abuse Act and, 29, 74
  border patrol funding and, 70
  CIR and, 98, 105, 108, 114–15,
    120, 122
  Defund Hate and, 142–45
  detention bed quota and, 51,
    133, 145
  DREAM Act and, 103, 110
  Freedom for Families Act and,
    161–62
  government shutdown and, 141
  HR 4437, 104–5
  IIRAIRA and, 36, 74
  Immigration Reform and
    Control Act, 28–29
  INS and, 37

National Origins Act and, 72
New Way Forward Act and, 195
Refugee Act and, 24
Title 42 and, 90
Undesirable Aliens Act and, 75
Violent Crime Control and Law
    Enforcement Act and, 31,
    34, 74
Contra Costa County, 163
Cook County Jail, 5
CoreCivic, 27, 70, 131, 140, 170
Corker, Bob, 113–14
Cornell Corrections, 40
Corporate Backers of Hate
    campaign, 136
Corrections Corporation of
    America (CCA), 27, 133, 134.
    See also CoreCivic
9/11 and, 40
Adams County Correctional
    Center, 138
Columbia University and, 136
Crete and, 169
Eloy Detention Center, 52, 131
Houston Processing Center, 4
Hutto Detention Center, 41, 156
Joliet, Illinois, 170
Laredo superjail and, 76
Lehman Brothers and, 134
Sodexho Marriott and, 133–34
South Texas Family Residential
    Center, 55
COVID-19, xiii–xiv, 87–88, 90, 143,
    150, 160, 177, 181, 195
Crete, Illinois, 169
crime bill. *See* Violent Crime Con-
    trol and Law Enforcement Act
Criminal Alien Program (now
    Criminal Apprehension
    Program), 56
Criminal Alien Requirement pris-

ons, 78–80, 137, 139–40
Critical Resistance, 7–8, 18, 152,
    190–91
Critical Resistance South, 7
Cruz, Ted, 81
Crystal City Internment Camp,
    159, 161
Cuba, 24–25, 28
Customs and Border Protection, 87,
    89, 109, 189
    "abolish ICE" and, 200
    creation of, 39
    deterrence strategy of, 74–75
    family separations and, 68–70, 83
    funding for, 12, 70, 113, 129,
        141–45, 153, 189, 191, 201,
        206–7
    Miller and, 87
    Operation Streamline and, 76–78
    Title 42 and, 88

Dallas, Texas, 206
D'Amato, Alfonse, 28–29, 74
Das, Alina, 30
Data for Progress, 200
Davis, Angela, 7–8
Davis, James, 72
Dean, Jesse Jerome, Jr., 1–3, 7
Deferred Action for Childhood
    Arrivals (DACA), 60, 111–12,
    115, 120, 124, 141, 195
Deferred Action for Parents of
    Americans and Lawful
    Permanent Residents, 118
Defund Hate, 129, 140–46, 206–7
DeGise, Tom, 179
Delaney Hall, 53
Del Rio, Texas, 76–77, 89, 198
Democratic Party, xii, 28, 67, 192, 195
    2022 elections and, 123
    "abolish ICE" and, 200–1

border enforcement and, 69, 85,
87–88, 92, 100
CIR and, 98–99, 102, 105,
113–15, 120, 122, 124
crime and, 27–28, 31, 33, 45,
80–82, 85, 189
Defund Hate and, 142–43
detention bed quota and,
50–51, 132
Illinois, 172
Nixon and, 23
private prisons and, 127, 167
Republican trifecta and, 141
Title 42 and, 90
trafficking and, 91
Democratic Socialists of America,
177
Denver, 59, 176
Department of Corrections
(Arizona), 48
Department of Corrections (New
York City), 50
Department of Defense, 154
Department of Homeland Security
(DHS), xvii, 93, 161, 195
287(g) and, 106
body cameras and, 190
CIR and, 113
creation of, 6, 39, 57, 75
Defund Hate and, 141–45
Etowah County Jail and, 150
family separations and, 83–85
ICE-NGO working group, 46
Mayorkas and, 89, 180
Obama and, 106
Operation Streamline and, 76, 83
private prisons and, 56, 129, 139,
146, 156–57, 165
reforms to, 45–46
Schriro and, 48
Secure Communities and, 56

Department of Justice (DOJ), 26,
39, 93, 154
CAR prisons and, 137
family separations and, 83–85
Office of the Inspector General,
137
Operation Streamline and, 76
private prisons and, 56, 80, 127,
138–39, 147, 167
SB 1070 and, 108
Section 1326 and, 89
Desis Rising Up and Moving, 176
Detention Watch Network (DWN),
xii, xiii, xv, 103, 105, 160
abolition and, 8–9, 102, 111, 153,
191–92
CAR facilities and, 137
CIR and, 105, 112–14
Communities Not Cages
campaign and, 154, 161, 175,
180–81, 201
Defund Hate and, 141–42, 145
Dignity Not Detention
campaign, 152
Dwight detention fight and, 171
End the Quota campaign and,
132, 142
Families for Freedom and, 102
founding of, 37
#FreeThemAll toolkit, xiv
ICE-NGO working group and,
46, 64
letter to ICE organized by, xiv
map of detention center
locations by, 47
in New Jersey, 173, 175
in New York City, 173, 175–76
Not1More campaign and, 115
shut down campaigns and, 111,
151–54
Tsao and, 172

We Are Home and, 122
Dickerson, Caitlin, 84
Dignity Not Detention, 165–66, 176, 180, 207
Dilley Family Detention Center, 131, 158–62
Dilley, Texas, 55, 198
The Dispossessed (Le Guin), 13
Dominguez, Neidi, 103, 109–11
DREAM Act, 103, 109–10, 207
Dream Defenders, 119
Dukakis, Michael, 82
Durbin, Richard, 51
Dwight, Illinois, 168, 170–71

Eagle Pass, 198
Eastern Europe, 72
Ecuador, 4
Ehrlichman, John, 23
Elizabeth Detention Center, 140
Elkhart County, Indiana, 170
Ellis Island, 24
Eloy Detention Center, 52, 131
El Paso, 83–84, 130
El Salvador, 155
End the Quota campaign, 132, 142
Essex County, 179
Essex County Jail, 54
Etowah County Jail, 148–50, 153, 181, 202
Europe, 20, 72, 134
Evans, Kate, 62
Expose and Close, 153, 155, 163, 173

Fagardo-Saucedo, Claudio, 79
Familia: Trans Queer Liberation Movement, 163
Families for Freedom, 102, 152, 173
Family Liberation Abolitionist Network, 161
Farmville Detention Center, 57–58

FBI, 56
Federal Bureau of Prisons, 7, 26, 78, 127–29, 137–39, 146, 154
Federal Emergency Management Agency, 143
Federal Law Enforcement Training Center, 55
Feinstein, Dianne, 33, 81
Ferguson, 99, 118–19, 138
First Ten to Communities Not Cages, 155, 161, 180
Fleming, Mark, 172
Florence, Arizona, 130
Flores, Jenny, 155
Flores settlement, 156, 158, 160–61
Florida, 1, 17, 25, 28, 54, 74, 85, 130, 163
Floyd, George, ix, xv, 2, 139, 150, 154, 177, 209
Foley, George, 63–64
Fox News, 85
Franco, Marisa, 112, 118–19
Freedom for Families Act, 162
Freedom for Immigrants, 163–64
Freedom Side, 119
Free Our Future, 201
#FreeThemAll, xiv, xv, 154

G4S, 70, 136
Gadsden, Alabama, 148
Galindo, Jesus Manuel, 138
Galveston County, 198
Gang of Eight, 113
Garcia, Carlos, 106
García-Mejia, Jorge, 52
García Zárate, José Inez, 81–82
Gary, Indiana, 170
Gee, Dolly, 158, 160
GEO Care, 64
GEO Group, xii, 27, 166–67. *See also* Wackenhut

Adelanto ICE Processing Center, 164–65, 167
ATDs and, 63–65
Broward Detention Center, 127
ICE-NGO working group and, 64
in Indiana, 170
in Jena, Louisiana, 41
Karnes County Civil Detention Facility, 54
Laredo superjail and, 76, 78
Moshannon Valley Correctional Center, 140
Northwest Detention Center and, 115, 132
Reeves County Correctional Center, 138
George Air Force Base, 164
Georgia, 85, 126, 152, 153
Georgia Detention Watch, 152
Ghana, 4
Ghandehari, Setareh, 191–92
Gideon v. Wainwright, 192
Gilmore, Ruth Wilson, 2, 7, 92, 135–36, 185, 192, 205
Giuliani, Rudolph, 26
Global South, 70
Golden Venture, 31–32
Golding, Karim, 148–49, 202
Goldwater, Barry, 19–20
Goodlatte, Bob, 51
Goodling, Bill, 32
Goshen College, 170
Gottlieb, Amy, 63
Graham, Bob, 28, 74
Grassroots Leadership, 6, 7, 75, 77, 103–4, 152, 159–60, 197, 204
Greenhouse, Linda, 108
Guadalupe-Gonzalez, Elsa, 52
Guantánamo Bay, 138
Gupta, Vanita, 157
Gurulé, Sophia, 176, 178

Haiti, 24–25, 28, 89, 160–61
Haitian Bridge Alliance, 161
Hall, Stuart, 92
Harris County, 4–5
Harris County Jail, 5
Harris, Kamala, 88
Hart-Celler Act, 20–22, 23, 29, 42, 101
HEAL (Healthy Economies Adapting to Last), 208
Helwig, Robert, 57
Hernández, Kelly Lytle, 71, 72, 89
Hernandez, Miguel, 97–98
Herzing, Rachel, 190
Hill, Randy, 76
Hines, Barbara, 157
Hobart, Indiana, 170
Hoeven, John, 113
Homan, Thomas, 55, 84–85
Homeland Security Investigations, 91
Honduras, 198
Horton, William, 82
House of Representatives, 104, 117, 120, 141, 200
Homeland Security Subcommittee for Appropriations, 143
HR 4437, 104
Judiciary Committee, 161
Houston, 3–5, 27, 57, 208
Houston Independent School District, 4
Houston Processing Center, 4
How Democracy Works Now, 102, 105
Hudson County, 174, 177, 179, 180
Hudson County Jail, 173, 176–78, 180, 192
Huling, Tracy, 33
Human Rights First, 173
Human Rights Watch, 47
Hutto: America's Family Prison, 158

Hutto Detention Center, 41, 48, 55,
    118, 156–58, 161

ICE Out of California Coalition,
    116
Idaho, 208
Illegal Immigration Reform and
    Immigrant Responsibility Act,
    35, 36, 40
Illinois, xi, 51, 107, 150, 167–72,
    179, 181, 196
Illinois Coalition for Immigrant
    and Refugee Rights, 168–72
Illinois Way Forward Act, 172
Immigrant Alliance for Justice and
    Equity, 121
Immigrant Defense Project, 102
Immigrant Legal Resource Center,
    165–66
Immigrant Youth Justice League, 109
Immigration and Customs Enforce-
    ment (ICE), xii, 93, 150, 153,
    166, 193–94
    287(g) and, 41, 56
    BOP prisons and, 154
    under Bush, 39–41, 121
    California shut down campaigns
        and, 163–67, 179, 196
    CAP and, 56
    COVID-19 and, xiv, xv
    Dean and, 1, 2
    demand to abolish, 69, 174, 176,
        176–77, 200–1
    demand to defund, 12, 141–47,
        153, 189, 191, 207
    Deportation 101 on, 102
    detention expansion, 53–56, 154,
        157, 168–72, 180, 196
    DWN-organized letter to, xiv
    family detention and, 41, 48, 55,
        144, 154–62

family separation and, 55, 69,
        84–85, 154, 200
    funding for, 129, 133, 141–46, 181
    García Zárate and, 81
    Harris County and, 5
    highest capacity of, 121
    Hutto Detention Center, 41
    infiltrators of, 110
    intergovernmental service agree-
        ments and, 130–31
    Irwin County Detention Center
        and, xvii
    Laredo superjail and, 78
    local police and, 5, 11, 56, 58, 59,
        81, 101, 103, 106, 120–21,
        142, 181, 193–94, 196, 204
    Maricopa County and, 41
    Mississippi raid of, 85, 121
    Morton Memo and, 59–61
    New Jersey raids of, 177
    New Jersey shut down campaigns
        and, 172–80, 196
    NGO working group, 11, 61–65
    Not1More campaign and, 115–16
    Office of Detention Oversight of,
        49, 50
    Operation Endgame of, 39
    Operation Return to Sender of, 40
    Operation Streamline and, 77
    private prisons and, 5, 40–41,
        127, 130–32, 139–40, 147,
        165–67, 171–72, 191, 205
    reforms and, 5, 9, 47–50, 56, 60,
        66, 88, 120, 152, 158, 172,
        188, 191
    Secure Communities and, 56, 58,
        107, 116
    sequestration and, 51, 97, 132
    "We are not criminals" and, 98
Immigration and Nationality Act,
    20, 73

Immigration and Naturalization
     Service (INS), 29, 39
     287(g) and, 36
     Clinton and, 31
     Congress and, 37
     detention and, 19, 24–26, 29,
          31–32, 37–38, 155–56
     Flores and, 155–56
Immigration Centers of America,
     57, 171
Immigration Reform and Control
     Act, 28–29, 101
Ina, Satsuki, 159, 161
India, 22
Indiana, 168, 170
Inland Coalition for Immigrant
     Justice, 165
Interfaith Community for Detained
     Immigrants, 168–69
Interfaith Movement for Human
     Integrity, 163
Iowa, 40, 102
Iraq War, 8, 38, 50
Irwin County Detention Center, xv,
     xvii, 85, 153
Ishii, Mike, 160

Jackson, Jesse, 25
Jadwat, Omar, 186
Jayapal, Pramila, 201
Jena, Louisiana, 40
Jim Crow, 20, 89
Johnson, Lyndon B., 19–20
Johnston, J. Bennett, 26
Joliet, Illinois, 170
Jozef, Guerline, 160–61
Justice Department. See Depart-
     ment of Justice (DOJ)
Justice Strategies, 77

Kaba, Mariame, 190, 199

Kang, S. Deborah, 74
Kankakee County Jail, 172
Karnes County, 54
Karnes County Civil Detention
     Facility, 54–55
Karnes Residential Center, 158–62
Katzmann, Robert, 174
Kilgore, James, 176
King, Martin Luther, Jr., 102, 197, 199
King, Rodney, 33
Kinney County, 198
Koulish, Robert, 62
Krome Detention Center, 17, 25
Krome, Florida, 130
Ku Klux Klan, 50

Landaverde, Reverend José, 169
Lara, Ricardo, 165
Laredo Immigrant Alliance, 160
Laredo, Texas, 75–76, 78, 80, 104,
     134, 197
Latin America, 20
Law Enforcement Assistance
     Administration, 20
Lawrence, Patrice, 207
The Least of These, 158
Leesport, Pennsylvania, 156
Legal Aid Society of New York, 174
Le Guin, Ursula K., 13
Lehman Brothers, 134
Lenoir, Gerald, 114
Libal, Bob, 75, 78, 103, 134, 157, 159
Little Village, Chicago, 169
Logan, Steve, 40
Loiselle, Mary, 64
Lorde, Audre, 188
Lorenzen-Strait, Andrew, 54, 64
Los Angeles, 33, 64, 102, 104, 107,
     155
Los Angeles Times, 28, 33
Louisiana, 26, 40, 89, 121, 204–6

Lutheran Immigration and Refugee
Service, 64

Macehualli Worker Center, 103
Macías-Rojas, Patrisia, 29
Mac, Juno, 91
Make the Road, 136
Maricopa County, Arizona, 23, 41,
    103, 106, 204
Mariel Boatlift, 25, 28, 217
Markowitz, Peter, 201
Marshall Project, 204
Martínez Rosas, Greisa, 119
Maryland, 167
Massachusetts, 82
Mass Immigration Emergency
    Plan, 26
Mattos, Tania, 176
May Day 2006, 39
May Day 2010, 108
Mayorkas, Alejandro, 89, 90, 180
Mbembe, Achille, 70
McElwee, Sean, 200
McHenry County Jail, 168–69, 172,
    181
McVeigh, Timothy, 35
Meissner, Doris, 37
Menendez, Robert, 106, 178
Mexico, 4, 19, 21, 23, 31–33, 72–73,
    88, 101, 140
Miami, 25, 53, 64, 110, 127
Michigan, 1, 168
Middle East, 186, 207
Migrant Border Crossing Study, 77
Migration Policy Institute, 143
Mijente, 119, 122, 201
Miller, Stephen, 85, 87
Miller, Todd, 70
Minidoka National Historic Site,
    208–9
Minneapolis, xv, 107

Minnesota, 168
Minority Report, 61
Mississippi, 85, 121, 138
Morawetz, Nancy, 35
Morgan County, Tennessee, 206
Morton, John, 51, 59
Morton Memo, 59
Moshannon Valley Correctional
    Center, 140
MoveOn, 143
Movimiento Cosecha, 177
MTC (private prison company), 170
Murakawa, Naomi, 67
Murguía, Janet, 117
Murphy, Sister Pat, 168–69
Muslim Ban, x, xvi, 84, 120, 186–87
Muslims for Just Futures, 207

Napolitano, Janet, 48, 51–52, 106
Nassau County, 63
Natchez, Mississippi, 121
National Coming Out of the
    Shadows Day, 109
National Council of La Raza, 101,
    112, 114, 117
National Day Laborer Organiz-
    ing Network, 102–3, 106–8,
    111–12, 115, 117, 118, 154
National Domestic Workers
    Alliance, 127
National Immigrant Justice Center,
    80, 141, 171, 172
National Immigrant Youth Alli-
    ance, 110
National Immigration Forum, 97,
    101, 114
National Origins Act, 72
National Priorities Project, 207
National Security Entry-Exit
    Registration System, 38
Nation, 82

NATO, 169
Nevada, 89, 187
Never Again Action, 177
Nevins, Joseph, 71
Newark, New Jersey, 53, 64
New Jersey, xi, xiv, 53, 63, 105–6,
    121, 140, 167, 173–80, 192,
    196, 205
New Jersey Alliance for Immigrant
    Justice, 177
Newman, Chris, 103, 106
New Mexico, 55
New Orleans, 7
New Right, 19
Newton County, Indiana, 170
New Way Forward Act, 195
New York, 28–29, 63–64, 74, 84, 113
    antidetention state legislation in,
        179–80
    Golden Venture and, 31–32
    ICE detention in, 130
    legal representation in, 174–75
    Not With Our Money! campaign
        and, 134
    Rockefeller Drug Laws in, 24
    Secure Communities and, 107
New York City, 31, 63, 64, 102,
    173–76
    DWN in, 173, 175–76
    Giuliani and, 26
    Rikers in, 5, 50
    sanctuary policy in, 177
New York City Council, 174
New York Immigrant Family Unity
    Project, 174–178
New York Police Department, 107
New York Times, 54, 84, 158, 185
Ngai, Mae, 22
Nixon, Richard, 23
Nofil, Brianna, 26
No More Deaths, 91

No New Jails, xi
Noorani, Ali, 97, 114
de Noronha, Luke, 124
North American Free Trade Agree-
    ment, x, 31–33, 39, 74, 113, 219
North Carolina, 103
Northrop Grumman, 70
Northwest Detention Center,
    115–16, 132
Not1More Deportation, 112,
    115–19, 154
Not With Our Money!, 133–34, 136
Nourn, Ny, 166
NWDC Resistance, 116

Oakdale, Louisiana, 26
Obama administration, 88, 159,
    181, 195
    ATDs and, 65
    CIR and, 120
    "civil" detention and, 48–49,
        54–56
    criminalization and, 11, 47,
        57–58, 66–67, 79–80, 83, 99,
        118–19
    detention bed mandate and, 50–51
    Expose and Close and, 152–53
    family separations and, 86
    formal deportations and, 57, 117,
        193
    guaranteed minimums and, 133
    Hutto Detention Center and, 48
    Morton Memo and, 59–60
    NWDC Resistance, 116
    private prisons and, 56, 127, 137,
        167
    reformist reforms and, 46–50, 189
    SB 1070 and, 107–8, 195
    Secure Communities and, 56–58,
        65–66
    Trump and, 55, 66, 149, 166

Obama, Barack, x, 8, 65
  287(g) and, 106
  "Address to the Nation on Immi-
    gration," 44, 90
  BLM and, 118–19, 138
  CIR and, 79, 99, 110, 112
  criminalization and, 44–45, 51,
    56–60, 66, 118, 166
  DACA and, 111, 124
  DAPA and, 118
  DHS and, 106
  DOJ and, 108
  Dreamers and, 110–11
  Hutto Detention Center and, 55,
    118, 158
  Karnes and, 54, 158
  Not1More campaign and, 115,
    117–18
  Operation Streamline and, 79
  Secure Communities and, 4, 116
  TUFF and, 157–58
Ocilla, Georgia, xv
Office of Detention Oversight, 49
Office of Detention Policy and
  Planning, 50
Office of Refugee Resettlement,
  83–84, 156
Office of the Federal Detention
  Trustee, 38–39
Office of the Inspector General, 137
Oklahoma, 26
Oklahoma City, 35
Online Detainee Locator System, 47
Operation Endgame, 39
Operation Intercept, 23
Operation Lone Star, 197–98
Operation Return to Sender, 40
Operation Streamline, 76–80, 84,
  113, 115, 198, 201
Orange County, 163
Oregon, 143, 154, 167, 193

Organized Communities Against
  Deportations, 171
Otero detention center, 208

Page Act of 1875, 21
Pasadena, 155
Paulos, Abraham, 152
Pax Christi, 169, 177
Pekoske, David, 188
Pembroke Township, Illinois, 170
Pennsylvania, 32, 140, 158, 162
Peoria, Illinois, 171
Persch, Sister JoAnn, 168–69
Personal Responsibility and Work
  Opportunity Reconciliation
  Act, 34
Phoenix, 108, 115
Phoenix New Times, 48
Piedras Negras, Mexico, 198
Pishko, Jessica, 41
Pocan, Mark, 200
Policing the Crisis (Hall et al.), 92
Polis, Jared, 153
Poor People's Campaign, 206
Port-au-Prince, Haiti, 89
Port Isabel, Texas, 130
Postville, Iowa, 40
Preciado, Karina Cisneros, 85–86
Prince Edward County, Virginia, 57
Pritzker, JB, 171–72
Proposition 184, 33–34
Proposition 187, 34, 163
Public Health Services Act, 87
Puente, 103, 106, 108, 152
Puerto Rico, 143
Purnell, Dereka, 187

Queens, New York, 31–32, 176
Queer Detainee Empowerment
  Project, 176

Ragbir, Ravi, 63
RAICES, 160
Raymondville, Texas, 138
Reagan, Ronald, 24–26, 28–29, 32,
    82, 101, 155
Reeves County Correctional
    Center, 138
Refugee Act, 24–25
Republican Party, xii, 69, 195
    "abolish ICE" and, 201
    Biden and, 88, 122, 189
    CIR and, 79, 112–15, 117–18, 120
    criminalization and, 27–28, 31, 39
    detention quota and, 51, 132
    Goldwater and, 19
    ICDI and, 169
    IIRAIRA and, 36
    moral panics and, 92
    Nixon and, 23
    Obama and, 45, 67
    sequestration and, 97
    trafficking and, 91
    trifecta of, 141
Reuters, 97
Reza, Salvador, 103, 106, 108
Richmond, California, 163
Rikers Island, 5, 50
Ritchie, Andrea, 190
Rivera, Jasmine, 162
Roberts, Dorothy, 86
Rockefeller Drug Laws, 24
Rocketto, Jess Morales, 127
Roe v. Wade, 186–87
Roybal-Allard, Lucille, 143
Ruiz, Grisel, 165–66

Saavedra, Marco, 110
San Antonio, 54
San Bernardino County, 165
Sanchez, Li Ann, 126
Sanctuary Promise Act, 193

San Francisco, 81
San Quentin State Prison, 160
Santa Ana, California, 163
Sarlin, Benjy, 114
SB 1070, 107–8, 195, 197
Schriro, Dora, 48–50, 53, 61, 65
Schumer, Chuck, 113
SCOMM. See Secure Communities
Seattle, 115, 133
Section 1324, 91
Section 1325, 73, 85
Section 1326, 73, 89
Secure Communities, x, 4, 49, 50,
    56–59, 65–66, 107
    ICE and, 107, 116
    ICE Out of California Coalition
        and, 116–17
    Not1More campaign and, 115
    Trump and, 121
SEIU, 143
Self, Jeff, 83
Senate, 34, 51, 112–14, 120, 141, 178
Sensenbrenner Bill, 104–5
Sensenbrenner, Jim, 39, 104
Sessions, Jeff, 68, 84, 139
Sharry, Frank, 102, 108
Shimoda, Brandon, 209
Shut Down Adelanto, 165
Shut Down Berks, 158, 160, 162
Shut Down Etowah, 150, 154
Sierra Blanca detention center, 208
Simon, Jonathan, 81
SmartLINK, 65
Smith, Molly, 91
Sodexho Marriott (now Sodexo,
    Inc.), 133–34
Solar, Alessandra, 41
Sound Strike, 108
South Africa, 108
South by Southwest, 158
South Carolina, 27, 73

Southern Border Communities
    Coalition, 141
Southern Europe, 72
South Texans Opposing Private
    Prisons Coalition, 76
South Texas Family Residential
    Center, 55
Staten Island, 206
State of Arizona v. United States, 108
State of the Union (1996), 67
Steinle, Kate, 81
St. Louis County, 118
Stop Cop City, xi
Supreme Court, 35, 73, 108, 186, 192
Syria, 186

Tacoma, Washington, 115, 132
Takei, Carl, 159
Taylor, Breonna, ix
Taylor, Texas, 41, 157
Tea Party, 51
Texans United for Families, 157–58
Texas, xi, 3, 81, 87, 91, 163, 208
    ACLU of, 156
    Biden administration and, 189
    BOP prisons in, 154
    CAR prisons in, 79–80
    Crystal City Internment Camp
        in, 159
    DAPA and, 118
    Dignity Not Detention
        campaign, 152
    ICE-owned and -operated
        detention in, 130
    Not With Our Money! campaign
        and, 134–35
    Operation Intercept and, 23
    Operation Lone Star and, 197–98
    Operation Streamline and, 75–76
    stopping prison expansion in, 6,
        103–4

Texas Criminal Justice Reform
    Coalition, 75
Texas National Guard, 197–98
Texas State Capitol, 6
Thurmond, Strom, 27
Time, 161
Title 42, 87–90, 123
Tornillo detention center, 208
Torres, Amy, 177–79
Transactional Records Access
    Clearinghouse, 59
Tri-County Detention Center, 172
Trinidad, 63
Trump administration, 68, 122, 187
    ATDs and, 64
    Biden and, 123
    CAR prisons and, 80, 139
    Defund Hate campaign and, 129
    family separations and, 68–69,
        83–86, 92, 200–201
    Flores settlement and, 160
    guaranteed minimums and, 133
    Muslim Ban and, 186
    Obama administration and,
        44–45, 66, 149, 166
    Pritzker and, 171
    sanctuary policies and, 177
    Title 42 and, 87
Trump, Donald, x, 1, 17, 99, 181
    2016 election of, 185
    CIR and, 120
    COVID-19 and, xiii
    Defund Hate and, 12, 140
    family separations and, xvi, 11,
        55, 60, 83–85, 154
    Giuliani and, 26
    moral panics and, 82
    Muslim Ban of, xvi, 186
    outwardly racist rhetoric of, 18,
        150, 189
    private prisons and, 127

Secure Communities and, 121
Steinle and, 81
TRUST Act, 117, 120, 194
Tsao, Fred, 168–72
Tsuru for Solidarity, 159–60
Tucker, Emily, 64
Tucson, 113

Undesirable Aliens Act of 1929,
    73–74, 75
UndocuBlack Network, 119, 207
United States Code, 73, 91
United We Dream, 104, 119, 141, 145
University of California, Santa
    Cruz, 103
University of Illinois at
    Urbana-Champaign, 171
University of Texas at Austin, 6,
    133–34
University of Texas Law School, 157
Unzueta, Tania, 109
USCIS, 39
US Conference of Catholic Bishops,
    64
US District Court, 158
US Marshals Service, 28, 38, 168,
    203, 204
    under Bush, 78
    family separations and, 83
    Laredo superjail and, 80
    Operation Streamline and, 77–78
    private prisons and, 75, 79, 127,
        130, 134
US-Mexico border, 125, 133
    Beyond the Enforcement
        Paradigm on, 206
    Biden on, 85, 88
    CIR and, 113–15
    Clinton on, 32, 75
    closure of, 150, 181
    Corker-Hoeven amendment on,

113–14
"crisis" at, 11, 21, 33, 69, 70, 83,
    114
crossing, 11, 68–69, 71, 73,
    76–77, 79, 84–85, 87, 93,
    101, 195, 197–98
deterrence and, 55, 70, 74, 88
enforcement focused on, 11, 71,
    74, 77, 79–80, 83, 88, 100,
    112, 113–15, 121–22, 144,
    189, 195, 204, 207
expulsions at, 57, 87, 123
family separations at, x, xvi,
    68–70, 83–86, 156
Harris on, 88
Japanese American incarceration
    and, 159–60
Mijente on, 201
militarization of, 11, 38, 70–71,
    88, 91–92, 99, 113, 114, 123,
    195, 200
moral panic around, 70, 90–92,
    181, 189, 199, 209
NAFTA and, 74–75
No More Deaths and, 91
Obama on, 79, 118, 121
Operation Intercept at, 23
Operation Lone Star and, 197–99
Reagan on, 28
Sessions on, 68, 84
Trump on, 140
wall along, 38, 70, 83, 113,
    140–141
U.S. News & World Report, 23
Utah, 208
Uvalde, Texas, 198

Val Verde County Detention
    Center, 198
Velasco, Bernardo P., 78
Venturella, David, 64

Vietnam, 4, 24
Vietnam War, 104
Villalpando, Maru Mora, 115–16
Villarreal, Carlos, 75
Violent Crime Control and Law
    Enforcement Act, 31, 34, 74, 82
Virginia, 26, 51, 57, 171

Wackenhut, 27, 40, 134. *See
    also* GEO Group
Walia, Harsha, 33
Warren, Scott, 91
Washington, DC, xiii, 12, 64, 99,
    101, 105–6, 110, 112, 117, 129,
    152, 157, 161
Washington State, xiv, 115, 154,
    167, 201
"We are America," 105
We Are Home, 122–23
Wessler, Seth Freed, 79
Western Hemisphere, 72
West Virginia, 50
Whitlock, Kay, 145
Willacy County Correctional Cen-
    ter, 138–39
Wilson, Darren, 118
Winnebago County, Illinois, 170
Wisconsin, 39, 104, 168, 200
Women's Refugee Commission,
    156–57
Woods, Julie Myers, 64
World Trade Center, 31
World Trade Organization, 133
World War II, x, 20, 159–60, 208–9

Yates, Sally, 137–39
York County Prison, 32
Yousef, Ramzi, 31

Zinn, Howard, 186–87

ABOUT HAYMARKET BOOKS

Haymarket Books is a radical, independent, nonprofit book publisher based in Chicago. Our mission is to publish books that contribute to struggles for social and economic justice. We strive to make our books a vibrant and organic part of social movements and the education and development of a critical, engaged, and internationalist Left.

We take inspiration and courage from our namesakes, the Haymarket Martyrs, who gave their lives fighting for a better world. Their 1886 struggle for the eight-hour day—which gave us May Day, the international workers' holiday—reminds workers around the world that ordinary people can organize and struggle for their own liberation. These struggles—against oppression, exploitation, environmental devastation, and war—continue today across the globe.

Since our founding in 2001, Haymarket has published more than nine hundred titles. Radically independent, we seek to drive a wedge into the risk-averse world of corporate book publishing. Our authors include Angela Y. Davis, Arundhati Roy, Keeanga-Yamahtta Taylor, Eve L. Ewing, Aja Monet, Mariame Kaba, Naomi Klein, Rebecca Solnit, Olúfẹ́mi O. Táíwò, Mohammed El-Kurd, José Olivarez, Noam Chomsky, Winona LaDuke, Robyn Maynard, Leanne Betasamosake Simpson, Howard Zinn, Mike Davis, Marc Lamont Hill, Dave Zirin, Astra Taylor, and Amy Goodman, among many other leading writers of our time. We are also the trade publishers of the acclaimed Historical Materialism Book Series.

Haymarket also manages a vibrant community organizing and event space in Chicago, Haymarket House, the popular Haymarket Books Live event series and podcast, and the annual Socialism Conference.

ALSO AVAILABLE FROM HAYMARKET BOOKS

Abolishing State Violence: A World Beyond Bombs, Borders, and Cages
Ray Acheson

Blood Red Lines: How Nativism Fuels the Right
Brendan O'Connor

The Border Crossed Us: The Case for Opening the US-Mexico Border
Justin Akers Chacón

Border and Rule
Global Migration, Capitalism, and the Rise of Racist Nationalism
Harsha Walia, afterword by Nick Estes, foreword by Robin D. G. Kelley

The Breakbeat Poets Vol. 4: LatiNext
Edited by Felicia Chavez, José Olivarez, and Willie Perdomo

Disposable Domestics: Immigrant Women Workers in the Global Economy
Grace Chang, foreword by Alicia Garza, afterword by Ai-Jen Poo

No One Is Illegal (Updated Edition)
Fighting Racism and State Violence on the U.S.-Mexico Border
Justin Akers Chacón and Mike Davis

Radicals in the Barrio: Magonistas, Socialists, Wobblies,
and Communists in the Mexican American Working Class
Justin Akers Chacón

Solito, Solita: Crossing Borders with Youth Refugees from Central America
Edited by Jonathan Freedman and Steven Mayers

ABOUT THE AUTHORS

Photo © Heather Posten

SILKY SHAH has been working as an organizer on issues related to racial and migrant justice for over two decades. Originally from Texas, she began fighting the expansion of immigrant jails on the US-Mexico border in the aftermath of 9/11. In 2009, she joined the staff of Detention Watch Network, a national coalition building power to abolish immigrant detention in the United States, and she now serves as its executive director. Her writing on immigration policy and organizing has been published in *Truthout, Teen Vogue, Inquest,* and the *Forge,* and in the edited volumes *The Jail Is Everywhere* (Verso, 2024), *Resisting Borders and Technologies of Violence* (Haymarket Books, 2024), and *Transformative Planning* (Black Rose Books, 2020). She has also appeared in numerous national and local media outlets including the *Washington Post,* NPR, and MSNBC.

AMNA A. AKBAR is a professor of law at the Ohio State University, Moritz College of Law. She writes broadly about left social movements today.